Mastering The LSAT

**How To
Prepare
Effectively
And Successfully**

Special Edition!
Includes the complete text of
John Richardson's
"Mastering The Personal Statement -
The Complete Marketing Manual for LAW"
$20.00 Value

Mastering The LSAT

How To Prepare Effectively And Successfully

Richardson Press

John Richardson, B.A., LL.B., J.D.

Richardson Press
Box 19602, Manulife P.O.
55 Bloor St. W.
Toronto, Canada
M4W 3T9

ISBN: 0-9696290-3-6

Printed and manufactured in Canada.

Forward To The Fourth Edition

I am excited that my **Mastering The LSAT - How To Prepare Effectively and Successfully** is now in its fourth edition. Every copy of the first edition in 1994, the second edition in 1998 and the third edition in 2000 has found its way into the hands of a "Law School Bound" student. It seems like just yesterday, that I wrote the Forward to the third edition. I am gratified by the many positive responses that have been generated by the book. Furthermore, I am pleased that the book has assisted so many students in navigating their way through the LSAT, the complete law school application process and into many Canadian and American law schools.

The first edition was published during a time of economic slowdown. The second edition was published during a time of economic vitality. The third edition was published at the height of the "dot com boom." This fourth edition is being published at the "end of the beginning" of the "dot com era." Regardless of the state of the economy, law continues to be a fascinating and exciting career.

There continues to be a healthy balance between the demand for and the supply of seats in law schools. Gaining admission to the best law schools will always be a challenge. But, the challenge is achievable and not impossible!

Our new millennium offers great opportunity for those who are hard working and forward looking. This includes lawyers. Some academics predict a shortage of lawyers in the early part of this new millennium. For those willing to embrace them, the opportunities for lawyers are tremendous.

In closing, I will repeat what I wrote in the "Forward" to the second edition of **Mastering The LSAT**:

"Your acceptance to law school is not a matter of luck. The road to law school is paved with the bricks of hard work and discipline. Stay on the road and an acceptance to law school will be yours! I wish you success in your academic and career goals!"

John Richardson, B.A., LL.B., J.D.

Everyone should firmly persuade himself
that none of the sciences, however abstruse, is
to be deduced from lofty and obscure matters,
but that they all proceed only from what is ...
easily understood.

- Rene Descartes -

CONTENTS

FEATURING:
"The Personal Statement Workbook"

PLUS:
• **Samples of winning personal
statements**
• **Tips for how to handle the
autobiographical sketch**
• **Samples of effective letters
of reference**
• **Inside perspectives from
admissions professionals**

From the Developer Of Canada's #1 Test PREP Program

**Mastering The
Personal Statement**

The complete marketing manual for
LAW - MBA - MED & GRAD Schools

FEATURING:
"The Personal Statement Workbook"
PLUS:
• Samples of winning personal statements
• Tips for how to handle the
autobiographical sketch
• Samples of effective letters of reference
• Inside perspectives from
admissions professionals

John Richardson, B.A., LL.B., J.D. - Author of Mastering The LSAT

Genesis

In the beginning the world of law admissions was without order and void, and uncertainty was upon its face. The spirit of a group of original wise old law professors was emerging to come to grips with the problem.

CREATING A UNIFORM NATIONAL
EXAMINATION FOR ADMISSION
TO LAW SCHOOL

Then, in 1947 a group of legal educators (acting under the authority of the group of wise old law professors) set out to create a uniform national examination for admission to law school. And this group of educators said, "Let us be called the Law School Admission Council"; and they were called the "Law School Admission Council" (LSAC) and they saw that they were good. And there was evening and there was morning, a first day.

And LSAC said, "Let there be an operating corporation through which we can conduct our activities." And LSAC created Law School Admission Services (LSAS) which became the operating corporation through which all their activities were conducted. And LSAC/LSAS said that the purpose of our operating corporation is to generate revenue and for that we need a product and we need customers for that product. And LSAC/LSAS saw that it was good. And there was evening and there was morning, a second day.

...SAW THAT IT WAS GOOD...

THE TEST HAD ESTABLISHED
A WELL DEFINED ROLL.

And LSAC/LSAS said, "Give us a product for our new corporation to sell!" And LSAC/LSAS created the Law School Admission Test (LSAT). And LSAC/LSAS thought that the areas that were likely to be useful on the LSAT included: paragraph reading, analogies, syllogistic reasoning, inconsistencies, practical judgment, "productivity of ideas," and quantitative reasoning. And LSAC/LSAS saw that it was good and that it was to be. And LSAC/LSAS said we need buyers for our product. The law schools responded and provided the market for the product by forcing law school applicants to pay for the LSAT. By the 1970's the LSAT had established a well defined role as a very important part of the admissions process in nearly every ABA approved law school in the United States and most law schools in Canada. And there was evening and there was morning, a third day.

And LSAC/LSAS said let there be consultants for the purpose of designing the LSAT format and questions. And it was so. By contracting with representatives of the College Board, and later the Educational Testing Service, and later still the American College Testing Program, LSAC/LSAS was able to generate the LSAT. And so the LSAT moved from being a theoretical concept to the reality that characterizes the life of young lawyers-to-be. And LSAC/LSAS saw that it was good. And there was evening and there was morning, a fourth day.

LET THERE BE CONSULTANTS...

··· AID IN ASSESSING THE ACADEMIC PROMISE
OF THEIR APPLICANTS

And LSAC/LSAS said, "Let the LSAT be designed as a test
to be used in determining basic competency for legal
education." And so it was so. The first LSAT was a multiple
choice exam designed to measure certain abilities important to
the study of law and, thus, to aid law schools in assessing the
academic promise of their applicants. The test was intended to
cover a broad range of academic disciplines. It was designed
to give no advantage to candidates from a particular academic
background. The multiple choice questions yielding the LSAT
score were designed to measure the ability to read, understand
and solve problems in matters and contexts thought to be
relevant to legal study. And LSAC/LSAS saw that it was good.
And there was evening and there was morning, a fifth day.

And LSAC/LSAS said, "Let all activities surrounding the development, questions and answers to questions on the LSAT be shrouded in secrecy." And it was so. All information concerning test development, the actual test questions and the answers to the questions was kept secret. LSAC/LSAS simply reported an LSAT score to test takers without giving any opportunity for test takers to know what sections they had performed poorly on. In addition, there was no opportunity to know what answers were credited as correct or any opportunity to challenge the wisdom of LSAC/LSAS. Many promising careers were ruined. And LSAC/LSAS saw that this was good. And there was evening and there was morning, a sixth day

MANY PROMISING CAREERS
WERE RUINED.

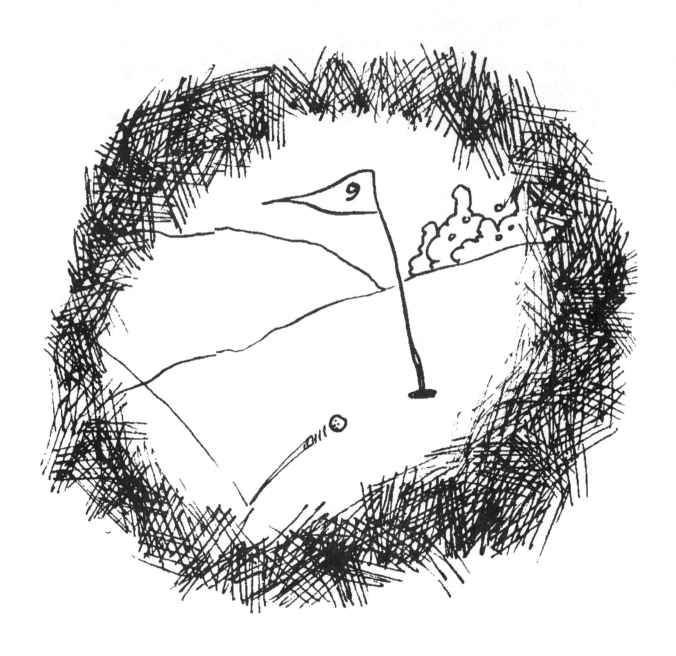

AND ON THE SEVENTH DAY...

Introduction

How To Use This Book

This book is very different from most other LSAT preparation guides. Most LSAT prep guides contain a large number of so-called "sample questions" and have very little "objective analysis." This book is the opposite. It is long on "objective analysis" and short on "sample questions." The reason is simple. Actual LSAT questions are written to a specific formula. Questions in commercially available books are not constructed according to that formula. But fear not! Law Services (the creator of the LSAT) publishes all of the recent LSAT exams. For practice you should use them. That way you will be assured that **every question that you practice with is an actual LSAT question!** These test questions may be ordered from Law Services (see the LSAT information book). They may also be available in your local bookstore.

The sample questions in this book have been carefully designed to accomplish the following goals:

- to demonstrate the different categories and subcategories of LSAT questions;

- to teach many of the background skills that are important for a high LSAT score;

- to teach some of the principles of approach that are important for a high LSAT score.

For the most part, Law Services does not provide any analysis of their practice questions. In addition, Law Services provides "few suggestions" for how to deal with the test or go about the questions. This is the role that this book has been designed to play.

What This Book Is And What It Is Not!

This book will encourage the "habits" that are **necessary** for a high LSAT score. I have taught and designed LSAT courses for eighteen years. Through my years of teaching LSAT preparation courses I have discovered that many students arrive at my courses having acquired a number of bad habits. These "bad habits" are a result of having practiced questions without any clear understanding of what the LSAT is about and how to go about preparing for it. The principal purpose of this book is to provide some proper coaching from the beginning.

How The LSAT Differs From Academic Exams

Throughout your academic career you have been taking exams. For the most part these exams have been designed to test your knowledge and understanding of a specific topic. When studying for these exams you have reviewed notes, attended lectures, and memorized information. This may have worked in the past.

The LSAT is not like other exams. It does not test understanding, memorization, or the acquisition of information. For that reason you must not prepare for the LSAT in the same way that you have prepared for these exams.

What The LSAT Has Been Designed To Test

The LSAT has been designed to test basic reasoning and reading skills and to test the application of those skills. The most important reasoning skill is the use of "conditional statements." For this reason I have included a whole chapter on "Conditional Statement Mastery." The application of these skills is tested specifically in the context of the logic games, logical reasoning and reading comprehension question types.

Your job is to become highly proficient at answering those specific question types **in the context of a multiple choice test!**
This will involve:

1. Learning specific techniques and strategies to apply to the multiple choice questions and answer choices; and

2. Practicing those techniques and strategies until they become internalized and are second nature!

LSAT preparation **is like training for an athletic event!** You practice the same kinds of things over and over until you become better and better at them!

Many Test Takers Know What To Do.
They Just Don't Do What They Know!

When preparing for the LSAT your goal should be to maximize your score - given your current level of reading and reasoning ability.

Training for the LSAT involves the "internalization" of a specific approach until that approach becomes "second nature."
Like anything else, practice counts!

Arnold (Red) Auerbach coached the Boston Celtics to become a basketball dynasty during the 1950s and 1960s. He was a coach who almost always **knew** a winning strategy. Do you think that he was capable of going out on the floor and implementing that strategy himself? Of course not. He had the players do it for him. The players were able to implement the coach's strategy because they:

- practiced that strategy day in and day out.

To put it simply:

There is a big difference between knowing what the strategies are and being able to implement them under the time constraints!

In the same way that the Celtics players practiced day in and day out to **internalize** the strategy that they had **learned,** you must practice to internalize the strategy that you will learn! Preparing for the LSAT is like training for an athletic event. Successful training requires a good training program.

The Bare Necessities

This book contains what I call "the bare necessities." (Have you seen the movie Jungle Book?) It contains the **minimal essentials** to prepare you for the test. Obviously, there are many levels to LSAT preparation. I have not included a number of advanced principles. Use this book to learn the **basic tools** and point yourself in the right direction. If you avoid the most common "bad habits" you will be able to improve your score.

The Toolbox Approach

This book uses a "toolbox approach." Your "toolbox" will contain many principles of approach. Think of each principle as being a "tool." As you progress through the book you will be offered many "tools" which if used properly will improve your performance. But, not every tool can be used for every question. Your job is to learn enough tools and get enough practice, so that when confronted with a question you will sense which tool works best for which question. Again, this will take practice!

Train Yourself To Be A Compass
Always Pointed Toward The Answer!

The LSAT is administered under very strict time constraints. Time slips by very quickly. There are approximately one hundred questions, each of which has five answer choices. This means that there is a total of approximately five hundred answer choices. It is impossible for anyone to deal with 500 answer choices during the limited time allotted. As a result, you must learn some basic principles to approach a question which will maximize your chances of identifying the answer quickly. Now, these basic principles must be principles that can never hurt but can only help. Some of these basic principles are discussed in the "Multiple Choice Mastery" chapter. At a minimum, for each question, your goal should be to eliminate three of the five answer choices.

The Importance Of Flexibility

I know that you are concerned about the LSAT. You should be. It will have a major impact on your chances of gaining admission to law school. Prospective test takers are always trying to find "one simple key" for finding the answers.

**Although there are "keys" for individual questions,
the same "key" will not work for every question!**

Be flexible. Think of your LSAT preparation period as a period in which you are going to enhance your awareness of the LSAT. Learn how it is constructed, why it must be constructed that way, and learn various principles of approach for every question type.

**It is important to be flexible!
If one approach doesn't work then try something else!
But, learn different ways of attacking each question type!**

The Importance Of Learning Principles Of Approach

A principle of approach is a method for finding the "best answer" to an LSAT question in a systematic way. It is a process which will work for most LSAT questions of that type.

**You will train by practicing generalized principles of approach
on LSAT questions in a consistent way!
Your job is to internalize these principles!**

The Importance Of Practice

Principles of approach should be practiced on actual LSAT questions. Make sure that you acquire all of the recent actual LSAT exams. They are available directly from Law Services or they may be available in your university or college bookstore.

What Skills Should You Master?

Follow this book. It will guide you through the mastery of the following essential skills:

- **Format Mastery**

- **Emotional Mastery**

- **Timing and Guessing Mastery**

- **Multiple Choice Mastery**

- **Conditional Statement Mastery**

- **Logical Reasoning Mastery**

- **Logic Games - Analytical Reasoning Mastery**

- **Reading Comprehension Mastery**

- **Writing Sample Mastery**

- **Practice Testing Mastery**

- **LSAT Training Period and Test Day Mastery**

- **Post-LSAT Mastery**

- **Application Process Mastery**

- **Career Choice Mastery**

- **Mastering The LSAT**

Let's begin.

Chapter One

Format Mastery

The Nuts and Bolts Of The LSAT - What Is It?

The letters **"L S A T"** stand for Law School Admission Test. The LSAT is required as part of the admissions process for almost all law schools in the United States and Canada.

When Can You Take The LSAT?

The LSAT is available to be taken four times a year. In general there will be a test in early October, early December, early February and mid June. Every administration except for the June administration is on Saturday mornings. The June administration is on a Monday afternoon. For Saturday Sabbath observers the October, December and February test dates are the Monday following the Saturday of the regular test date. Special arrangements can also be made for the physically challenged. See the **Law Services Information Book** for full details.

The form to register for the LSAT may be found in the **Law Services Information Book**. This book may be obtained free of charge from your local law school, career counseling center or from Law Services directly. You may write to Law Services and request one at:

Law School Admission Services
Box 2006
Newtown, PA 18940-0963
U.S.A.

(215) 968-1001
http://www.LSAC.org

They do not have a toll-free telephone line.

You must register to take the LSAT and there is a fee. To see how to register you should refer to the **Law Services Information Book**. At the present time there are three ways to register for the LSAT.

1. Regular Registration by Mail, Telephone or Online - approximately five weeks before the test date.

2. Late Registration by Mail - a "window period" that extends for approximately one week after the deadline for regular registration expires.

3. Late Registration by Telephone and Online - a "window period" that extends for approximately eleven days after the deadline for regular registration expires.

The most inexpensive way to take the LSAT is through "Regular Registration."

You will find that the LSAT is administered at most universities in the United States and Canada. It is up you to select the location at which you wish to take the test.

Warning!! It is very common for certain test centers to fill up. Hence, it is to your benefit to register as early as possible!

There are both Canadian and U.S. editions of the **Law Services Information Book**. Both have basic information about the LSAT. The Canadian edition also includes information on each of Canada's common law schools. Information on U.S. schools may be obtained in the **Official Guide To U.S. Law Schools** which is available from Law Services.

What Kind Of Test Is The LSAT?

The LSAT is a multiple choice test. It presently consists of five thirty-five minute sections and a separate writing sample section. Four of the five sections count towards your LSAT score. The remaining section is experimental. Its purpose is to allow the test designer (LSAC/LSAS) to try out questions for future use. The four sections that count are as follows:

1. **Reading Comprehension** - four passages - approximately 28 questions

2. **Logic Games** - four sets of conditions - approximately 24 questions

3. **Logical Reasoning** -   approximately 16 arguments and
                             approximately 24 questions

4. **Logical Reasoning** - same as number 3 above

The four sections are in no specific order. Different test takers will encounter the four sections in different orders. The experimental section will be a repeat of one of these four sections.

The writing sample is administered separately either before or after the main LSAT is over. It is a thirty minute exercise. A copy of the writing sample is sent along with your LSAT score to every school that receives a copy of your LSAT score. The writing sample is not graded and is placed in your file for possible consideration.

How Is The LSAT Used?

The LSAT score which is **based on the number of questions you answer correctly is reported on a scale of 120 - 180.** There is no penalty for guessing or putting the wrong answer. The LSAT is not a pass or fail exam. Your score is simply a reflection of how you perform relative to everybody else taking the test. Each school is free to decide how to use the LSAT and to decide what score will satisfy its admissions requirements.

How Many Times Can You Take The LSAT?

You may not take the LSAT more than three times in any two year period. You should, however, be aware that **some schools will take the average of your LSAT scores and some will take the highest. Clearly, the LSAT should never be taken for practice!**

What Does The Score Mean And What Is A Good Score?

Your scaled score from 120 - 180 is a reflection of how you performed relative to all test takers. You need not get all the questions right to get a score of 180. It is possible to get three or four questions wrong and still get a score of 180.

Your score report will also give the percentile ranking that your scaled score (120 - 180) is equivalent to. For example a score of 180 would mean that you scored better than 99.9% of all test takers.

When And How Do Law Schools Receive Your LSAT Score(s)?

Until you apply to a law school your LSAT score will be known only to you. After you submit your application to a law school, the school will request your score from Law Services. In the case of multiple LSAT scores, Law Services will report multiple scores. **The policy on the number of scores reported, changes from year to year.**

May I Take The LSAT and Not Receive the Score?

It is important for you to know that, **at the present time**, it is possible to take the LSAT and choose to not have the test scored. The information for when and how to cancel your score may be found in the **Law Services Information Book**. Please note that if you cancel your score, you will still have used one of your three attempts at the LSAT.

When To Take The LSAT

You should take the LSAT as early in the year as possible. By taking the LSAT earlier you will be leaving yourself an opportunity to take the test again (should that option be desirable). By doing the test in June or October you will be doing the test:

At a time when you will have the least pressure from other academic commitments.

Many schools require that the LSAT be taken no later than December. It is important that you check the requirements for every school that you are applying to! Even if it is an option don't leave your first LSAT attempt until the February administration. The first problem you will face is that your application will not be complete until the February LSAT scores are released. This will be sometime in March. The second reason for not doing the LSAT **for the first time** in February is emotional. While you are actually taking the LSAT it is important for you to know that you have another attempt at the test. If you take the LSAT in February it should be a "follow up attempt."

How To Prepare - Getting Organized

In addition to this book you should have the **Law Services Information Book**. Read it from cover to cover. It is also important that you obtain as many actual past exams as possible. Information about how to order them may be found in the **Law Services Information Book**. You may also wish to take a formal LSAT preparation course. Make sure that you investigate all options that may be available to you. They vary tremendously in quality.

LSAT Watch - Brave New World!!

It is likely that the current "paper and pencil" version of the LSAT will soon be a relic of the past. Computers have transformed our lives. The LSAT will soon be administered on computer in the form of a Computer Adaptive Test (CAT). Early indications suggest the following as possible changes:

- the LSAT CAT will contain both multiple choice and non-multiple choice question types;

- there will be entirely new question types including the possibility of a "listening comprehension" test.

The LSAT CAT will (at least initially) be less predictable and harder to prepare for. Tell your friends to take the LSAT now and avoid the new test format!

Chapter Two

Emotional Mastery

I have taught LSAT preparation courses since 1979. During that time period I have learned that Mastering The LSAT is about seventy percent "emotional mastery" and about thirty percent the mastery of specific principles of approach.

LSAT Reality - How To Think About The LSAT

The Only Thing You Have To Fear Is Fear Itself

The LSAT is a very important test. There is no test in your academic career that is as big a factor in determining whether you will be admitted to law school. So, there is reason for **concern** but there is no reason to experience incapacitating fear. People frequently fear what they do not know and do not understand.

I once heard it said that fear is : **F**alse
Evidence
Appearing
Real.

The key to conquering fear is understanding. Once you understand a bit of LSAT reality you will understand why the LSAT feels difficult for everyone, and why this feeling of difficulty should not be a particular concern for you. So, let's begin by exploring where the test comes from, its role in the admissions process, what the test measures, how it is constructed, and how it is scored.

Where Does The LSAT Come From?

The responsibility for the development and administration of the LSAT is that of Law Services. Law Services is based in Newtown, Pennsylvania. In the same way that Ford builds and markets cars, Law Services designs and markets the LSAT. In the same way Ford can stay in business only as long as it sells cars, Law Services can stay in business only as long as it sells the LSAT. To sell the LSAT, Law Services requires customers. By using the LSAT as part of their admissions criteria, the law schools have become the customers for the LSAT. Law school applicants pay for the law schools' decision to purchase the LSAT.

So Why Is The LSAT Part Of The Admissions Process?

There are two reasons.

First, the cost to apply to law school is very low relative to the time that it takes an admissions committee to review the file and the secretarial costs required to process the file from beginning to end. By using the LSAT the law schools have an excuse for spending less time on the rest of the applicant's file.

Second, the LSAT is the great equalizer. The debate can go on forever about which undergraduate school has the hardest grading standards and the most difficult courses. The debate can go on forever about which kind of undergraduate program is most challenging. But, the LSAT is an objective test. When interpreting an LSAT score an admissions committee need only understand that a higher number is greater than a lower number. The LSAT makes the evaluation of part of an applicant's file quite easy.

What Does The LSAT Measure?

Law Services and the law schools claim that one's LSAT score is indicative of one's ability to do law school work. Although it is likely that LSAT scores that are extremely high or extremely low are indicative of something, most LSAT scores are in the middle range, and are probably indicative of nothing.

The LSAT is not a measure of what kind of law student you will be. It is a measure of only your ability to do the LSAT! And to that I should add (since test takers' multiple scores fluctuate) that the LSAT is a measure of your ability to do the LSAT - **on that particular day.**

Therefore, you should proceed on the assumption that there is no merit in a high LSAT score (other than increasing your chances of getting into law school) and there is no shame in a low LSAT score. Aside from law admissions there is no market for people who score high on the LSAT.

Your LSAT Score - Reported On A Scale Of 120 - 180

Your score from 120 - 180 is a reflection of how you performed relative to all people taking the LSAT. The score corresponds to a percentile ranking. For example, a score of approximately 151 means that you scored in the 50th percentile. A score of 165 means that you scored in approximately the 95th percentile.

The Good News About Percentile Rankings

There is both good news and bad news about receiving a percentile ranking. First the good news. **There is a guarantee that each of you will score better than a lot of people taking the LSAT!**

The Bad News About Percentile Rankings

Now the bad news. **There is a guarantee that each of you will score worse than a lot of people taking the LSAT!** There is only one way to score worse than a lot of people. That is to get a reasonable number of wrong answers. Everybody gets a reasonable number of wrong answers. In fact, you should assume (on the current format of the LSAT) that it is possible to get 20 wrong answers and still come through with a very good score!

The fact that you are getting wrong answers will make you **feel bad! For all people, the "feel" of the LSAT is one of varying degrees of incompetence.** Therefore, you should not become discouraged if you are having difficulty and are behind schedule. This is normal!! It is how everybody experiences the LSAT.

The Character Of The LSAT

The LSAT has three principal characteristics.

1. The questions (given enough time, which you don't have) are answerable by anybody.

2. The test must be completely predictable.

3. Law Services will go out of its way to disguise the right answer.

Questions Must Be Answerable By Anybody (Given Enough Time)

The customers for the LSAT are the law schools. In the final analysis law schools must be accountable for the admissions criteria that they use. If they use a test that contains questions that are answerable by only a small number of people, the LSAT as a criterion for law admissions is sure to come under attack. Therefore, nearly every question on the LSAT must be answerable by almost anybody. The LSAT is made difficult by giving test takers a limited amount of time to do the test.

The Test Must Be Completely Predictable

The LSAT is administered four times a year. An admissions committee will base its admissions decisions on LSAT scores from LSATs written in June, October, December and February. No matter which of these four tests you take your score will be reported on a scale of 120 - 180. It is essential that a given score (for example 160) mean the same thing **irrespective of the test date.** This requirement can be satisfied if and only if each LSAT is designed to test the same things in the same ways. Hence, the passages, questions, and answer choices must be designed the same way for each test! LSAT questions are written to satisfy specific format and design requirements.

**Since the LSAT is very predictable
it is also highly susceptible to preparation!**

Law Services Must Disguise The Correct Answer

It is a hard job to design the LSAT. On the one hand every test must have exactly the same characteristics. On the other hand, every test must have different questions. Law Services must do its best to disguise the correct answer. After all, the integrity of the test requires that a large number of people get wrong answers. Law Services will disguise the answer in two ways.

First, by making other answer choices seem attractive.

Second, by making the right answer seem unattractive.

To put it simply, the test designer must design the test in order to:

Attract you to the answer if it is wrong; and

Repel you from the answer if it is right!

All LSAT wrong answers can be understood in terms of these principles!

Test Taker Reality - How To Think About "You"

The Necessity Of A Winning Attitude

Perhaps you have heard the saying:

"Your Attitude Determines Your Altitude!"

You need a positive attitude toward the LSAT. A positive attitude is a function of two things.

1. Confidence that you understand and can do most of the questions; and

2. A realistic emotional attitude and goal.

You Will Get Answers Wrong!

Everybody gets answers wrong on the LSAT. You will be one of them. In fact, for many LSATs, it is possible to get as many as twenty-five wrong answers and still score in the 80th percentile.

Be A Realist! Not A Perfectionist!

There can be few test takers who see the LSAT as a test that exists to help them get into law school. For most test takers, the LSAT is seen as a possible impediment to their law degree and to their plans to become a lawyer. With good reason, most people are concerned about their LSAT scores. People typically react to this concern in one of two ways depending on whether they are high achieving perfectionists or whether they are high achieving realists. The realist keeps things in perspective.

Profile Of A Perfectionist

The perfectionist will take the position that he or she **must** get close to a perfect LSAT score. The effect of this will be a heightened anxiety level which will get in the way of an optimal performance. Since everyone gets a number of questions wrong, and the person is a perfectionist, the person will **never feel ready to take the LSAT!** This lack of confidence will almost always result in a less than optimal score.

Profile Of A Realist

The realist is more practical and realizes that he or she is a human being, and that human beings will get answers wrong on the LSAT. As long as the realist knows that he or she is a human being then he or she is satisifed that wrong answers are a part of the test. The realist is not concerned with getting all the answers right. The realist is concerned only with getting an LSAT score that is high enough so that he or she will not be rejected on the basis of that LSAT score. This is a much more sane and workable attitude toward the LSAT.

Therefore, I suggest that you should be happy to:

**Get A High Enough LSAT Score So That You Won't Be Rejected
On The Basis Of That Score!!!**

How To Think About The Test Taker In Relation To The Test

Let's Establish A Workable Goal

A workable goal must be deeply rooted in the reality of the LSAT. It must reflect emotional considerations, multiple choice considerations, background skills considerations, and considerations specific to each section.

Your goal should be to:

Identify the best answer to as many questions as you can.

The key words are:

Identify - In multiple choice four of the five choices are wrong.

Best Answer - The directions tell us to select the "best answer."

As Many Questions As You Can - Many test takers do better by working fewer questions.

It is within the abilities of each and every one of you to achieve this goal. It doesn't mean that you will all achieve the same score. But, it does mean that you will be focusing on the right kinds of things and using your time productively.

A Few Emotionally Comforting Suggestions

1. Don't Listen To People Talk About Their LSAT Scores

There is a great deal of interest in other peoples's scores (to put it mildly). **The problem is that the only people who talk about their scores are those who do well. Their sole purpose in talking about their scores is to upset other students!** Have you ever heard someone walking around the campus talking about his or her low LSAT score? Therefore, whenever you hear someone talking about a high LSAT score either:

i) Ignore them; or

ii) Remember that for every person who scores high there is someone else who scores low!

2. Take The LSAT At An Optimal Time.

i) Take the LSAT at a time when conflicts with academic commitments are at a minimum.

ii) Take the LSAT at a time which will you allow you at least one more crack at it!

The best times to take the LSAT are in June or October.

3. Remember The Worst Thing That Can Happen

The worst thing that can happen is that you do not attain an LSAT score that is high enough and that you have to do the test again. Remember that you do not have to have the test scored. Under no circumstances should you view the LSAT as being a "one shot deal!" It will be comforting for you to remember this while you are actually taking the test.

4. Remember That It Is Possible To Cancel Your Score

Yes! You can go through the whole test and decide that you do not wish to have it scored. You will never know what the score is. There is a strict time limit on exercising this option.

5. Know That It Is Common For People To Retake The LSAT

Know that many people increase their scores by doing the LSAT a second time. You should however, try to make your first score a good score because many law schools will average multiple LSAT scores. Hence, the LSAT should never be done just for practice.

6. Know That It Is Possible To Improve Your LSAT Score

I have seen many people improve their LSAT scores. As you know small differences in LSAT scores can mean the difference between acceptance and rejection. For some LSATs as few as five additional right answers will **significantly increase your score!** If you do not score high enough the first time, make it your goal to improve the second time!

So Much For So Little

The following chart is based on the June 1993 LSAT. There were 101 questions on the test.

Minimum Correct Answers	Maximum Wrong Answers	Number Scaled Score	Percentile Ranking
99	2	180	99.9
94	7	175	99.6
89	12	170	98.3
81	20	165	93.8
73	28	160	83.7
64	37	155	66.7
57	41	151	50.3

Notice the following points :

1. You can get 20 wrong answers and score in the 93rd percentile.

2. The difference between the 66th and 83rd percentile is only 9 more right answers.

3. The difference between the 50th and 66th percentile is only 7 right answers.

Conclusion : Most test takers score well below the 93rd percentile. Below the 93rd percentile an extra 7 right answers will dramatically increase your percentile ranking. Through the right kind of preparation you will be able to get at least 7 additional right answers.

Chapter Three

Timing
And Guessing
Mastery

Timing Isn't Everything - It's The Only Thing!

If you ask anybody who has taken the LSAT why the test was difficult they will come back with the same answer.

Not enough time!!

The most important principle of the LSAT
is that you will always be behind schedule.
You will never have enough time!

The consequence of this disturbing fact is that you will be forced to select an answer to each question when you are not sure what the answer is! This is a rather technical way of saying that you will be guessing! Don't worry. That is just part of the reality of the test.

There is no penalty for putting the wrong answer on the test. Therefore,

Make sure that you have an answer filled in for every question!

You must concern yourself with the following issues:

1. Speed Versus Accuracy;

2. The Correct Order To Approach Different Parts Of The Test;

3. The Mechanics For Guessing When You Are Not Sure.

Speed Versus Accuracy

There is a difference between putting an answer to a question (which requires only that you fill it in) and "actively interacting" with a question (which means that you read the question and try to identify the answer to it). Although you will put an answer to each question you will not necessarily "actively interact" with every question. Your goal is to get the largest number of correct answers that you can. The faster one works the more mistakes a person will make. It is entirely possible that you will get a larger number of correct answers **if you actively interact with fewer questions or fewer sets of questions.**

Many test takers are able to raise their scores by "actively interacting" with fewer *questions* or *fewer sets of questions*.

Working With Fewer Questions

Every question on the LSAT counts the same as any other. There are few questions that can be defined as objectively hard or objectively easy. But, for each individual there will certainly be some questions that are harder then others.

Avoid the individual questions that are hard for you until you have done all the individual questions that are easy for you.

Many test takers are attracted to the hardest questions on the test. That kind of attraction is fatal. Learn to avoid questions that you find difficult. Never do anything hard when there is something easy to do. Let's put it this way.

1. All test takers will get answers wrong.

2. You are a test taker.

Therefore, you (Yes, even you) will get some answers wrong.

Avoid actively interacting with questions that are too hard for you.

Working With Fewer Sets Of Questions

It is possible to view each 35 minute section of the LSAT as consisting of four mini tests. For example:

1. In logic games there are four sets of conditions followed by questions. Each of these sets of conditions should be thought of as a mini test.

2. In reading comprehension there are four reading passages followed by questions. Each of these passages should be thought of as a mini test.

3. In logical reasoning there are four sets of six questions each. Each of these four sections should be thought of as a separate mini test. Although the test maker has not divided the section into four smaller mini tests, there is no reason why you cannot.

Let's look at it this way:

Logic Games	Set 1	Set 2	Set 3	Set 4	Total
Number of questions	6	6	6	6	24

Reading Comp	Passage 1	Passage 2	Passage 3	Passage 4	Total
Number of questions	7	7	7	7	28

Logical Reasoning 1	Group 1	Group 2	Group3	Group 4	Total
Number of questions	6	6	6	6	24

Logical Reasoning 2	Group 1	Group 2	Group 3	Group 4	Total
Number of questions	6	6	6	6	24

If for any of these sections you were to *actively interact* with all four mini tests you would spend approximately nine minutes on each one. On the other hand, you could actively interact with only three of the four mini tests and spend twelve minutes on each one. You would of course guess on the remaining section. (Assume there are six questions in one of the mini tests. If you were simply put all "B" the chances are that you would guess at least one of them right.) The point is that by spending twelve minutes on each of three mini tests you might very well get more right answers on the whole section than you would by spending nine minutes on each of four mini tests. Consider slowing down. Sometimes by slowing it down you will do a better job.

How Can You Know How Long To Spend On A Mini Test

Again, the issue is whether you will do better on the section as a whole by slowing down and "actively interacting" with fewer *questions* or *sets of questions*. This can be determined *only* by practicing with **actual recent LSAT exams**.

Why Actual Recent LSAT Exams?

Actual LSAT exams are written to a very specific formula. If you don't practice with **actual** recent exams you will be cheating yourself in two ways.

First : You will think that somebody else's imitation
of the LSAT is the real LSAT.

Second : You will never get a sense of the "true feel"
of the LSAT.

The Mechanics Of Time Allocation During Practice

Ideally your goal would be to be able to handle all four mini tests in the 35 minutes. With practice you will be able to gradually increase your speed. Here are two ways to determine whether you should do three or four mini tests.

Option 1

Begin by spending twelve minutes on each mini test in the following way:

1. Work for the first nine minutes. At the end of the nine minutes clearly indicate how far you have gotten and what answers you have selected.

2. Work for three more minutes. Your goal should be to see whether you are able to increase your score in that second three minutes. Some people can and some people can't. If you consistently find that the extra 3 minutes does not help you, then you should do all four mini tests spending nine minutes on each.

Option 2

Begin by spending twelve minutes on each mini test. Through practice you gradually work your way down to eleven minutes, ten minutes and finally to nine minutes.

How To Learn To Work Within The 35 Minute Time Frame

Although it is convenient to think of the LSAT as consisting of a series of 9 minute tests, it is in fact a series of 35 minute tests. After deciding how long you will spend on each mini set of logic games or reading comprehension you must practice doing the mini tests back to back. First do two mini tests together. Then do three mini tests together. If you have decided that you are going to do four mini tests in the 35 minutes, you should work your way up to doing four in the 35 minutes.

Warning!! What Your Goal Should Not Be!

You will **NEVER** feel comfortable with the time constraints of the LSAT. Remember, that is how the test designer makes the test hard. Feeling comfortable with the time is not a prerequisite for answer identification. So, practice until you are comfortable with the feeling of being uncomfortable (Yes, you can do that).

To put it simply, **you don't have to be comfortable with timing to be able to identify the answer.**

The Correct Order To Do Different Parts Of The Test

Time Isn't Everything - It's The Only Thing.

Once again, you will run out of time. You should not do the reading comprehension and logic games questions in the order that they appear on the test. Why not?

In reading comprehension each of the passages will be about different topics. Test takers are different and have different strengths and interests. You will do better on passages that are of greater interest to you.

Hence, take a quick "taste test." Number the passages in the order that you like them best. Then do them in that order. This will ensure that you run out of time when you are hitting the passage that you like the least.

The same principle applies to logic games. The four sets of conditions will not be of the same type. Through practice you will develop a feeling for the type of game that you like best and the type of game that you like least. There is no universally hard or universally easy kind of logic game.

Hence, take a quick "taste test." Number the sets of conditions in the order that you like them best. Then do them in that order. This will ensure that you run out of time when you are hitting the set of conditions that you like least.

Your strategy should be to put yourself under the most severe time pressure when you are hitting the questions that are most difficult for you.

In logical reasoning the questions are (for the most part) independent. You should be careful to not spend an undue amount of time on any one question.

A Comforting Piece Of Information

LSAT questions **do not** get progressively more difficult. When you encounter a question that you cannot do, simply keep going and find something that you can do.

Some Mechanics For Guessing When You Are Not Sure

You Need A Positive Attitude Toward Guessing.

Everybody guesses on the LSAT. If you are able to eliminate three of the five choices and get it down to a fifty-fifty guess, you are approaching the test properly. You should be happy and have **a positive attitude toward that guess.** I have never known a person who had a negative attitude toward guessing who scored well on the LSAT. Time is the currency of the LSAT. One can easily **spend far too long** analyzing which of the remaining two choices is better. Have you heard of **The Paralysis Of Analysis?**

I Have It Narrowed Down To A Fifty-Fifty Guess. Now What?

First : reread the question itself.
  Be clear on what you are being asked.

Second : read every word of each answer choice.
  Try to give meaning to each word.

Third : ask which of the two choices is **better.**

It's Better To Be Decisive Than To Be Right - The Paralysis Of Analysis

It is almost never appropriate to spend a lot of time deciding between two remaining choices. If you can't make a reasonable choice in a reasonable amount of time, cut your losses and guess. The realist will do this naturally. The perfectionist will have to learn to do this. Remember, be a realist.

Any "Active Interaction" Means You Put An Answer Then And There

One of the biggest mistakes made by test takers is that they begin a question, then stop working on it, thinking they will have time to return to it. This is almost always a mistake. Test takers rarely have time to return to questions that they miss.

Hence, it is vital that you always put an answer at the point of having had any exposure to the question. Don't leave it blank. At the end you will be forced to enter a "blind guess." You may actually guess something which you could have easily determined to be (or knew at the time) was wrong.

Use The Same Letter For All "Blind Guesses"

If you have not had time to look at a question, you must put an answer. For some people this will amount to a substantial number of questions. Use the same letter for all "blind guesses." For example, choose "C."

Is There A Letter Than Appears More Frequently Than Another?

What follows is an analysis of the eight disclosed tests from June 91 to June 93. The December 1992 LSAT was not disclosed. Here is a summary for the distribution of answers to all 808 questions.

A was the answer **142 times.**
B was the answer **161 times.**
C was the answer **168 times.**
D was the answer **174 times.**
E was the answer **163 times.**

Does that make the letter "D" the best blind guess? Not necessarily. On three of the eight tests, "D" was not the most prevalent answer. "A" appeared the least number of times. Should your blind guess be anything but "A?" Probably not. On four of eight tests the letter "A" did not appear as an answer choice the least number of times.

No reasonable inference can be made. For blind guesses, simply be consistent in your choice of letter.

It Is Rare For The Answer To Be The Same Letter Four Times In A Row.

For the eight disclosed tests from June 91 to June 93 (December 92 was not disclosed) there was only one instance of the same letter appearing as an answer choice as many as four times in a row. From this we may conclude that is rare for the answer to be the same letter four times in a row.

Transferring Your Answers In Groups - Is This A Timesaver?

Many books and prep courses offer the following piece of advice:

*First circle your answers in the test book and then transfer them
in groups to the answer sheet.*

For many people this is not good advice. What would you do if the time for the section had run out and you still had not filled in your answer sheet? I have seen this happen to a number of people. Don't be one of them.

**My advice to you is to fill in the answer sheet
at the time of doing the question.
This will ensure that you do have the answer sheet filled in.
You will have one less thing to worry about.**

Take Timing Issues Seriously From The Beginning.

Remember - Timing Isn't Everything, It's The Only Thing.

Summary

Begin by becoming familiar with the question types. It is then important that you time yourself from the beginning. You have to decide whether or not you will do better by "actively interacting" with fewer questions. For many test takers doing fewer questions results in a higher score.

Chapter Four

Multiple Choice Mastery

The Character Of Multiple Choice

Multiple Choice Is Your Friend - The General Model!

An LSAT multiple choice question consists of the following three parts.

1. A "Statement" which provides information for the question to refer to.

2. A "Question" which the test taker is to identify the best answer to.

3. The "Answer Choices" - one of which is to be identified as best.

Here is an example.

Statement

The director of personnel at Columbia Airlines is assigning five female flight attendants - F, G, H, I, and J - and five male flight attendants - P, Q, R, S, and T - to five sections of the plane. The five sections are adjacent to one another starting at the front of the plane and continuing to the rear, and are numbered in numerical order.

Exactly one female attendant and exactly one male attendant must be assigned to each of the five sections, subject to the following constraints:

G must be assigned to section two.

R must be assigned to section four.

I and S must be assigned to the same section.

F must be assigned to a section that is immediately adjacent to G's section.

H and P cannot be assigned to the same section.

Question

Which of the following is a complete and accurate list of the females who could be assigned to section five?

Answer Choices

(A) F, I
(B) F, J
(C) H, I
(D) F, H, I
(E) H, I, J

How Multiple Choice Differs From Non-Multiple Choice

Non-Multiple Choice - The Test Taker Makes Up The Answer

If a test is **not** multiple choice the onus is on the test taker to construct an answer. This is often difficult. The consequence is that the test taker must focus on the questions!

Multiple Choice - The Test Maker Designs The Answer Choices!

If a test is multiple choice the onus is on the test taker to *identify one of the answers already constructed by the test designer* as right!

The consequence is that the test taker must focus on the answer choices.

Many students taking the LSAT have had little experience with multiple choice. As a result, they tend to focus on the question and try to construct answer choices themselves. They then try to match their work with one of the available choices. **This is a huge mistake.**

You Can See The Answer - Look For It.

Multiple choice is unique. It is the only kind of test where the correct answer is right before your eyes. All you need to do is *identify that answer*. There is often a difference between *answer identification* and *answer understanding*. You will not get any extra credit for having any understanding of why that answer is correct or why it is the best. **In order to identify the answer you must look for it.**

What Should You Look For When You Look At The Answer Choices?

Your job is to identify one of the five answer choices. One of the five choices must qualify as being the "credited response." When you look at the answer choices you should both **look for what is right** and **look for what is clearly wrong**. Why look for what is wrong? By eliminating four of the five choices you will have identified the remaining choice as being correct.

The Power Of Elimination

It is easier to identify answers that are wrong than to identify answers that are right. Learn to be very aggressive in eliminating wrong answers.

Test takers who are not aggressive about eliminating wrong answers are failing to take full advantage of the multiple choice format. Notice that your focus should be on the answer choices and not on the questions.

The Terrible Consequences Of Not Focusing On The Answer Choices

Solve and Match - The Ultimate Quest For Enlightenment

The wrong way to approach multiple choice is to use what I call the "solve and match" method. It works like this. The test taker begins by reading the question. After having read the question the test taker starts to think about and to analyze the question without paying any attention to the answer choices. (Of course three of the five choices are so stupid that they are practically screaming out - don't choose me.) The test taker refuses to look at the answer choices until he or she has deduced an answer. Following that, the test taker tries to match the answer that he or she has deduced with one of the five choices. There is no answer choice that is remotely close to what the test taker has deduced as the answer. The "solve and match" approach results in three horrible things.

1. The test taker gets the answer wrong.

2. The test taker wastes a lot of time getting the answer wrong.

3. The test taker is not in a strong guessing position because he or she has not focused on the answer choices.

"Solve and match" is characterized by a focus on **understanding the question** rather than on the **identification of the answer. Always focus on the identification of the best answer.**

In Search Of The Answer - The Correct Approach.

In multiple choice your emphasis must be on the identification of the answer.

This is an easy statement to make, but a hard one to implement. It raises two questions. They are:

1. What is meant by the best or correct answer?

2. How do we go about the identification of the best answer?

The answers to these questions will be explored in the context of introducing some fundamental principles of multiple choice.

Unfortunately there is no one rule, procedure or process which will allow you to identify the answer quickly. Identification of the answer is a combination of a number of skills. Some of these skills are applicable to all questions and some are applicable to fewer questions. It is important that you be flexible in your approach. Nevertheless, there are some fundamental principles which **will never lead you astray.**

The Fifteen Basic Principles Of LSAT Multiple Choice

 Principle 1 : Make sure that you fill in an answer for every question.

Commentary - At the present time there is no penalty for selecting the wrong answer. Fill in an answer to every question.

 Principle 2 : Once you spend time on a question, select an answer before leaving it.

Commentary - It is usually easy to eliminate some answers as a result of spending any time on a question. Select one of the "possible answers" before moving on. You probably won't have time to return to the question. You will be forced to guess. It is possible that you could guess one of the answer choices that you had previously eliminated.

 Principle 3 : Never do a hard question if there is an easy question to do.

Commentary - LSAT questions are of varying degrees of difficulty. Some are hard and some are easy. Furthermore, the questions are not in any order of difficulty. Harder questions take up more of your time. Don't "rise to the challenge" of hard questions when there are easier questions to do.

 Principle 4 : If you are going to get an answer wrong, get it wrong fast.

Commentary - Your LSAT score is a reflection of how you perform relative to all test takers. You will do better than some and worse than some. You can only do worse than some test takers if you select wrong answers. Therefore, each of you will be selecting wrong answers. Do it quickly.

Principle 5 : LSAT directions instruct you to select the "best answer." Understand what "best answer" means for each question type.

Commentary - The directions to each section instruct the test taker to select the "best answer." Only in Analytical Reasoning (logic games) does "best answer" mean **objectively correct.**

In Analytical Reasoning you eliminate choices that are objectively incorrect.

In Logical Reasoning and Reading Comprehension, "best answer" means better than the other choices.

In Logical Reasoning and Reading Comprehension you eliminate choices that are "worse" in favor of those that are "better."

The "best answer" may be far from optimal. It will however, be the best provided.

 Principle 6 : Underline the "operative words" of each question.

Commentary - The "operative words" of the question define the conditions that the "best answer" will satisfy. The strength of every answer choice must be measured against the "operative words" of the question. Your job is to eliminate the choices that fail to meet the condition of the question, as defined by the "operative words."

What follows are some sample questions with the "operative words" italicized and underlined.

1. Which one of the following *conclusions is best supported* by the passage as a whole?

2. If all of the above statements are true, which one of the following *must also be true*?

3. Which of the following statements *would be inconsistent* with the advertisement above?

4. Which of the following if true would *increase the probability* of John's enjoying his new car?

5. Which one of the following arguments has a *logical flaw most similar to* the one in the passage above?

6. Which one of the following arguments *most closely parallels* the reasoning above?

7. Which one of the following, if true, *most seriously weakens* the author's argument?

8. If N is assigned to space 5, which of the following *can* be true?

9. Which one of the following would be the *most appropriate title* for the passage?

 Principle 7 : Always understand the relationship between the right and the wrong answers.

Commentary - Effective answer elimination requires that you understand the characteristics of both the right and the wrong answers. This relationship is defined by the "operative words" of the question.

What follows are some examples.

If the question asks for what **must** be true, the wrong answers fail to satisfy the requirement because they don't have to be true. This could be either because they could be false or because they are always false.

**You would eliminate the choices that
either could be false or are always false.**

If the question asks for what **could** be true, the wrong answers fail to satisfy the requirement because they could never be true. They must be false.

**You would eliminate the answers that could never be true
because they violate the conditions given.**

If the question asks for what **must be true except**, the wrong answers fail to satisfy the condition because they must be true.

You would eliminate everything that must be true.

If the question asks for what **could be true except**, the wrong answers fail to satisfy the condition because they could be true.

You would eliminate everything that could be true.

There are many other things that questions could ask. You must aggressively eliminate any answer choice that fails to satisfy the condition specified in the question.

 Principle 8 : Eliminate answer choices systematically.

Commentary - There are better and worse methods of eliminating answer choices. It would be dangerous to establish *hard and fast rules* for effective answer elimination. There are, however, some approaches that are *usually better than others*.

Exercise : Eliminate your way to the answer with the following general multiple choice question.

> P, Q, R, S, T, and U represent six consecutive positive integers, not necessarily in that order. If P is 2 more than Q, P is 3 less than T, and R is 2 less than S, which of the following is the correct ordering, from least to greatest, of the numbers?
>
> (A) PRQSUT
> (B) PRQTSU
> (C) QRPTSU
> (D) QRPSUT
> (E) QUPRST

The question includes three important conditions. They are:

1. P is 2 more than Q.

2. P is 3 less than T.

3. R is 2 less than S.

The Correct Method Of Elimination

Test takers typically approach this question in three different ways. Let's look at each one.

1.　　Solve And Match - The Worst Possible Approach

Under this scenario a test taker will ignore the answers, read the conditions in the question, then try to determine the order, and finally try to match the order determined with one of the five answer choices.

This is a recipe for disaster. Don't do it.

2.　　Analyzing From Answer Choice To Condition
Better (At Least There Is Focus On The Answer Choices)
But Still Not Good Enough.

Under this scenario a test taker is oriented towards seeing if an answer choice satisfies the conditions given (and is therefore the correct answer). The test taker will simply focus on an answer choice and see if it conflicts with any of the conditions in the question. If so, the test taker will eliminate it. If not the test taker will assume it is correct.

**This approach is still deficient because
you may well have to analyze each condition more than once.**

3.　　Analyzing From Condition To Answer Choice

Under this scenario the test taker is focused exclusively on elimination. Here is how it could work with the exercise on page 40.

1) Focus on the first condition - P is two more than Q.

　　Choices (A) and (B) are inconsistent with this. Hence, they are both
　　　wrong. *Notice how by doing just this one thing we have
　　　eliminated two answer choices.* We are left with choices
　　　(C), (D), and (E).

2) Focus on the second condition - P is three less than T.

　　Choice (C) is inconsistent with this condition. Hence, we are left
　　　with choices (D) and (E).

3) Focus on the third condition - R is two less than S.

Choice (E) is inconsistent with this condition. Hence, we eliminate (E) and are left with (D).

**Notice also how by doing one small thing at time
we are always able to eliminate at least one answer choice.**

 Principle 9 : Do one and only one thing at a time. Eliminate wrong answer choices after having "done that one thing."

Commentary - Your job is to quickly eliminate answers that are wrong. The result should be that you are either able to identify the correct answer or turn it into a fifty fifty guess. By doing one thing at a time you will be consistently moving yourself in the direction of the right answer.

 Principle 10 : Keep your eyes on the answer choices.

Commentary - None of the preceding principles will be of any help to you if you stray from the answer choices for too long. Many test takers "overwork the questions." (They find that they have gone much further than was required to identify the answer. Have you had this experience in logic games?) This is the result of not paying attention to the answer choices.

 Principle 11 : The content of the answer choices will allow you to determine what is relevant and what is not. Look to it for guidance.

Commentary - In the same way that you use a road map to find your way through a strange city, you use the contents of the answer choices to guide you to the best answer. Stay focused on the answer choices. When you look at the answer choices, ask how are they the same? How are they different? You must learn to take advantage of their differences to identify one as being better than the other.

Principle 12 : Learn to ask the right questions based on the content of the answer choices.

Commentary - You have limited time on the test. Hence, every thought that runs through your mind and every question you undertake to ask **must have a focus.** The questions you ask **must be based on the content of the answer choices.** Your job is to ask questions that will distinguish one choice from another. Hence, the questions you ask must be constructed on the basis of the differences among the answer choices.

The following two examples will illustrate the interaction of the first twelve principles.

Example 1   The director of personnel at Columbia Airlines is assigning five female flight attendants - F, G, H, I, and J - and five male flight attendants - P, Q, R, S, and T - to five sections of the plane. The five sections are adjacent to one another starting at the front of the plane and continuing to the rear, and are numbered in numerical order.

> Exactly one female attendant and exactly one male attendant must be assigned to each of the five sections, subject to the following constraints:
> G must be assigned to section two.
> R must be assigned to section four.
> I and S must be assigned to the same section.
> F must be assigned to a section that is immediately adjacent to G's section.
> H and P cannot be assigned to the same section.
>
> Which of the following is a complete and accurate list of the females who could be assigned to section five?
>
> (A)   F, I
> (B)   F, J
> (C)   H, I
> (D)   F, H, I
> (E)   H, I, J

The operative word is **could.**

Hence, we eliminate what could never be true.

Let's do one thing at a time. Since, F is beside G it follows that F must be assigned to section 1 or section 3. Hence, F cannot be assigned to section 5.

Eliminate (A), (B), and (D).

We keep our eyes on the remaining answer choices. They are (C) and (E). We also note how those answer choices are the same and how they are different.

Let's ask the right question. Choices (C) and (E) are the same in that they both include H and I. Hence, it would be a tremendous waste of time to consider whether H or I were possible. They obviously are.

Based on the difference between (C) and (E) the appropriate question to ask is:

"Could J be in section 5?"

Since, the answer is yes, the answer to the question is (E).

Example 2   Three women - Helen, June, and Sharon - and four men - Edward, Greg, Lance, and Richard - are eligible to serve on a three-member committee. No other people are eligible.

> June and Greg are the only people in the group who are related to each other.
> People who are related to each other cannot serve together.
> Richard cannot serve with any of the women.

> If Helen and Sharon have been appointed, which of the following is a complete and accurate list of those people who could possibly be selected as the third member?

> (A)   June
> (B)   June, Edward, Lance
> (C)   Edward, Greg, Lance
> (D)   June, Greg, Edward, Lance
> (E)   June, Greg, Edward, Lance, Richard

Let's keep our eyes on the answer choices. The sensible way to approach this question is by reading the answer choices and noting how they are the same and how they are different. For example, all of the choices except (C) have June.

Let's ask a focused question. It would be very focused to begin by asking whether June is a possibility for the third person. Helen, Sharon and June is a possible group of three. The question asks for a "complete and accurate" list. Since, June is not in choice (C), (C) is wrong.

But, we must keep our eyes on the remaining choices. Let's look again at (A), (B), (D), and (E). Note that it is only choice (E) that includes Richard.

Let's ask the right question. Ask, if Richard is possible. No. (Richard cannot serve with a woman.)

Remember we do one thing at time. Hence, we eliminate (E) and are now left with (A), (B), and (D).

Let's keep our eyes on the remaining answer choices. What do they have in common? How are they different? You will select one of (A), (B), or (D) based on a determination of whether Lance, Edward or Greg can be in the answer.

Let's ask a focused question again. On which of the three should you direct your attention? By looking at the answer choices you should realize that:

If Greg is in the answer then the answer must be (D).

(Only choice (D) includes Greg.)

If either Edward or Lance is not in the answer then the answer must be (A).

(Both choices (B) and (D) include Edward and Lance.)

Helen, Sharon and Greg is a possible group. Hence, Greg is in the answer and the answer is (D). Don't waste time considering whether Edward or Lance is possible. It is not necessary.

 Principle 13 : Think down. Look for the simple and obvious.

Commentary - Remember LSAT questions must be answerable by anybody. Don't complicate the questions by trying to do too much or asking how a genius would approach the questions. Simply, look for what is simple and basic. Ask what a person with a simple mind would realize was obvious.

EXERCISE :

What follows is an example of a set of questions that is easy if you look for what is simple and obvious, but is hard if you try to do too much. Begin by constructing a diagram in which you incorporate the "simple and obvious," one condition at a time. Spend nine minutes trying the questions. Then notice how the explanatory discussion highlights our general principles of approach.

5 Questions - 9 Minutes

1. Six people - H, I, J, K, L, and M - comprise two sets of triplets.

2. Four of the six are female and two are male.

3. Each set of triplets contains at least one male and one female.

4. None of the six can marry either a sibling or some one of the same sex.

5. H and K are married to each other.

6. I is L's only sister.

  1.   Who cannot be brother and sister?

      (A) H and L
      (B) J and M
      (C) K and L
      (D) K and M
      (E) L and M

  2.   M must be male if

      (A) H and L are siblings.
      (B) J and M are siblings.
      (C) K and L are siblings.
      (D) J is K's brother-in-law.
      (E) J is K's sister-in-law.

  3.   Which of the following statements must be false?

      (A) J is K's brother-in-law.
      (B) L is K's brother-in-law.
      (C) I is K's sister-in-law.
      (D) J is K's sister-in-law.
      (E) L is K's sister-in-law.

4. If L and M are married to each other, which of the following must be true?

    (A) J is a female.
    (B) M is a female.
    (C) H is a male.
    (D) I is a male.
    (E) K is a male.

5. If K and M are sisters, which of the following must be true?

    (A) H and J are siblings.
    (B) I and K are siblings.
    (C) H is a female.
    (D) J is a male.
    (E) L is a male.

Explanations And Discussion

Begin by reading the conditions. (I have numbered the conditions from 1 to 6 so that I may refer to them by number.) We are told that we are dealing with two sets of triplets. In order to visualize this you would want to begin to develop each of the two sets.

What is the most simple piece of information that would allow us to develop two sets of triplets? Let's look at conditions 4 and 6 together. We are told that siblings can't marry and that H and K are married. Therefore, one simple thing we know for sure is that **H and K are in different sets of triplets.**

Set 1	Set 2
H	K

The next piece of basic information we are given is that "I is L's only sister." A number of important things can be inferred.

First, we know that I and L are part of the same group of triplets. Therefore, I and L both are with H, or I and L are both with K. Look at the following picture.

Set 1	Set 2	Set 1	Set 2
H	K	H	K
I			I
L			L

Second, we know that if I is a sister then I is female. Let's add that it now.

Set 1	Set 2	Set 1	Set 2
H	K	H	K
I (F)			I (F)
L			L

Third, we know that I is L's *only sister*. This means that I cannot have another sister and that the third person paired with I and L must be male. Let's add this to our picture.

Set 1	Set 2	Set 1	Set 2
H (M)	K	H	K (M)
I (F)			I (F)
L			L

Fourth, we know that if H and K are married that they are of the opposite sex. Let's add this to our picture.

Set 1	Set 2	Set 1	Set 2
H (M)	K (F)	H (F)	K (M)
I (F)			I (F)
L			L

Fifth, we know that J and M will be in the same set of triplets and that they will be in the set where I and L are not. Let's add this in.

Set 1	Set 2	Set 1	Set 2
H (M)	K (F)	H (F)	K (M)
I (F)	J	J	I (F)
L	M	M	L

Sixth, conditions 2 and 3 tell us that there are four females and two males and that there is at least one male in each group. This means that in each set of triplets there are two females and one male. From this we can conclude that L is always female and that one of J or M is male and the other is female. We don't know which of J or M is male and which of J or M is female. Let's see what this looks like now.

Set 1	Set 2	Set 1	Set 2
H (M)	K (F)	H (F)	K (M)
I (F)	J	J	I (F)
L (F)	M	M	L (F)

One of J or M is male and the other is female.

Now that is an example of how by working with very simple pieces of information we were able to organize the information. It is simple if you take it obvious piece-of-information by obvious piece-of-information. It is very difficult if you try to do too much at once.

Let's try the questions using our basic rule of multiple choice.

Question 1 - The operative word is **cannot.**

We eliminate everybody who can be or are brother and sister

(A) H and L can. Eliminate. See the diagram on the left.
(B) J and M always are. Eliminate. See either diagram.
(C) K and L can. Eliminate. See the diagram on the right.
(D) K and M can. Eliminate. See the diagram on the left.

(E) is the answer. L and M cannot. The diagrams indicate they are in separate sets of triplets.

Question 2 - The operative word is **must.**

Eliminate any choice that does not have to be true.

(A) H and L can be siblings when M is a female. Eliminate. See the diagram on the left.
(B) J and M are always siblings. In neither diagram does M have to be male. See either diagram. Eliminate.
(C) K and L can be siblings when M is a female. See the diagram on the right. Eliminate.
(D) If J is K's brother-in-law then J is male and M is female. See the diagram on the right. Eliminate.

(E) This is correct. First because this is multiple choice and you have eliminated the other four choices. Second, because if J is K's sister-in-law then J must be female which would make M male.

Set 1	Set 2	Set 1	Set 2
H (M)	K (F)	H (F)	K (M)
I (F)	J	J	I (F)
L (F)	M	M	L (F)

Question 3 - The operative words are **must be false**.

We eliminate anything which either could be true or must be true.

> (A) It is possible for J to be K's brother-in-law. See the diagram on the right. Eliminate.
>
> (C) It is possible for I to be K's sister-in-law. See the diagram on the left. Eliminate.
>
> (D) It is possible for J to be K's sister-in-law. See the diagram on the right. Eliminate. (Note also that "J is K's sister-in-law" was the answer to the second question. The answer to the second question would have to be possible.)
>
> (E) It is possible for L to be K's sister-in-law. See the diagram on the left. Eliminate.

> **(B) This is the answer. It is not possible for L to be K's brother-in-law because L must be female.**

Question 4 - The operative words are **must be true**.

We will eliminate any choice that is either always false or could be false.

What does the fact that "L and M" are married to each other mean? Given that L is female, it means that M is male. This of course would mean that J would be female.

> (B) Eliminate. M is male.
>
> (C) Eliminate. It is possible that H could be female. See the diagram on the right.
>
> (D) Eliminate. I is always female.
>
> (E) Eliminate. It is possible that K could be female. See the diagram on the left.

> **(A) This is the answer. Take the money and run.**

Set 1	Set 2	Set 1	Set 2
H (M)	K (F)	H (F)	K (M)
I (F)	J	J	I (F)
L (F)	M	M	L (F)

Question 5 - The operative words are **must be true.**

We will eliminate anything that either could be false or is false.

What does the fact that "K and M" are sisters mean? First, it directs us to the diagram on the left where K and M are part of the same set of triplets. Also, if K and M are sisters it means that they are both female. Hence, J must be male.

- (A) Eliminate. We are working with the diagram on the left. H and J are not siblings on that diagram.
- (B) Eliminate. We are working with the diagram on the left. I and K are not siblings on that diagram.
- (C) Eliminate. We are working with the diagram on the left. H is not a female on that diagram.
- (E) Eliminate. We are working with the diagram on the left. L is not male in that diagram (or under any circumstances.)

(D)This is the answer. This is consistent with the diagram on the left.

 Principle 14 : Spend at least as much time looking at the answer choices as at the questions.

Commentary - The answer to a multiple choice test question does not necessarily mean the same thing as the answer to a question that is not multiple choice. If the question is not a multiple choice question the onus is on the test taker to construct his or her own answer. In multiple choice the onus is on the test taker **not to construct an answer** but to identify the answer already constructed that comes closest to satisfying the conditions specified in the question.

In multiple choice:

1. The test maker designs the answer choices *which may or many not be objectively correct*; and

2. It is the job of the test taker to *identify* which of the answer choices already designed *comes closest to satisfying the conditions specified in the question.* **Notice that it is the job of the test taker to focus on the answer choices.** Notice also that there is no requirement that any of the answer choices actually satisfy the condition required in the question. Test takers may be forced to select the best of a number of weak answers.

The most important thing to realize about the job of the test taker is that he or she is required to focus on the answer choices.

Principle 15 : Be flexible. Whatever works reasonably quickly is the right way to do the question.

Commentary - There is no one approach or method that will always work. When preparing for the LSAT strive to develop a number of ways of going about different questions. When you are confronted with the question simply try as many things as are necessary for identification of the answer. Through the conscious application of these principles of multiple choice you will develop the basic tools for Mastering The LSAT.

Remember the toolbox approach to LSAT preparation.

Multiple Option Mastery

Historically most LSAT questions have had "single option" answer choices. The following question is an example of a "single option" answer choice.

> If Tracy dances in the rumba studio, who must dance with Oren?
>
> (A) Roma
> (B) Sharon
> (C) Tracy
> (D) Ursula
> (E) Vera

A minority of LSAT questions have been of the "multiple option" variety. The following question is an example of a "multiple option" question.

> If Oren dances with Vera, where may Peter dance?
>
> I.   The waltz studio
> II. The cha-cha studio
> III. The tango studio
>
> (A) I only
> (B) II only
> (C) III only
> (D) I and II only
> (E) II and III only

At first blush this question type can look intimidating. Don't worry! The test designer has a great deal of difficulty in hiding the answer from those who have practiced the proper approach to them.

The Wrong Way To Approach This Question Type!

As always the worst approach is "solve and match." It is particularly destructive with "multiple option" question types. In other words, you should not, independently assess each of the options (I, II, and III) and then try to match your work with one of the available choices.

The Right Way To Approach This Question Type

As always, we will stay with our general principles of multiple choice. The general principles of multiple choice that are most applicable are:

Principle 8 :   Eliminate answer choices systematically.

Principle 9 :   Do one and only one thing at a time. Eliminate answers after having done that one thing.

Principle 10 : Keep your eyes on the answer choices.

Principle 11 : The content of the answer choices will allow you to determine what is relevant and what is not. Look to that content for guidance.

Principle 12 : Learn to ask the right questions based on the content of the answer choices.

Let's put these principles to work with the following exercise.

EXERCISE :

On a particular evening, four men—Mike, Ned, Oren, and Peter—and five women—Roma, Sharon, Tracy, Ursula, and Vera—will take a dance class at the same dance school. The dance school consists of five private studios. Each of the men must dance with one of the five women in one of the five private studios.

Each private studio can accommodate at most one couple.

Each private studio is used exclusively for one of the following dances: waltz, foxtrot, tango, cha-cha, rumba.

Ned will not dance with Roma, and Mike will not dance with Ursula.

Oren must dance with either Tracy or Vera.

Mike dances only in the rumba studio.

Ned must dance in the foxtrot studio, and Vera must dance in the waltz studio.

1. If Oren dances with Vera, where may Peter dance?

   I.   The waltz studio
   II. The cha-cha studio
   III. The tango studio

   (A) I only
   (B) II only
   (C) III only
   (D) I or II only
   (E) II or III only

2. If Ned dances with Sharon, with whom may Mike dance?

   I.   Roma
   II. Tracy
   III. Ursula
   IV. Vera

   (A) II only
   (B) I or II only
   (C) I or IV only
   (D) I, II, or IV only
   (E) I, II, III, or IV

3. If Tracy dances in the foxtrot studio, who may dance in the rumba studio?

   I.   Roma
   II. Sharon
   III. Ursula
   IV. Vera

   (A) I only
   (B) IV only
   (C) I or II only
   (D) II or IV only
   (E) I, II, or III only

ANSWERS AND ANALYSIS ON NEXT PAGES

Multiple choice principle 9 tells us that we must do one and only one thing at a time. But, where do we begin? With which Roman numeral do we begin? The answer is that we begin with the Roman numeral that is easiest for us to work with. The one that we are most certain is either in the answer or not in the answer.

> **Begin with the Roman numeral that you are most certain
> is in the answer or is not in the answer!**

Let's analyze these three questions.

A diagram will be useful in answering any of these questions. A preliminary diagram based only on the initial conditions would look like this.

	W	F	T	C	R
Men		N			M
Women	V				

This diagram can be used as the starting point for any of the three questions.

Question 1 - The operative word is "may." Eliminate studios where Peter may not dance.

The variable information (information supplied for use with this question only) is that Oren dances with Vera. The addition of the variable information looks like this.

	W	F	T	C	R
Men	O	N			M
Women	V				

Now, which of "I, II, or III" is easiest to work with?

It is clear that since Oren is dancing with Vera, the waltz studio is not available for Peter. It is easiest to know that "I" cannot be in the answer. Hence, we must eliminate choices (A) and (D). We are left with choices (B), (C) and (E). A look at the diagram reveals that the cha-cha studio is available to Peter. Hence, we know that "II" is in the answer. Eliminate (C). We are left with (B) and (E). The difference between (B) and (E) is that (E) includes "III." Hence, you must ask:

May Peter dance in the tango studio?

A look at the diagram reveals that the tango studio is available.

Hence, the answer is (E).

Question 2 - The operative word is "may." Eliminate any choice that includes people that Mike may not dance with.

The variable information (information supplied for use with this question only) is that Ned dances with Sharon. The addition of the variable information looks like this.

	W	F	T	C	R
Men		N			M
Women	V	S			

Which of Roman numerals "I, II, III, or IV" is easiest to work with?

A quick look at the diagram reveals that Vera can never dance with Mike. Hence, we eliminate any answer choice that has "IV" in it. Choices (C), (D), and (E) may be eliminated. We are left with (A) and (B). The only difference between (A) and (B) is that (B) includes "I."

Ask, may Roma dance with Mike?

A look at the diagram reveals that this is possible.

Hence, the answer is (B).

Question 3 - The operative word is "may." Eliminate any choice that includes people who may not dance in the rumba studio.

The variable information (information supplied for use with this question only) is that Tracy dances in the foxtrot studio. The fact that Tracy dances in the foxtrot studio means that Oren must dance in the waltz studio. (Remember that Oren must dance with either Vera or Tracy.) The addition of the variable information looks like this.

	W	F	T	C	R
Men	O	N			M
Women	V	T			

Which of Roman numerals "I, II, III, or IV" is easiest to work with?

A look at the diagram reveals that Vera can never dance in the rumba studio. Hence, we eliminate any choice with "IV" in it. (B) and (D) must be eliminated.

The conditions tell us that Mike will not dance with Ursula. Hence, we eliminate any choice with "III" in it. Hence, (E) must be eliminated. We are left with (A) and (C).

The only difference between (A) and (C) is that (C) includes "II."

Ask may Sharon dance in the rumba studio?

A glance at the diagram reveals that there is no reason why not.

Hence, the answer is C.

SUMMARY TEST - TOPICAL EXERCISE

Questions 1 - 6

Twelve politicians A, B, C, D, E, F, G, H, I, J, K, and L, are lined up waiting for government perks. They are lined up according to degree of dishonesty with the least dishonest politician on the left and the most dishonest politician on the right. The higher the "Dishonesty Quotient" (D.Q.) the greater the degree of dishonesty. The following information is known about the order in which the politicians are standing:

A is the least dishonest politician and E is the most dishonest politician.
Both I and L have D.Q.s of exactly 90 and both C and F have D.Q.s of exactly 110.
No other politician has the same D.Q. as any other politician.
J is more dishonest than D and less dishonest than I.
L is less dishonest than B and C.
D stands next to J and H.
B stands next to either C or F.
The positions are numbered 1 through 12, from left to right.

1. Which of the following politicians could stand next to A?

    I.   H
    II. J
    III. K

    (A) I only
    (B) II only
    (C) I and II only
    (D) I and III only
    (E) I, II, and III

2. Which of the following combinations depict possible occupants for positions 5, 6, 7, and 8, respectively?

    I.   L I C B
    II. L I G F
    III. I L K B

    (A) I only
    (B) II only
    (C) III only
    (D) I and II only
    (E) II and III only

3. If K were standing in position 2, in which of the following positions could L be standing?

    I.   7
    II. 8
    III. 9

    (A) I only
    (B) II only
    (C) I and II only
    (D) II and III only
    (E) I, II, and III

4. Which of the following orderings depict possible occupants for positions 9, 10, and 11, respectively?

    I.   C F B
    II. C B K
    III. F B C

    (A) I only
    (B) III only
    (C) I and II only
    (D) II and III only
    (E) I, II, and III

5. Which of the following orderings depict possible occupants for positions 7, 8, 9. 10, and 11, respectively?

    I.   B F C G K
    II. F B C G K
    III. I B C F K
    IV. I L G C F

    (A) I and II only
    (B) I and III only
    (C) II and IV only
    (D) III and IV only
    (E) I, III, and IV only

GO ON TO NEXT PAGE

6. If K is more dishonest than G and if D is in position
    4, who of the following CANNOT be in position 6?

    I. G
    II. I
    III. K
    IV. L

    (A) I only
    (B) III only
    (C) I and III only
    (D) II and IV only
    (E) II, III, and IV only

Answers And Commentary

This is a set of basic ordering questions. It is an excellent set of practice questions because each of the six questions is a multiple option question. Questions 1 to 4 give us three options and questions 5 and 6 give us four options.

Remember that we must distinguish between fixed information and variable information.

Fixed Information - This is the information that is either given in the initial conditions or is deducible from the initial conditions. In other words, unless otherwise stated, it applies to all six questions.

Variable Information - This is the information that is added to a specific question for the purpose of that question only. It is not to be carried to any other question.

Fixed Information

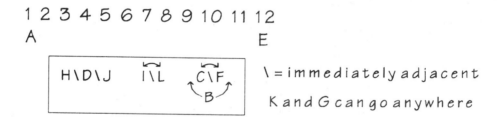

Remember that for these multiple option questions it is essential that you do one and only one thing at a time. Where should you begin? **Always begin with the Roman numeral that is the easiest for you to work with!** Keep your eyes on the answers.

1. The operative word is "could" stand next to A. A is on the far left.

First, J could never be next to A. This is because H and D are to the left of J. Hence, "II" is not in the answer. Eliminate (B), (C), and (E).

Second, we are left with (A) and (C). Since "I" is in each of these choices, the only issue is the possible inclusion of "III" in the answer. Can K stand next to A? There is no reason why not. Hence, the answer must contain both "I and III."

(D) is the correct answer.

2. The operative word is "possible."

First, "I" is not in the answer. Remember that C must be beside F. Hence, eliminate (A) and (D).

Second, "II" is possible and is in the answer. Eliminate (C).

1 2 3 4 5 6 7 8 9 10 11 12
A H D J L I G F C B K E

Hence, the possible answers are (B) and (E).

Third, is "III" possible? Yes. See the following diagram.

```
1  2  3  4  5  6  7  8  9  10  11  12
A  H  D  J  I  L  K  B  C  F   G   E
```

Hence, "II" and "III" are in the answer.

(E) is the correct answer.

3. The operative words are "could L be standing." We are told that K is in position 2. **What is the effect of the variable information?** Let's do one thing at a time.

First, could L be in 7? Yes. See the following diagram.

```
1  2  3  4  5  6  7  8  9  10  11  12
A  K  H  D  J  I  L  B  C  F       E
```

Since, "I" is in the answer, eliminate (B) and (D). The possible answers are (A), (C) and (E).

Second, could L be in 8? Yes. See the following diagram.

```
1  2  3  4  5  6  7  8  9  10  11  12
A           H  D  J  I  L  B  C   F   E
```

Since "I" and "II" are in the answer it is (C) or (E).

Third, could L be in 9? No. This would leave only two places for C, B, and F, and three places are required. See the following diagram.

```
1  2  3  4  5  6  7  8  9  10  11  12
A                       L       E
```

B, C, and F cannot
fit in two spaces

Hence, "III" is not in the answer.

(C) is the correct answer.

4. The operative word is "possible." Notice that there is no variable information.

First, "III" is not in the answer. C and F must be beside each other. See the fixed information diagram. Hence, we eliminate (B), (D), and (E). We are left with (A) and (C). Notice that each of (A) and (C) has "I" in it. Hence, we need only concern ourselves with the possible inclusion of "II."

Second, it is possible to put C, B, and K in positions 9, 10, and 11. See the following diagram.

```
1  2  3  4  5  6  7  8  9  10  11  12
A  G  H  D  J  I  L  F  C  B   K   E
```

(C) is the correct answer.

5. The operative word is "possible." Notice that there is no variable information.

First, "IV" is not in the answer. One cannot place I, L, G, C, and F in positions 7, 8, 9, 10, and 11. There is no space left for B. Remember: B must be beside either C or F. See the following diagram.

```
1 2 3 4 5 6 7 8 9 10 11 12
A           I L G C  F  E
           (no space left for B)
```

Since "IV" is not in the answer, we eliminate (C), (D), and (E).

We are left with (A) and (B). Each of (A) and (B) has "I." Don't worry about "I." At this point we need only check one of "II" or "III." If we check "II" and it is in the answer, then the answer is (A). If not, the answer is (B). Let's check "II." No, it violates the rule that C and F must be side by side. Hence, the answer must include both "I" and "III." **Notice that we know this without having specifically considered either of them.**

(B) is the correct answer.

6. The operative words are "CANNOT be in position 6." We are told that K is more dishonest than G and that D is in position 4. **What is the effect of this variable information?**

First, let's consider "I." Can G be in position 6? The answer is no. See the following diagram.

```
1 2 3 4 5 6 7 8 9 10 11 12
A   H D J G|_____|  E
         5 spaces for 6 people
         There is no room for K
           to the right of G
```

If G is in position 6 then spaces 7 - 11 must be taken up by I, L, B, C, and F. This would leave no room for K. Remember that K must be to the right of G.

Hence, "I" is in the answer. The only possible answers are (A) and (C).

The issue is whether "III" is in the answer. Can "K" be in position 6? The answer is yes. See the following diagram.

```
1 2 3 4 5 6 7 8 9 10 11 12
A G H D J K I L B C  F  E
```

Since "K" **can** be in position 6, "III" is **NOT** in the answer.

(A) is the correct answer. Notice that we are able to identify the answer without checking each of "I, II, III and IV!"

Chapter Five

Conditional Statement Mastery

Conditional statements permeate the LSAT. The correct application of conditional statements is tested directly in both logic games and logical reasoning. The incorrect applications of conditional statements appear as the **wrong answer choices** in both sections. To put it simply:

> **The understanding of conditional statements is the single most important background skill on the LSAT! Understanding conditional statements is a necessary but not a sufficient condition for a high LSAT score!**

So, let's begin with the basics.

What is a conditional statement?

A conditional statement is a *hypothetical statement*.

For example:

If a person suffers a stroke **then** he will die.

The statement is a hypothetical. It does not state that anybody has suffered a stroke. It should be interpreted to mean that:

Should it for some reason be determined that **a person suffers a stroke** then it would follow from that determination that **the person would die.**

A Bit Of Technical Language

The words "a person suffers a stroke" are called the **antecedent**. The words "he will die" are called the **consequent**.

Rule : A conditional statement asserts that the **antecedent** implies its **consequent**. It does **not** assert that the antecedent is true or that the consequent is true, but only that **if** the antecedent is true, **that then** the consequent is true.

How To Identify The Antecedent And The consequent

The antecedent implies the consequent. Therefore, it is essential that we are able to identify each of the antecedent and consequent. Here are two simple principles.

1. The antecedent is what always follows the "antecedent indicator."

2. The consequent is what always follows the "consequent indicator."

The LSAT is principally a test of language. Although the word "if" is an antecedent indicator, there are others. Although the word "then" is a consequent indicator, there are others. In addition, the consequent may appear before the antecedent or vice-versa. The order of the "if" and the "then" can be reversed. It is your job to discern the intended meaning from the language on the test! Avoid being overly mechanical. Meaning always is to be given a priority over form.

**In fact, not every use of the word "if" on the LSAT
implies a conditional statement!**

**The connective "If ... then" can be replaced
by a wide variety of antecedent and consequent indicators.**

What follows is a **partial** list of antecedent and consequent indicators.

Some Antecedent Indicators
- if
- when
- whenever
- in the event that
- in case
- provided that
- any

Some Consequent Indicators
- then
- the word "then" omitted
- it follows that
- entails
- results in
- is a condition for

Conditional Indicators In Action

EXERCISE : Rewrite the following conditionals in "If ... then" form.

1. The roads are wet if it is raining.

2. Any U.S. citizen has the right to enter the U.S.

3. Provided that Susan takes the LSAT, the
   admissions committee will consider her file.

4. In the event that I can rent a car, I can visit you
   this weekend.

5. Whenever the Detroit Pistons hold their
   opponents to under 100 points the Pistons win.

6. His having a good lawyer entails his acquittal.

What Inferences Are Valid From Conditional Statements?

The next section will include some technical language. **It is not necessary for you to know the technical language in order to take the LSAT. It is not even necessary for you to know the technical language in order to understand this next section.** What is necessary is that you understand the pattern of reasoning involved. I am using the technical language for the sole purpose of refreshing the memory of those who have studied these concepts in a formal setting. If you have never studied formal logic, simply pay attention to the patterns.

A. The Rule Of Modus Ponens

Premise 1. If Jack suffers a stroke then he will die.

Premise 2. Jack suffers a stroke.

Conclusion : Jack will die.

The general form of this rule is:

Premise 1. If A then B.

Premise 2. A

Conclusion : B.

EXERCISE : Try the following question in LSAT format.

7.   Frank is short, dark and ugly, but not gifted.
People who are short and ugly are popular.
Popular people either have money or are gifted.
Jane would like to meet anyone with money.

If the statements above are true, which of the following statements must also be true?

  I.   Frank is popular.
 II.   Frank has money.
III.   Frank is someone Jane would like to meet.

(A) I only
(B) II only
(C) III only
(D) I and II only
(E) I, II, and III

B. The Rule Of Modus Tollens

Premise 1. If Jack suffers a stroke then he will die.

Premise 2. Jack will not die.

Conclusion : Jack has not suffered a stroke.

The general form of this rule is:

Premise 1: If A then B.

Premise 2: Not B

Conclusion : Not A.

EXERCISE : Try the following two questions in LSAT format.

8. If Dave goes to Holland, then Sarah will go. If Tina goes to Holland, so will Mike. If Sarah does not go to Holland, Tina will go.

    If Sarah does not go to Holland, which of the following statements must be true?

    I. Dave goes to Holland.
    II. Mike goes to Holland.
    III. Tina goes to Holland.

    (A) I only
    (B) II only
    (C) III only
    (D) II and III only
    (E) I, II, and III

GO ON TO NEXT PAGE

9. Whenever the air is humid and the temperature is high, Dave takes a hay fever pill. Whenever the air is humid and the temperature is not high, Dave carries his hay fever pills with him. Some times the temperature is high when the air is not humid.

If the statements above are true, and it is true that Dave has NOT taken a hay fever pill, which of the following claims must be true?

(A) Dave is carrying his hay fever pills with him.
(B) The air is not humid.
(C) The air is not humid and the temperature is not high.
(D) The air is not humid and/or the temperature is not high.
(E) The air is humid and/or the temperature is not high.

C. The Rule Of Contraposition

The conditional statement:
> If it is raining then the roads are wet.

is logically equivalent to the statement:
> If the roads are not wet then it is not raining.

The general form of this rule is:
> If A then B

is logically equivalent to:
> If Not B then Not A.

➡ **EXERCISE** : Convert the following conditionals into their logical equivalents.

10. The car will run provided that there is gas in the tank.

11. They'll make it, provided that they don't get lost.

12. He could not read without his glasses on.

13. If the Smiths come to dinner, we won't have chicken.

14. If today is Thursday then tomorrow is payday.

D. How To Interpret The Words "Only If"

Warning!! Warning!! The word "only" has kept more people out of law school than any other word in the English language!!

Consider the following statement from a mythical law school's admission brochure.

"Only those students with a straight A average will be considered for admission to law school."

You will note that the statement cannot be interpreted to mean that anyone with a straight A average will be admitted, but rather that only those with straight A averages will be **considered** for admission. Hence, the above statement can be expressed in "If ... then" form in the following way:

If a person is considered for admission then that person has a straight A average.

The general form of the rule is:

Only if A then B

is logically equivalent to

If B then A.

EXERCISE : Rewrite the following statements in conventional "if ... then" format.

15. None but the brave will be awarded a medal.

16. Only Socialists are eligible for government employment.

17. The only time the Smiths serve wine is when guests come to dinner.

E. If and Only If - The Bi-Conditional

There are few bi-conditionals on the LSAT. We will consider them only for the purposes of completeness. Consider the following statement:

If and only if the landfill's capacity to hold liquids is exceeded will pollutants escape.

The effect of the words "If and only if" is that the above statement can be broken into two conventional conditional statements. They are:

1. If the landfill's capacity to hold liquids has been exceeded then pollutants will escape.

2. If pollutants escape then the landfill's capacity to hold liquids has been exceeded.

The general form of the rule is:

If and only if A then B

implies both

If A then B **and** If B then A.

➤ **EXERCISE :** Break each of the following bi-conditionals into two statements in conventional "if ... form."

18. Those and only those with a straight A average will be admitted to law school.

19. The Federal Court has exclusive jurisdiction over copyright cases.

20. A student may take the LSAT provided he has paid the appropriate fees and fee waivers are not possible.

F. The Hypothetical Syllogism - Multiple Conditional Statements

Consider the following two conditional statements.

1. If rent controls are enacted then builders won't construct rental property.

2. If builders won't construct rental property then there will be a shortage of rental property.

If it is determined that rent controls are enacted it follows from this that:

there will be a shortage of rental property.

The general form of the rule is:

If A then B.

If B then C.

Therefore, If A then C.

G. The Constructive Dilemma

Consider the following statements.

1. If I get good grades I will go to law school.

2. If I don't go to law school the government will employ me sorting mail.

3. Either I will get good grades or I won't go to law school.

On the basis of these three statements it may be concluded that:
either I will go to law school or I will sort mail for the government.

The general form of the rule is:

If A then B.

If C then D.

Either A or C.

Therefore, either B or D.

H. The Destructive Dilemma

Consider the following statements.

1. If Malone goes back to Philadelphia then the 76ers will win the championship.

2. If Winfield goes to the Blue Jays then the Blue Jays will win the championship.

3. Neither the 76ers nor the Blue Jays will win the championship.

On the basis of these statements it may be concluded that:
   Malone did not go to Philadelphia and Winfield did not go to the Blue Jays.

The general form of the rule is:

If A then B.

If C then D.

Neither B nor D.

Therefore, neither A nor C.

Two Inferences That Are Not Valid
But That Are Commonly (And Wrongly) Made

I. Denying The Antecedent

1. If Jack suffers a stroke then he will die.

2. Jack does not suffer a stroke.

On the basis of the above two statements, what if anything, may be concluded?

Wrong Conclusion : Jack will not die.

We know that **if** Jack suffers a stroke **then** he will die. But clearly it would be stupid to conclude that since he does not suffer a stroke that he will not die (and will live forever). THERE ARE MANY OTHER REASONS WHY HE COULD DIE! Statement one gives us ONE SPECIFIC INSTANCE IN WHICH JACK WILL DIE! IT DOES NOT SAY THIS IS THE ONLY INSTANCE IN WHICH JACK WILL DIE!

Therefore, on the basis of statements 1 and 2 nothing may be concluded.

Many people wrongfully conclude that since Jack has not suffered a stroke that Jack will not die. To mistakenly make this inference is to commit the fallacy of denying the antecedent.

To generalize, the conditional:

If A then B

does not imply

If Not A then Not B.

J. Affirming The Consequent

1. If Jack suffers a stroke then he will die.

2. Jack will die.

On the basis of the above two statements, what if anything may be concluded?

Wrong Conclusion : Jack will suffer a stroke.

We know that **if** Jack suffers a stroke **then** he will die. It would be stupid to conclude that just because Jack will die that he suffers a stroke. The statement provides ONE SPECIFIC INSTANCE IN WHICH JACK WILL DIE! IT DOES NOT SAY THAT THIS IS THE ONLY INSTANCE IN WHICH JACK WILL DIE.

Therefore, on the basis of statements 1 and 2, nothing may be concluded.

To mistakenly conclude that Jack has suffered a stroke is to commit the fallacy of "affirming the consequent."

To generalize, the conditional:

If A then B

does not imply

If B then A.

EXERCISE : An undergraduate student by the name of Quon is trying to decide whether to join a fraternity. What follows are conditionals and information. Your job is to:

First : Put the information in conditional statement form.

Second : Decide if the conditional statement and the information will allow you to answer the question of whether Quon will join the fraternity.

Third : In the event that you decide that you can answer the question of whether Quon joins the fraternity, then decide whether he will in fact join.

21. Quon will join a fraternity if they are democratic. They are democratic. Will Quon join?

22. Quon will join a fraternity only if they are democratic. They are democratic. Will Quon join?

23. Only if fraternities are democratic will Quon join. Fraternities are not democratic. Will Quon join?

GO ON TO NEXT PAGE

24. Which of the following arguments draws the most reliable inference?

  (A) All people who are good at math make good computer programmers. Dick is not good at math and consequently will not make a good computer programmer.
  (B) If Dave won the lottery then his wife would not divorce him. Dave's wife is not divorcing him; therefore Dave won the lottery.
  (C) All Democrats are in favor of subsidizing medicare. Jim is not a Democrat and is therefore not in favor of subsidizing medicare.
  (D) My stockbroker is either negligent or stupid. He is not stupid; therefore, he is negligent.
  (E) Any day that my housekeeper cleans, my kitchen shines. Since my kitchen is shining today, my housekeeper must have cleaned today.

25. When it snows the roads become slippery; but since it has not snowed for some weeks, the roads are not slippery.

Which of the following is logically most similar to the argument above?

  (A) When people are educated, they criticize their state owning corporations; but our state owns no corporations, so it must have no critics.
  (B) When a state owns corporations, it inevitably has critics; our state owns many corporations, so it has critics.
  (C) When people are educated they criticize their state owning corporations; but one can be critical of state ownership of corporations and not be educated.
  (D) When people are critical of their state owning corporations they are educated; but no one is criticizing our state owning corporations, so our state must have no educated persons.
  (E) If a state has critics, it must also own corporations; our state has critics so it must also own corporations.

A Bit More About LSAT Language!

K. Double Negatives

Double negatives appear on the LSAT. Hence, it is critical that you know exactly how to interpret them.

The statement "It is **not** the case that **not** proposition P," is equivalent to "proposition P."

For example the statement "There is not a single person in this room who does not intend to go to law school," is equivalent to the statement "Everybody in this room intends to go to law school."

EXERCISE : Rewrite the following statements to get rid of the double negative.

26.   There is no person who can't make his or her dreams come true.

27.   No person would refuse this job offer.

28.   There is not a single member of our club who does not drive a Jaguar.

L. The Word "Some" (Does Not Mean "Not All")

The word "some" has a very technical meaning in texts on formal logic and on the LSAT. Many students misinterpret the word. To put it simply, the word "some" means:

There is at least one that ....

As you know, "some applicants to law school are admitted to law school."

This statement simply means that there is **at least one** applicant who is accepted. In addition, the word "some" might include "all."

How Do Test Takers Misinterpret The Word "Some?"

Many students interpret the word "some" to mean **not all**. This is wrong for the following two reasons.

1. "Not all" might mean **none**! This is inconsistent with the definition of some which says that there is **at least one**.

2. "Not all" precludes **all**. Strictly speaking the word "some" might include **all**. For example, the statement "Some of you reading this book will be taking the LSAT" is a true statement. This is so even though it is probable that "All of you reading this book will actually be taking the LSAT."

Watch out! The word "some" should not be interpreted to mean that "Some will" and "Some won't." The word "some" might mean that "all will."

EXERCISE : Consider the following statement:

Some law students study contracts.

What follows are a number of possible inferences. Your job is to decide which of the inferences **must** follow from the statement, which ones **could** follow from the statement and which **could not** follow from the statement.

29.   No law student studies contracts.

30.   There are 100 law students. 70 do study contracts and 30 do not.

31.   Every law student studies contracts.

32.   Out of 100 law students most of them study contracts.

33.   Any student who studies contracts is a law student.

34.   Some people who study contracts are law students.

M. Categorical Syllogisms

You may have seen these questions before. They use "all" and "some" language. We have already explored the meaning of the word "some." The word "all" means each and every one. What inferences can be made? Consider the following statement:

All lawyers are corrupt.

If this statement were expressed in conditional statement form it would read:

If one is a lawyer then one is corrupt.

It would be wrong (remember the fallacy of affirming the consequent) to reason backwards **always** concluding that:

If one is corrupt then one is a lawyer.

There are many other groups of corrupt people that are not lawyers (for example politicians).

A Quick And Dirty Way To Diagram

Some As are Bs   A - - - - - - - -> B   (broken line)

All Bs are Cs   B ───────> C   (solid line)

What follows is a sample of what these two statements would look like in the form of a diagram.

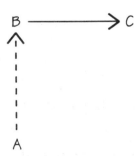

➡ **EXERCISE :** Each of the following statements relates to the above two statements. For each of the following statements decide whether it must follow from, could follow from, or could never follow from.

35. All Cs are Bs.

36. Some As are Cs.

37. Some Cs are As.

38. No As are Cs.

39. Some Bs are As.

40. All As are Cs.

41. All Cs are As.

Questions 42 and 43

All students are subsidized from public funds.
All people who get subsidies from public funds are public charges.
All people on welfare are public charges.
Most students are Democrats.
Some people who are permanently employed are students.
Some public charges are Democrats.
All Democrats are believers in subsidized medicare.

42. On the basis of the above information it must be concluded that:

   (A) Some people who are permanently employed are Democrats
   (B) Some Students are on welfare
   (C) Some permanently employed people are public charges
   (D) All believers in subsidized medicare are students
   (E) The class of persons who are students is identical to the class of persons on welfare.

43. On the basis of the above information it must be concluded that:

   (A) All people on welfare believe in subsidized medicare.
   (B) Some public charges believe in subsidized medicare.
   (C) All permanently employed people are public charges.
   (D) Some people who are permanently employed are on welfare.
   (E) All public charges are on welfare.

Questions 44 - 46

All A's are B's.
All C's are B's.
All B's are C's or A's, but not both.
Some B's are D's.
Not all D's are B's.
All E's are D's.

44. Which of the following must be inferred from the statements above?

   (A) Some D's are A's.
   (B) All E's are A's.
   (C) All E's are C's.
   (D) All E's are either A's or C's.
   (E) Some D's are either A's or   C's.

45. Which of the following is NOT possible, given the statements above?

   (A) Some E's that are A's are also C's.
   (B) Some B's that are C's are also E's.
   (C) Some B's that are E's are also A's.
   (D) Some D's are not C's.
   (E) Some E's are A's.

46. If an E is an A it must also be

   (A) a D only
   (B) a B only
   (C) a C only
   (D) a C and a B
   (E) a D and a B

Questions 47 and 48

All of those who voted to increase the offer, hoped that the offer, after being increased, would not be accepted.
Some of those who wanted the offer to be accepted abstained from voting on whether the offer should be increased.
None of those who voted against increasing the offer thought the offer would be accepted, whether increased or not.
Smith abstained from voting on whether the offer should be increased, and Jones voted against increasing the offer.

47. It can be inferred that Smith

   (A) wanted the offer to be accepted.
   (B) thought the offer would be accepted.
   (C) wanted the offer to be accepted, but thought that it would not be.
   (D) may have wanted the offer to be accepted.
   (E) could not have wanted the offer to be accepted.

48. It can be inferred that Jones thought which of the following would happen?

   I.   The offer would be increased.
   II. The offer would not be increased.
   III. The offer would be accepted.
   IV. The offer would not be accepted.

   (A) I only
   (B) II only
   (C) IV only
   (D) I and III only
   (E) II and IV only

N. Summary

This is an attempt to summarize our rules in the form of easy symbols. Although it is possible to answer many questions through the application of these mechanical rules, I urge you to try to **interpret the language.** Try to understand what the statements are intended to mean in everyday language. **The LSAT is first and foremost a test of language!**

A, if B = If B then A.

A, only if B = If A then B.

If A, B = If A then B.

Only if A, B = If B then A.

Not Not A = A.

If A then B = If not B then not A.

If and only if A then B = If A then B **and** If B then A.

SUMMARY TEST - TOPICAL EXERCISES

Premises :

Only dishonest people can be politicians.
No well read people are lovers of Shakespeare.
No well read people can be LSAT historians.
There are no dishonest people who are not lovers
  of Shakespeare.

Conclusion :

Therefore all politicians are LSAT historians.

49. Which one of the following cannot be inferred
    from the premises?

    (A) All politicians are dishonest people.
    (B) Politicians are not well read people.
    (C) People who are not well read are LSAT
        historians.
    (D) Lovers of Shakespeare are not well read
        people.
    (E) Dishonest people are lovers of Shakespeare.

GO ON TO THE NEXT PAGE

Conditional Statements As Logic Games

Game 1

Questions 50 - 56

Larry, Martha, Noreen, Oren, and Peter are eligible to run for political office, but none of them ever runs for office without being nominated.

A candidate must be nominated before he or she can run.
If Larry is nominated he will run.
If Martha is nominated she will run, but only if Peter also runs.
If Noreen is nominated, she will run, but only if Oren also runs.
If Oren is nominated he will run, but only if Larry does not run.
If Peter is nominated he will run, but only if Noreen does not run.

50. If Larry, Martha, Noreen, Oren, and Peter are all nominated, how many of them will run?

    (A) 1
    (B) 2
    (C) 3
    (D) 4
    (E) 5

51. If only Martha, Noreen, Oren, and Peter are nominated, how many of them will run?

    (A) 0
    (B) 1
    (C) 2
    (D) 3
    (E) 4

52. If only Larry, Noreen, Oren, and Peter are nominated, how many of them will run?

    (A) 0
    (B) 1
    (C) 2
    (D) 3
    (E) 4

53. If only Martha, Noreen, and Peter are nominated, which of them will run?

    I.   Martha
    II. Noreen
    III. Peter

    (A) I only
    (B) II only
    (C) III only
    (D) I and III only
    (E) I, II, and III

54. If only Larry, Martha, and Noreen are nominated, which of them will run?

    I.   Larry
    II. Martha
    III. Noreen

    (A) I only
    (B) II only
    (C) III only
    (D) I and II only
    (E) I and III only

55. Which one of the following pairs of people could NOT both run for political office?

    (A) Larry and Martha
    (B) Larry and Noreen
    (C) Larry and Peter
    (D) Martha and Peter
    (E) Noreen and Oren

56. In order for Martha and Oren to run for office, which of the following people would have to be nominated?

    (A) Larry, Martha, and Oren only
    (B) Martha, Noreen, and Oren only
    (C) Martha, Noreen, and Peter only
    (D) Martha, Oren, and Peter only
    (E) Martha and Oren only

GO ON TO THE NEXT PAGE

Conditional Statements As Logic Games

Game 2

Questions 57 - 61

Five coins from five countries are lying in a display case. Each of the five coins has the face of only a man or only a woman on one side, and only a lake or only a city on the reverse side. The coins are arranged in a row and are numbered one through five consecutively from left to right.

> Coin one has a side with a man showing.
> Coin two has a side with a woman showing.
> Coin three has a side with a lake showing.
> Coin four has a side with a city showing.

57. If coin five has a city showing and no coins with men on one side have lakes on the other side, which coins must be turned over to determine how many coins with women on one side there are?

   (A) Coin three only
   (B) Coin four only
   (C) Coins three and five only
   (D) Coins four and five only
   (E) Coins three, four, and five

58. If there are exactly two coins with a woman on one side and at least three coins with a city on one side, and if all the coins with a man on one side have the same thing on the other side, which of the following must be true?

   (A) Coin one has a lake on one side.
   (B) Coin three has a man on one side.
   (C) Coin five has a lake on one side.
   (D) Both coins one and two have a lake on one side or both coins one and two have a city on one side.
   (E) Coins four and five have a man on one side.

59. If coin five has a woman showing, and if all coins with a woman on one side have the same thing on the other side, which of the following must be true?

   (A) There are at least two coins with a man on one side.
   (B) There are at least two coins with a city on one side.
   (C) There are exactly three coins with a woman on one side.
   (D) Coin two has a city on one side.
   (E) Coin four has a woman on one side.

60. If all the coins with a man on one side have the same reverse side, and all the coins with a woman on one side have the same reverse side, which of the following can be true?

   I.   The reverse side of coin one has a lake, there are three coins with lakes, and coin five has a lake.
   II. Coin five has a lake and there are three coins with lakes.
   III. Coin five has a woman and there are three coins with cities.

   (A) I only
   (B) II only
   (C) III only
   (D) II and III only
   (E) I, II, and III

61. If exactly three coins have a lake on one side and exactly three coins have a man on one side, and if all coins with a man on one side have the same thing on the reverse side, all of the following must be true EXCEPT:

   (A) Coin three has a man on one side.
   (B) Coin five has a lake on one side.
   (C) Coin five has a woman on one side.
   (D) All of the coins with a city on one side have a woman on the other side.
   (E) All of the coins with a man on one side have a lake on the other side.

ANSWERS AND COMMENTARY ON NEXT PAGE

ANSWERS AND COMMENTARY

1. If it is raining then the roads are wet.

2. If U.S. citizen then right to enter the U.S.

3. If Susan takes the LSAT then the admissions committee will consider her file.

4. If I can rent a car then I can visit you this weekend.

5. If the Detroit Pistons hold their opponents under 100 points then they win.

6. If he has a good lawyer then he will be acquitted.

7. This is a multiple option question. Do one thing at a time.

   1.   We know that Frank is short and ugly. We also know that peole who are short and ugly are popular. **Therefore, we know that Frank is popular.** Hence, "I" is in the answer. Eliminate (B) and (C).
   2.   We know that Popular people either have money or are gifted. **The fact that Frank is not gifted means that he has money.** Hence, "II" is in the answer. Eliminate (A).
   3.   We are left with (D) and (E). The issue is "III." We have concluded that Frank has money. We are told that Jane would like to meet anyone with money. **Therefore, Frank is someone Jane would like to meet.**

   (E)   is the correct answer.

8. This is multiple option. Do one thing at a time. The question tells us that Sarah does not go to Holland.

   1.   Look at the first conditional. The fact that Sarah does not go to Holland means **Dave will not go.** Hence, "I" is not in the answer. Eliminate (A) and (E).
   2.   Look at the third conditional. If Sarah does not go to Holland then **Tina will go.** Hence, "III" is in the answer. Eliminate (B). We are left with (C) and (D).
   3.   Look at the second conditional. If Tina goes to Holland **Mike will go to Holland.** Hence, "II" is in the answer.

   (D)   is the correct answer.

9. The question tells us that Dave has NOT taken a hay fever pill. The first sentence in conditional statement form is as follows.

   If (the air is humid and the temperature is high) then Dave takes a hay fever pill.

   The fact that Dave has not taken a hay fever pill means that:

   It is not the case that both the air is humid and the temperature is high.

   In other words both of these things cannot be true together. There are three ways that these things cannot be true together.

1. The air is humid and the temperature is not high.
2. The air is not humid and the temperature is high.
3. The air is not humid and the temperature is not high.

The correct answer must capture all three of these possibilities.

(A) is wrong. This would follow from the second conditional if we were to establish that "the air is humid and the temperature is not high." We don't have these facts.
(B) is wrong. The air may or may not be humid.
(C) is wrong. The air may be humid or the temperature may be high.
(E) is wrong. The air might not be humid.

(D) is correct. It is the only choice that captures all of the above possibilities.

10. Conditional: If there is gas then the car will run.
Contrapositive: If the car does not run then there is no gas.

11. Conditional: If they don't get lost then they will make it.
Contrapositive: If they don't make it then they got lost.

12. Conditional: If no glasses then no read.
Contrapositive: If he can read then he has his glasses on.

13. Conditional: If the Smiths come to dinner then we won't have chicken.
Contrapositive: If we have chicken then the Smiths did not come to dinner.

14. Conditional: If today is Thursday then tomorrow is payday.
Contrapositive: If tomorrow is not payday then today is not Thursday.

15. If awarded a medal then brave.

16. If eligible for government employment then Socialist.

17. If the Smiths serve wine then guests have come to dinner.

18. If straight A average then admitted to law school.
    If admitted to law school then straight A average.

19. If copyright jurisdiction then Federal court.
    If Federal court then copyright jurisdiction.

20. If a student has paid the fees then the student may take the LSAT.
    If a student takes the LSAT then the student has paid the fees.

21. If a fraternity is democratic then Quon will join.

    The fact that they are democratic means that we can determine if Quon will join.
    (Modus ponens) Quon will join.

22. If Quon joins a fraternity then they are democratic.

    We know that the fraternity is democratic. No inference is possible. To make an inference is to commit the fallacy of affirming the consequent.

23. If Quon joins then the fraternity is democratic.

The fact that they are not democratic means that we can determine whether Quon will join. (Modus Tollens) Quon will not join.

24. This question provides a review of our basic patterns.

To commit the fallacy of denying the antecedent is to reason from:

If A then B to If not A then not B.

(A) is wrong. This is the fallacy of denying the antecedent.
(C) is wrong. This is the fallacy of denying the antecedent.

To commit the fallacy of affirming the consequent is to reason from:

If A then B to If B then A.

(B) is wrong. This is the fallacy of affirming the consequent.
(E) is wrong. This is the fallacy of affirming the consequent.

(D) is the correct answer.

25. This is a parallel reasoning question. The pattern of reasoning is the fallacy of denying the antecedent.

If A then B, therefore If not A then not B.

(A) is wrong.
(B) and (E) are both wrong. The reasoning pattern in both is:

If A then B, A, therefore B. (Modus Ponens)

(C) is wrong. It consists of two hypotheticals and no concrete facts.

(D) is correct. It is an example of denying the antecedent.

26. Anybody can make his or her dreams come true.

27. Anyone would accept this job offer.

28. All our club members drive Jaguars.

29. could not

30. could

31. could

32. could

33. could (if you make the assumption that all students are law students but otherwise could not).

34. must

35. could

36. must

37. must

38. could not

39. must

40. could

41. could

42. The operative words are "must be concluded." Generally students select either (A) or (C).

(A)   is wrong. It qualifies as a could follow from. Although we know that some permanently employed people are students and some students are democrats, we don't know if any of the students who are democrats include any of the students who are permanently employed.

(C)   is correct. All students are public charges. There is at least one permanently employed person who is a student. Hence, there is at least one permanently employed person, who by virtue of being a student is a public charge.

43. The operative words are "must be concluded."

(C)   is wrong. It could be true.
(A)   is wrong. It could be true.
(D)   is wrong. The reasoning involved in selecting (D) is equivalent to: Cats have fur. Dogs have fur. Hence, cats are dogs.
(E)   is wrong. It is affirming the consequent.

(B)   is correct. All Democrats believe in subsidized Medicare. Some public charges are democrats. Therefore, some public charges, by virtue of being democrats are believers in subsidized Medicare.

44. The operative words are "must be inferred."

(A)   is wrong. Some Ds are Bs. All Bs are Cs or As. But the Ds that are Bs could all be Cs.
(B)   is wrong. If any Ds go on to be As, we don't know that they include any of the Ds that are also Es.
(C)   is wrong. See the explanation for (B).
(D)   is wrong. See the explanation for (B).

(E)   is right. All Bs are As or Cs, and Some Ds are Bs. Hence, some Ds, because they are Bs, qualify as As or Cs.

45. The operative words are "not possible." Hence, we eliminate anything that is possible.

(B), (C), and (E) are wrong because they are possible. See the explanation for choice (B) of the previous question.

(D) is wrong because it is possible. A D can be a C by first being a B. Some Ds may not be Bs.

(A) is correct because it is not possible. The only way that an E can be an A, is if it is first a B. But, a B can't be both an A and a C. Therefore, an E that is an A can't also be a C.

46. The operative word is "must." We eliminate choices that must not be true. See the explanation for choice (A) of the previous question.

(E) is correct. The only way that an E can be an A is by first being both a D and a B.

47. The operative words are "can be inferred." We are given three conditionals. We know as a matter of fact that Smith abstained from voting and that Jones voted against increasing the offer. The second statement tells us what happens when one abstains. **Some who abstained wanted the offer to be accepted.** This is the only thing that can be inferred.

(A), (B), (C), and (E) are wrong because there is no basis for inferring any of these things one way or the other.

(D) is correct. The most we can responsibly infer is that Smith may or may not have wanted the offer to be accepted.

48. The operative words are "can be inferred." Jones voted against increasing the offer. The third conditional tells us what happens if one votes against increasing the offer. **Jones thought the offer would not be accepted whether increased or not.** This is multiple option. Do one thing at a time.

1. Jones thought the offer would not be accepted. "IV" is in the answer. Eliminate (A), (B), (D). This leaves (C) and (E).
2. The issue is whether "II" should be included. Did Jones "think the offer would not be increased?" Jones doesn't think anything about this one way or the other. Hence, "II" is not in the answer.

(C) is correct.

49. This question is an excellent review question. You are to identify the inference that cannot be inferred from the premises. Let's interpret each of the four statements. They should be interpreted as follows.

The statement: Only dishonest people can be politicians.
translates into
If politician then dishonest.

(pay attention to the word "only.")

The statement: No well read people can be lovers of Shakespeare.
translates into
If lover of Shakespeare then not well read.

The statement: No well read people can be LSAT historians.
translates into
If LSAT historian then not well read.

The statement: There are no dishonest people who are not lovers of Shakespeare.
translates into
If dishonest then lover of Shakespeare.

(play on double negatives)

Now let's put our translated statements into a more logical order.

1.   If politician then dishonest.
2.   If dishonest then loves Shakespeare.
3.   If loves Shakespeare then not well read.
4.   If LSAT historian then not well read.

(A)   is wrong. All politicians are dishonest.
(B)   is wrong. Politicians by virtue of being dishonest and loving Shakespeare
        are not well read.
(D)   is wrong. Lovers of Shakespeare are not well read.
(E)   is wrong. If dishonest then lover of Shakespeare.

**(C)   is correct. To infer that "People who are not well read are LSAT historians"
        is to affirm the consequent and is not a permissible inference.**

Questions 50 - 56

Preliminary Discussion - The conditions make it clear that there is a difference between
being nominated and determining whether the candidate actually runs. Let's number
the conditions from 1 to 6 as follows.

1. A candidate must be nominated before he or she can run.
2. If Larry is nominated he will run.
3. If Martha is nominated she will run, but only if Peter also runs.
4. If Noreen is nominated she will run, but only if Oren also runs.
5. If Oren is nominated he will run, but only if Larry does not run.
6. If Peter is nominated he will run, but only if Noreen does not run.

Conditions 2 to 6 are the rules that define whether a candidate runs if nominated. Most
of the questions will be explained with diagrams. Below each arrow is a notation.
For example: ②Y-4. This means that the person is considered as the second step of
our reasoning, that the person will be running and that this is determined by using
condition 4. For example:③N-5 means the following. The person is considered as
the third step of our reasoning. The person will not be running and this is determined
by the fifth condition.

50. See the following diagram.

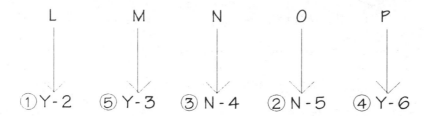

L   M   N   O   P

① Y-2   ⑤ Y-3   ③ N-4   ② N-5   ④ Y-6

(C)   is the correct answer.

51. See the following diagram.

M   N   O   P

④ N-3   ② Y-4   ① Y-5   ③ N-6

(C)   is the correct answer.

52. See the following diagram.

L   N   O   P

① Y-1   ③ N-4   ② N-5   ④ Y-6

(C)   is the correct answer.

53. This is multiple option. Do one thing at a time. See the following diagram.

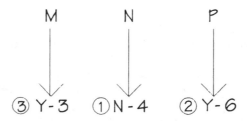

M   N   P

③ Y-3   ① N-4   ② Y-6

(D)   is the correct answer.

54. This is multiple option. Do one thing at a time. See the following diagram.

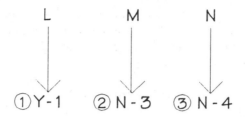

(A) **is the correct answer.**

55. The operative words are "could NOT both run." We must eliminate the pairs that could run for office together. Let's use the diagrams from our previous questions to identify the pairs that can run together.

(A) is wrong. Larry and Martha can run together. See our diagram for question 50.

(C) is wrong. Larry and Peter can run together. See our diagram for question 50.

(D) is wrong. See the diagram for question 50. Martha and Peter can run together.

(E) is wrong. Noreen and Oren can run together. See our diagram for question 51.

(B) **is the correct answer. Larry and Noreen cannot run together.**

56. See the following diagram.

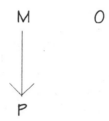

(D) **is the answer. Martha requires Peter. Oren does not require anybody else.**

Questions 57 - 61

Preliminary Discussion - This set of questions is good practice. In each case, the additional information provided in each question is in the form of a conditional statement. An analysis of the fixed conditions reveals that the following information is fixed for all questions.

Fixed Information

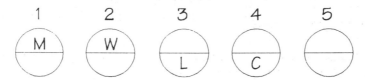

57. The statement "no coins with men on one side have lakes on the other side" means: **if man then city.** This means that coin 1 has a city and coin 3 has a woman.

   (D) is the answer. The diagram reveals that only coins 4 and 5 must be turned over.

58. The conditional is "If the coin has a man on one side then it has the same thing on the other side as all the other coins with men on one side." This statement coupled with the fact that there are exactly three coins with a man on one side and at least three coins with a city on one side means that: If a coin has a man on one side then it has a city on the other. **This does not mean that if it has a woman on one side then it has a lake on the other!** From this it follows that coins 4 and 5 have a man on one side and a city on the other. We do not know what is on each side of coin 2.

   (E) is the answer.

59. The conditional tells us, that if a coin has a woman on one side, on the other side it has the same thing as all the coins with a woman on one side. It is clear that not both of coins 3 and 4 can be women. **But they could both be men!** Therefore, there are either two or three men.

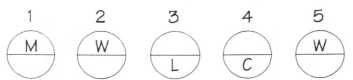

   (A) is the correct answer.

60. The operative word is "can." This is multiple option. Do one thing at a time. Let's look at "I." This scenario is entirely possible. See the following diagram.

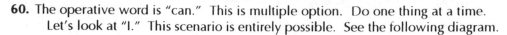

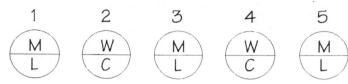

Eliminate (B), (C), and (D). We are left with (A) and (E). Let's look at "II." You will note that it is drawn in the above diagram. Therefore, "II" is in the answer as well.

(E) **is the correct answer. Once we see that the answer includes both "I and II" we know that the answer must be (E). It is the only choice that includes both "I and II." Furthermore, we need not concern ourselves with "III."**

61. The operative words are "must be true EXCEPT." We must eliminate anything that must be true. Notice that the information in the question is descriptive of the diagram we developed for question 60. Rather than draw a new diagram, let's use the diagram that we have already drawn.

(A), (B), (D), and (E) all can be eliminated. They are consistent with the diagram for question 60.

(C) **is the answer. It is the only choice that is inconsistent with the diagram for question 60.**

Chapter Six

Logical Reasoning Mastery

Format

Currently there are two 35 minute sections. Each section has approximately twenty-four questions. You should think of each section as containing either four 9 minute tests or three 12 minute tests. Each of the mini tests should be thought of as containing six questions.

If you choose to do three of the four tests,
leave out any six questions along the way!

Think of each logical reasoning section as being a series of four tests!

Timing Considerations

The issue is speed versus accuracy. Once again, the issue is whether you should answer three of the tests spending 12 minutes on each, or four of the tests spending 9 minutes on each. This should be determined by your performance on actual tests.

Directions

Directions: "The questions in this section are based on the reasoning contained in brief statements or passages. For some questions, more than one of the choices could conceivably answer the question. However, you are to choose the **best answer**; that is, the response that most accurately and completely answers the question. You should not make assumptions that are by commonsense standards implausible, superfluous, or incompatible with the passage. After you have chosen the best answer, blacken the corresponding space on your sheet."

A Sample Question

The Statement

A comparison of the salary structures of the state police force and the municipal police force indicates that municipal policemen are well below state policemen in pay. It would take immediate pay increases of $7.0 million in order to re-establish the relative positions that existed in 1975 between state policemen's and municipal policemen's power to purchase goods and services.

The Question With The
Operative Words In Italics

1. Which of the following can *most reliably be inferred* from the passage above?

The Answer Choices

(A) Since 1975 the municipal police force has reduced the number of policemen on its payroll.

(B) A $7.0 million increase in pay to municipal policemen would bring about equality of earnings between municipal and state policemen for comparable jobs.

(C) The total number of dollars spent by municipal policemen on goods and services has decreased annually since 1975.

(D) Municipal police forces are risking the loss to the state police force of policemen who are seeking higher pay.

(E) Pay increases to teachers during the last half of the 1970s have absorbed funds once available for municipal policemen.

What Does The Test Maker Say This Section Is About?

According to Law Services, logical reasoning questions test:

"... a variety of abilities involved in reasoning logically and critically."

Examples include:

■ recognizing the point or issue in an argument or dispute;

■ the identification of assumptions involved in an argument;

■ drawing reasonable conclusions from evidence;

■ the identification and application of principles;

■ the detection of reasoning errors and misinterpretations;

■ determining the impact of additional evidence on an argument;

■ the identification of explanations of conflicting arguments;

■ the recognition of resolutions to conflicts.

What Is This Section Testing?

The description of this section in the **Law School Admission Information Book** indicates that the "questions sample a variety of abilities which might appropriately be described as subtypes of the ability to reason logically and reason critically." In other words, this section is to test your ability to **analyze arguments**.

What The Section Will Require The Test Taker To Do

For the most part, the Logical Reasoning Sections will require the test taker to:

1. Identify the conclusion of an argument.

2. Identify a supporting premise of an argument.

3. Identify a missing premise of an argument.

4. Identify what may follow from an argument.

5. Identify what must follow from an argument.

6. Identify the logical structure of an argument.

7. Identify what best objectively describes the argument.

8. Assess the reasonableness of an argument.

Obscuring The Answer.
How The Test Maker Accomplishes It

It is your job to identify the best answer and it is the job of Law Services to hide the answer. Since the LSAT is a predictable test, Law Services will attempt to obscure the "best answer" in predictable ways. Here are **some of the most common ways.**

Obscuring The Answer By Focusing On Elements Of The Statements

Law Services will "pad" the statement with irrelevant information!

1. Law Services will try to get you to confuse the premise with the conclusion.

2. Law Services will invite you to confuse irrelevant information with a premise.

3. Law Services will invite you to focus on one or more facts that are irrelevant to the argument.

Obscuring The Answer By Focusing On The Answer Choices

Law Services will attempt to attract you to the answer if it is wrong and repel you from the answer if it is right!

4. Law Services will invite you to focus on information that is a true statement but is irrelevant to what is being asked.

5. Law Services will invite you to focus on "value judgments" that are outside the internal structure of the argument.

6. Law Services will invite you to select an answer choice before having read every word of that choice.

7. Law Services will attract you to answer choices that are the opposite of the "best answer choice."

8. Law Services will include "provocative language" in the answer choices. Examples are words like "all," "some," "requires," "sufficient," etc.

Ten General Principles Of Approach For Logical Reasoning

 Principle 1 : There may not be an argument at all!

Commentary - Many people refer to this section as "arguments." Although there are many questions that do deal with arguments, there are some which do not. For example, conditional statement questions are not arguments. Therefore:

If you are having difficulty identifying an argument in one of the questions you may be right. There may not be an argument at all.

 Principle 2 : Don't waste your time looking for "trick questions."

Commentary - LSAT questions do not involve hidden tricks or meanings. Therefore:

Simply read the statement, passage, or argument the way you would read the morning paper.

Principle 3 :   Operative words aren't everything - they're the only thing!

Commentary - The "operative words" of the question define the part of
the "statement" that is relevant. They also define the
relationship between the "best" and "not best" answers.

The point is that you must pay attention to the question asked!

As a reinforcement exercise I have italicized the "operative words" in
each of the following questions.

1.   Which of the following *most closely parallels*
     the kind of reasoning used in the argument
     above?

2.   The author's *method of reasoning* may be best
     described as

3.   Which of the following, if true, would *most
     weaken* the argument above?

4.   All of the following would be an *appropriate
     attack* on the above argument *except*

5.   The author's conclusion logically depends on
     the *assumption* that

6.   The above argument would be *most effectively
     used as*

7.   Which of the following is the most reasonable
     inference that can be drawn from the above
     argument?

8.   Which of the following is *logically deducible
     from* the above argument?

9.   It may be *validly inferred from* the above
     argument that

The following question is a dramatic example of what happens if you
fail to pay attention to the operative words. (Please note that this particular
question format has not been on the test since the early 1980s.)

10. Judging from the tenor of the following
     statements and the apparent authoritativeness
     of their sources, which is the most reasonable
     and trustworthy?

     (A) Meteorologist: A ferocious hurricane
          which will destroy all of the world is
          presently over the Gulf of Mexico.

> (B) English teacher: My daughter has failed
> her last five English courses, but she is
> really a good student of English.
> (C) Life-long smoker: I know that my smoking
> is the reason why I have managed to
> keep my weight down. I will never quit
> smoking.
> (D) Small aircraft salesman to customer: Small
> airplanes are safer than cars. There are
> fewer accidents per thousand miles
> flown than per thousand miles driven.
> (E) Law Professor: In my judgment Buddha
> was a wiser man than Christ.

Many test takers answer the question as though it read:

Which statement is most reasonable and trustworthy?

That is simply not what the question asks. Rather, the question asks the test taker to identify what is **most** reasonable and trustworthy in terms of two specific criteria. They are:

1. Tenor - Is there bias? Is there a lack of objectivity?

2. Apparent Authoritativeness - Is it apparent by virtue of the person's title that he or she would know what he or she is talking about?

Let's start our analysis from the bottom up.

(E) Fails because of no apparent authoritativeness. Although it is possible that a law professor might know about religion, it is not apparent by virtue of his title.

(D) Fails because of a tenor problem. The salesman is speaking to his or her customer! (Do you believe everything, or for that matter anything, a salesman tells you?)

(C) This is a weak answer for two reasons. The first is a lack of apparent authoritativeness. There is nothing about smoking that qualifies one to talk about the effects of smoking on weight. The second is a tenor problem. It sounds as though he or she is trying to justify his or her bad habits.

(B) This is a weak answer. There is no apparent authoritativeness problem. A parent talking about a daughter does give rise to a tenor (bias) problem.

(A) is the answer. Yes, it is a very stupid statement. But we do have a meteorologist talking about weather. So, there is no apparent authoritativeness problem. In addition, there is no evidence of bias or any other kind of tenor problem.

 Principle 4 : Therefore, begin by reading the question and underlining the operative words!

Commentary - Remember the last question.

 Principle 5 : The fact that an answer is "best" doesn't make it right!

Commentary - In this section, "best answer" simply means better than the other answer choices. For the most part "best answers" will not be objectively correct. Therefore:

When you read answer choices think in terms of one answer being better than another. Don't think in terms of one answer being correct and another being incorrect.

You may end up selecting the best of a number of bad answers!

 Principle 6 : Therefore, use the approach of comparing and contrasting answer choices!

Commentary - Never ask if an answer choice is correct. Ask only, how it compares to the other choices. You should not analyze an answer choice on a non-comparative basis unless you are required to do so. The problem with analyzing an answer choice by itself is that you may be ambivalent with respect to whether it is the answer. Let's look at the following example which illustrates the interaction of principles 5 and 6.

1. A comparison of the salary structures of the state police force and the municipal police force indicates that municipal policemen are well below state policemen in pay. It would take immediate pay increases of $7.0 million in order to re-establish the relative positions that existed in 1975 between state policemen's and municipal policemen's power to purchase goods and services.

Which of the following can most reliably be inferred from the passage above?

(A) Since 1975 the municipal police force has reduced the number of policemen on its payroll.

(B) A $7.0 million increase in pay to municipal policemen would bring about equality of earnings between municipal and state policemen for comparable jobs.

(C) The total number of dollars spent by municipal policemen on goods and services has decreased annually since 1975.

(D) Municipal police forces are risking the loss to the state police force of policemen who are seeking higher pay.

(E) Pay increases to teachers during the last half of the 1970s have absorbed funds once available for municipal policemen.

The question asks you to identify which of the five choices **can most reliably be inferred**. Note that there is no requirement that any choice **must** follow from the passage. Let's consider the extent to which each choice is a reliable inference.

(A) There is no basis for inferring that the municipal police force has reduced the number of people on it's payroll.

(B) This choice says that the increase would bring about **equality** of earnings. This would require the assumption that the municipal and state police were in a position of equality in 1975. **This is a very weak assumption. In fact by using the words "relative positions" in the passage, the opposite is implied.**

(C) This could not possibly be an inference. It would require the assumption that municipal policemen were actually getting a decrease in pay. That would be a very unreasonable assumption.

(D) This is a reasonable inference. It is based on the perfectly reasonable assumption that **all other things being equal - people would rather be where the money is.**

(E) This choice talks about "teachers." It is irrelevant and is not the answer.

(D) is the best choice and is therefore the answer. It is the only one that is possible and is not based on an unreasonable assumption. But, note that it is not a particularly reliable inference. It is not a strong answer. This question is a good example of how you must sometimes choose the best of a number of weak answers.

Principle 7 : Read every word of every choice!

Commentary - Answer choices consist of single words, phrases, or sentences. The phrases and sentences can involve compound thoughts. Be on the lookout for words that indicate compound thoughts. The complete sentence or phrase must qualify as an answer.

Consider the following two answer choices in which the word that indicates the "compound thought" has been italicized.

> "The threat of local extinction imposes no obligation to try to prevent that extinction, *whereas* the threat of global extinction does impose such an obligation."

If this choice qualifies as an answer then it must be true that:

1. The threat of local extinction must impose no obligation to try to prevent that extinction: and

2. The threat of global extinction must impose such an obligation.

> "They considered porpoise teeth to be valuable, *and* these were generally threaded on strings to be worn as jewellery."

If this choice qualifies as an answer then it must be true that:

1. Porpoise teeth must be considered to be valuable; and

2. They were generally threaded as jewellery.

 Principle 8 : Be on the lookout for "restrictive language" in the answer choices.

What follows are some answer choices. The "restrictive word" in each of the choices has been italicized.

> (A) It *requires* confirmation that the change is representative of the change of students in general.

> (B) It offers *no* proof to the effect that the teacher is an accurate judge of math ability.

(C) From what has happened in the past, it is
     impossible to infer with certainty that ...

(D) The *only* sufficient justification for
     experimenting is that ...

(E) *All* people who want decent jobs go to
     high school.

(F) Good jobs are obtained *only* by people
     who have gone to technical school.

Commentary - The fact that "restrictive language" is in an answer choice
            does not guarantee that the answer choice is wrong. It
            does mean that you should pay attention to that word and
            decide what impact it has on the possible correctness of
            the choice.

 Principle 9 : There is a consistent vocabulary to logical reasoning.

Commentary - This follows from the fact that LSAT exams must be consistent
            from test to test. What follows are **some** words and phrases
            that have repeated themselves, year after year, on test after
            test. A failure to understand this vocabulary will mean a
            failure to understand the answer choice in which it appears.

How To Read Answer Choices - The Essential Vocabulary

Many test takers have difficulty eliminating answer choices because of
a lack of sensitivity to the meaning of the language in those choices. What
follows is the essential vocabulary of answer choices.

1. Analogy

Reasoning by analogy is a form of reasoning in which similarities between things are inferred from a similarity of those things in certain par-
ticulars. Remember, to reason by analogy is to reason from characteristics
about one specific thing to characteristics about another specific thing. **It
is not to reason from specific to general!** The following are examples of
the language used when Law Services constructs answer choices.

■ arguing by analogy

■ based on a dubious analogy

2. Generalization

To generalize is to infer a general principle from specific facts. Remember that it is reasoning from a statement about a specific thing to a statement about a group. The following are examples of the language used when Law Services constructs answer choices.

■ generalizing from a specific instance

■ draws a general conclusion on the basis of evidence of a particular instance

■ supports the conclusion by overgeneralizing from a piece of evidence

■ discredits Cameron's evidence and then generalizes from new evidence

3. Citing Specific Evidence

To cite or offer specific evidence is different from saying that specific evidence exists! Before choosing an answer choice that specifies that evidence is offered or cited, make certain that the evidence was cited! It is not good enough to say that evidence exists without saying what the evidence actually is! The following are examples of language used by Law Services when constructing answer choices.

■ presenting evidence that implies a conclusion

■ stating a conclusion and then providing evidence

■ providing statistical evidence

■ supports a commonly held point of view by providing additional evidence

■ Evidence is provided that the legislation is feasible and necessary.

4. A Contradiction

To contradict a claim involves much more than saying that it is wrong. To contradict a claim is to assert its opposite. Many test takers confuse disagreeing with a claim with contradicting the claim. Be careful to select a choice that describes a **contradiction** when and only when the opposite of the claim has been asserted! The following are examples of language used by Law Services when constructing answer choices.

- She reveals a contradiction in a position generally believed to be correct.

- John accuses Ann of contradicting herself.

- The author's premises are shown to lead to a contradiction.

5. Language That Suggests A Value Judgment

A "value judgment" is a claim that is outside the structure of the argument. This means that it has little (if anything) to do with the premises or the conclusion. The most common value judgments on the LSAT are claims that one thing is "better than" another or that "premises are not relevant to a conclusion." This type of claim rarely has anything to do with the internal structure of the argument given. Before selecting this type of choice you must be extra careful to ensure that it is the best answer. Some examples of the way Law Services introduces this type of claim are:

- It is **better** to be wealthy then to be virtuous.

- He names factors that are **more important** than ...

- Singers have **more conventional** cars than do other kinds of performers.

- National laws are **more effective** than local laws.

The inclusion of "value laden" language does not mean that a choice is wrong. It simply means that you should pay particular attention to that language and decide what impact it has on the answer!

6. Ambiguous Term

Most answer choices that state that a term is ambiguous are wrong. They are designed to play on test takers emotionally. The test taker's response operates like this.

1. I don't understand what is going on! Help!! Things just aren't clear to me!

2. This answer choice talks about a word being unclear.

Since I am unclear and this choice talks about being unclear, this choice is right!

It is a rare instance where the "ambiguous term" choice is correct. What follows are some ways that Law Services constructs these choices.

■ The author uses a medical term and does not clarify its meaning.

■ fails to define the critical term "satisfied"

■ uses the term "student" equivocally

■ depend on the ambiguity of the term "ancient"

■ pointing out that there is an ambiguous use of the term "disposable" in the argument

■ the use of an ambiguous term

7. Confusing Cause And Effect

An answer choice that suggests the confusion of cause and effect is rarely correct. Once again, it is there to play on the emotions. People respond to it in the following way.

1. Boy, I find this question and these answer choices confusing.

2. Look!! This choice talks about being confused.

Since, I am confused and this choice talks about a confusion, it must be right!

Law Services has played out the "confusing cause and effect" choice in some of the following ways.

■ It confuses earlier and later events

■ The author confuses an effect for a cause.

8. Restrictive Language - All, Some, Most, None, Necessary, etc.

The "best answer" in logical reasoning cannot be overly contentious. It cannot be easy to criticize. Language that is overly restrictive or that limits conditions too severely makes the answer choice easy to criticize.

> **Warning!! It is not true that all answer choices
> with restrictive language are wrong!
> It's just that they are wrong enough of the time so that,
> when you read an answer choice,
> you should direct your attention to those words!**

Examples of answer choices with this kind of language are:

■ **All** parents who are generous are wealthy parents.

■ **Some** parents who are poor are not young parents.

■ **Most** parents who are poor are generous.

■ **Many** of the most active participants and benefactors are themselves lawyers.

■ **No** treatment plants are capable of handling sewage.

■ a well paid police force is **sufficient** for establishing law and order.

■ Addressing the difficult issues facing the country **requires** an understanding ...

■ Nitrogen is currently the **only** chemical that must be supplied by ...

9. The Word "Some" Specifically

The word "some" means "there is at least one that ....." Note that this guarantees at least one. The word "some" could also include "all." For example the statement:

"Some readers of this book are thinking about the LSAT"
is a perfectly true statement even if, in fact,
"all readers of this book are thinking about the LSAT."

Be Careful!! The word "some" does not mean "Not all." This is true for two reasons.

    1. "Not all" might mean none.

    2. "Not all" precludes all!

10. The Words "Sufficient" and "Necessary"

A "sufficient condition" is a condition which will by itself guarantee a certain result. Imagine the following statement from a mythical law school calendar.

"Anybody who scores 180 on the LSAT will be automatically admitted!"

A score of 180 and nothing more will **guarantee** admission!

A "necessary condition" is a condition which is required for a certain result but will not by itself guarantee the result. For example:

"Oxygen is a necessary condition for fire."

Note that oxygen is not sufficient for fire. But, in order to have fire you must have oxygen!

11. The Percentage Versus Number Problem

In some questions the "text" of the argument will speak of either percentages or actual numbers. If the "text" speaks of a percentage beware of answer choices that speak of actual numbers. If the "text" speaks of actual numbers beware of answer choices that speak of percentages.

12. Circular Reasoning

Circular reasoning is the logical fallacy of "begging the question." It is an argument where the author of the argument proceeds by simply reiterating the conclusion rather than by offering supporting evidence. **In other words one is assuming as a premise for an argument the very conclusion that one wishes to prove.** For example, the following argument was once reported by Whately:

"To allow every man unbounded freedom of speech must always be, on the whole, advantageous to the state, for it is highly conducive to the interests of the community that each individual should enjoy a liberty, perfectly unlimited, of expressing his sentiments."

Law Services has directed test takers to consider this style of reasoning in the following examples of excerpts from answer choices.

- ■ it exhibits circular reasoning

- ■ argues circularly by assuming the conclusion is true in stating the premises

- ■ The argument presupposes the desirability of socialized medicine, which is what the argument seeks to establish

- ■ assuming at the outset what the argument claims to establish through reasoning

13. Attack On The proponent Of The Claim Rather Than The Claim

Some of you may recognize this as an "Argument ad Hominem." This is an argument which is directed against the person making the claim rather than at the claim itself. There are two forms of this argument. The first is abusive and the second is circumstantial. Let's look at each of these.

Abusive : In this case instead of trying to disprove the argument, one attacks the person making the argument on a personal level. For example, somebody should be denied a promotion because he is a bad person.

Examples of Law Services playing on this kind of attack are:

- John unfairly directs his argument against Ann personally.

- an attack on Dr. Lincoln's character

Circumstantial : In this case instead of attacking an argument the person charges that the proponent of the argument is so prejudiced that his alleged reasons are mere rationalizations or conclusions dictated by self interest. This is the more common type on the LSAT. Consider the following.

> "The arguments of manufacturers for tariff protection should not be taken seriously. After all, as manufacturers they will gain through the imposition of tariffs."

In other words, it is because of the special circumstances of manufacturers that they are making the argument that they are. An example of Law Services playing on this second type would be:

> "A physician's argument against the Clinton's health plan may sound persuasive. But, **imagine how much he stands to lose** if the plan is implemented."

14. Appealing To Authority

One who appeals to authority argues that a conclusion is correct because it is the view of an expert. An excellent example may be found in the debate over NAFTA between Vice President Gore and Ross Perot. Gore argued that NAFTA was a good thing **because it had the support of every living president.**

Law Services has referred to "appeal to authority" in the following ways.

- appealing to authority

- appealing to authority, even when different authorities give conflicting advice about an issue

15. Assumptions

Assumptions are things that the author of the argument **takes for granted**. On the LSAT you should think of an assumption as being an unstated premise.

16. Inferences

Inferences are conclusions that may be drawn from the information in the argument.

 Principle 10 : The Best Answer Has Predictable Characteristics.

The "best answer" is generally easily understandable, descriptive and hard to effectively criticize.

Anatomy Of The Logical Reasoning Question Process

1. Read the question and note the "operative words."

2. Read the argument or statement. You should be sensitive to:

    A. What is he/she saying? (The conclusion); and

    B. Why is he/she saying it? (The premises)

3. Read the question again to re-emphasize the operative words.

4. Think about the relationship between the "right" and "wrong" answers. For example, if the operative words are "could" then none of the wrong answers **could be true**. Why not? The wrong answers must **conflict with the information in the passage!**

5. Read **every word of every choice** of the answers one at a time. Your job is to eliminate all the choices that are wrong leaving you with one or two remaining choices. Eliminate choices that are:

    Answer opposite - the opposite of what you want

    Answer neutral - have no relationship to what is asked and are wrong

This will leave you with one or more choices that are:

Answer possible - choices that are not clearly wrong and bear some relation to what is asked.

6. You will probably have two "answer possible" choices left. At this point you should:

First : Go back and note the operative words of the question.

Second : Think "better" versus "worse."

Third : **Read every word of each remaining choice.**

Fourth : Select one. It may not be objectively correct. It should be hard to criticize.

The Approach Applied - A Sample Question

Every question must be analyzed in terms of each of the text, question, and answer choices. Let's begin by analyzing the following question.

The costs of legal services are as high as they are because there is no competition among those who provide legal services. One in need of legal services is in the position of a traveler in a city whose only hotels are expensive ones.

1. The analogy above serves to make which of the following points?

    (A) Legal services are a commodity few can afford.
    (B) People in need of legal services can choose only among expensive services.
    (C) Inexpensive legal services are every bit as good as expensive legal services.
    (D) Competition among expensive hotels helps keep hotel prices lower than they would otherwise be.
    (E) The cost of legal services keeps up with the rate of inflation.

The Question

 Principle : In logical reasoning you should begin by reading the question. Identification of the "operative words" will define what is most relevant in the argument!

Be clear on the operative words and the relationship between the right and wrong answers.

> 1. The *analogy* above serves to make which of the following *points*?

The "operative words" have been italicized. The relationship between the right and wrong answers is that one of the five choices comes close to, or actually does identify the point made by the analogy. The other four do not. Our job is to eliminate the choices that do not.

The Statement (Text)

Law Services will do its best to obscure the part of the statement (text) that is most important for answering the question. Your job is to "strip" the text down to its bare essentials. In most questions a major portion of the text is irrelevant. Focus on the premise and conclusion.

> The costs of legal services are as high as they are because there is no competition among those who provide legal services. One in need of legal services is in the position of a traveller in a city whose only hotels are expensive ones.

In this case it is only the second sentence that is relevant. The first sentence is simply filler or commentary. We know this because the "operative words" refer us to the analogy! The analogy is in the second sentence. Hence, for all practical purposes the text reads:

> One in need of legal services is in the position of a traveler in a city whose only hotels are expensive ones.

The Answer Choices

The principle rule of answer choice construction is that Law Services will try to attract you to the answer if it is wrong and repel you from it if it is right. Make sure that you read every word of every choice.

> (A) Legal services are a commodity few can afford.
> (B) People in need of legal services can choose only among expensive services.
> (C) Inexpensive legal services are every bit as good as expensive legal services.
> (D) Competition among expensive hotels helps keep hotel prices lower than they would otherwise be.
> (E) The cost of legal services keeps up with the rate of inflation.

Let's analyze our choices.

(E) There is no justification for this at all. It is wrong and is completely outside the scope of what the text is talking about.

(D) This is wrong. It is interesting for two reasons. First the word "competition" is in the statement. Test takers are often attracted to choices which have language that is the same as that in the text. Second, the choice focuses us on the first sentence of the text which is not the relevant part of it.

(C) This is a "value judgment." It has nothing to do with the text and is wrong. Value judgments are very often true statements but they have nothing to do with what is asked. Test takers are often attracted to value judgments simply because they are often true judgments. In addition, value judgments often appeal to test takers on an emotional level.

We now have it down to a choice of (A) and (B). You should now ask yourself:

**Which of (A) or (B) comes closer
to identifying the point made by the analogy?**

The analogy makes the point that legal services are expensive and not that few people can afford them. At best, (A) would be a possible inference from the fact that legal services are expensive. But the point made by the analogy alone is only that legal services are expensive.

(B) Is the better choice, and is the right answer.

Argument Analysis - The Bare Necessities

Arguments on the LSAT are not complicated and should be analyzed the same way that you would analyze any argument. An argument consists of a conclusion which is supported by one or more premises.

Conclusion - This is the bottom line or main point.

Premise - The why or the justification for the conclusion.

Reasoning - The relationship or linkage between the premise and the conclusion.

It can be complicated to identify which is the premise and which is the conclusion. But, there are words that often signal premises and conclusions.

Conclusion Indicators
- it follows that
- which shows that
- in consequence
- which implies that
- which allows us to infer that
- points to the conclusion that
- which means that
- which entails that
- therefore
- we may infer
- proves that
- I conclude that
- accordingly
- consequently
- hence
- thus
- so

Premise Indicators
- as
- for
- since
- because
- follows from
- as shown by
- as indicated by
- the reason is that
- for the reason that
- may be inferred from
- may be derived from
- may be deduced from

Where Are The Premises And Where Is The Conclusion?

On the LSAT you will not find the premise in any specific place. Each of the following forms of argument is possible.

premise, premise, conclusion

conclusion, premise, premise

premise, conclusion, premise

Argument Stripping - How To Read The Text

Let's begin by considering the following argument.

> If it is wrong to kill a one-month-old infant but not a six- month fetus, there has to be a difference between them — not just some difference or other, but a morally relevant difference: there has to be something true of the six-month fetus but not of the one-month-old infant that makes it permissible to kill the former. Surely, though, there is no significant developmental difference, somatic or psychological. True, the six-month fetus is dependent on its mother for its life. But so, normally, is the one-month-old infant — in a different way, of course, but to no less a degree. Apparently there is no morally relevant difference. Therefore, if it is not wrong to kill a six-month fetus, it is not wrong to kill a one-month-old infant. But the latter is wrong. Hence, so is the former.

What is the conclusion? Think in terms of one sentence.

Remember that you don't have time to be overly analytical. The general conclusion is that:

abortion is wrong

Some of you may wish to use more technical language or be a little more specific. An example of being more specific would be to identify the conclusion as being:

it is wrong to kill a six-month fetus

What are the premises?

**what is true of an infant is true of a fetus
and it is wrong to kill an infant**

How can this argument be restated in a smaller number of words?

1. What is true of a one-month old infant is true of a six-month old fetus.

2. It is wrong to kill a one-month old infant.

   Therefore, it is wrong to kill a six-month old fetus.

EXERCISE : For each of the following arguments identify and underline the premises and conclusion.

1. Being married, rather than restricting him, provides a man even greater freedom than being single because he need not worry about day-to-day chores, cleaning the house, making dinner, spending long hours with the children, or anything else to do with the home.

2. In a primitive society in which each family can raise only enough food for itself, everybody lives on the land. When farm productivity doubles, each farm family can grow enough for two, and half the population is freed to work in industry. When each farm family can grow enough food for three, only a third of the population need stay on farms, and so on. It follows as almost a matter of simple arithmetic that the percentage of total population on farms must be inversely proportional to the productivity of farm labor.

3. By a rough rule of thumb, economists reckon that to secure one unit of income you have to invest three times as much capital. So, even to keep pace with a three-percent increase in population, a nation has, roughly speaking, to invest nine percent of its national income each year.

4. There is no position which depends on clearer principles than that every act of a delegated authority, that is contrary to the tenor of the commission under which it is exercised, is void. No legislative act, therefore, contrary to the Constitution, can be valid. To deny this would be to affirm that the deputy is greater than his principle; that the servant is above his master; that the representatives of the people are superior to the people themselves; that men acting by virtue of powers may do not only what their powers do not authorize, but what they forbid.

5. Since all judges first were lawyers, since lawyers are notorious for their low tolerance of criticism, and since lawyers-become-judges were first law students on a steady diet of the adversary system, it is a rare judge who will admit that this process is often inappropriate for solving social and political problems.

6. Wealth is not sought except for the sake of something else, because of itself it brings us no good, but only when we use it, whether for support of the body or for some similar purpose. Now the highest good is sought for its own, and not for another's sake. Thus wealth is not the highest good.

7. In general, the laws of a democracy tend toward the good of the greatest number, for they spring from the majority of all the citizens, which may be mistaken but which cannot have an interest contrary to its own. But those of an aristocracy do tend to monopolize power and wealth in the hands of a few, because in the nature of things an aristocracy is a minority. One can therefore say in general terms that democracy's aim in its legislation is more beneficial to humanity than that of aristocracy in its lawmaking.

What follows are the arguments with the premise indicated in italics and the conclusion indicated in bold type.

1. **Being married**, rather than restricting him, **provides a man even greater freedom than being single** *because he need not worry about day-to-day chores, cleaning the house, making dinner, spending long hours with the children, or anything else to do with the home.*

2. In a primitive society in which each family can raise only enough food for itself, everybody lives on the land. *When farm productivity doubles, each farm family can grow enough for two, and half the population is freed to work in industry. When each farm family can grow enough food for three, only a third of the population need stay on farms, and so on.* **It follows as almost a matter of simple arithmetic that the percentage of total population on farms must be inversely proportional to the productivity of farm labor.**

3. *By a rough rule of thumb, economists reckon that to secure one unit of income you have to invest three times as much capital.* **So, even to keep pace with a three-percent increase in population, a nation has, roughly speaking, to invest nine percent of its national income each year.**

4. There is no position which depends on clearer principles than that *every act of a delegated authority, that is contrary to the tenor of the commission under which it is exercised, is void.* **No legislative act, therefore, contrary to the Constitution, can be valid.** To deny this would be to affirm that the deputy is greater than his principle; that the servant is above his master; that the representatives of the people are superior to the people themselves; that men acting by virtue of powers may do not only what their powers do not authorize, but what they forbid.

5. *Since all judges first were lawyers, since lawyers are notorious for their low tolerance of criticism, and since lawyers-become-judges were first law students on a steady diet of the adversary system,* **it is a rare judge who will admit that this process is often inappropriate for solving social and political problems.**

6. *Wealth is not sought except for the sake of something else,* because of itself it brings us no good, but only when we use it, whether for support of the body or for some similar purpose. *Now the highest good is sought for its own, and not for another's sake.* **Thus wealth is not the highest good.**

7. In general, *the laws of a democracy tend toward the good of the greatest number, for they spring from the majority of all the citizens,* which may be mistaken but which cannot have an interest contrary to its own. *But those of an aristocracy do tend to monopolize power and wealth in the hands of a few,* because in the nature of things an aristocracy is a minority. **One can therefore say in general terms that democracy's aim in its legislation is more beneficial to humanity than that of aristocracy in its lawmaking.**

Assessing Reasonableness

Have you seen question types that read:

Which of the following, if true, most weakens the above argument?

Which of the following, if true, most strengthens the above argument?

These question types appear on the LSAT. When Law Services uses the words "weaken" and "strengthen" they mean "more or less convincing."

For an argument to be convincing you would expect that:

1. The premise(s) is/are true.

2. The conclusion is true.

3. The truth of the premise(s) provide(s) support for the truth of the conclusion.

Therefore, choices that "weaken" an argument do so because they weaken the premise, conclusion or the linkage between the premise and the conclusion. Choices that "strengthen" an argument do the opposite.

SUMMARY TEST - TOPICAL EXERCISES

Conclusions

Tip : This is like a "main idea" question in the reading comprehension section. The answer will be found in the argument itself.

1. Reasoning is good if it is such as to give us a true conclusion from true premises but not otherwise. The question of whether reasoning is good is purely one of fact and not of thinking. "A" being the premises, and "B" being the conclusion, the question is whether the premises and conclusion are so related that if "A" is, "B" is. It is not the least the question whether, when the premises are accepted by the mind, we feel an impulse to accept the conclusion also. It is true that we do generally reason correctly by nature. But that is an accident; the true conclusion would remain true if we had no impulse to accept it; and the false one would remain false though we could not resist the tendency to believe in it.

The author of the above passage would probably LEAST agree with which of the following claims:

(A) Beauty is in the eye of the beholder.
(B) Because nobody says that a basket full of garbage smells nice, garbage does not smell nice.
(C) Because we have discovered no life on Mars, there is no life on Mars.
(D) Even though Americans believe that all of their Presidents have been honest, there is no such thing as an honest President.
(E) A rose would be beautiful even if there were nobody there to appreciate it.

2. George: For when the one great scorer comes
    To write against your name,
    He marks - not that you won or lost-
    But how you played the game.

   Vince: Winning isn't everything.
    It's the only thing.

Which one of the following statements may most reasonably be made about the disagreement above?

(A) George and Vince are in agreement that winning is important.
(B) George and Vince disagree on what it means for one to win.
(C) George and Vince agree on the necessity to win at all cost.
(D) George and Vince agree on the necessity to always use best efforts to win.
(E) George and Vince disagree on the relative importance of winning.

GO ON TO THE NEXT PAGE

Assumptions - Unstated Premises
Tip : An assumption is unstated and provides the evidence necessary for the argument's conclusion to be drawn.

3. Ninety percent of the letters published in the Globe during the air traffic controllers' strike assert that air traffic controllers do not have the right to strike. These letters published in the Globe reflect public opinion on the matter.

Which of the following is one of the assumptions on which the argument above logically depends?

(A) The air traffic controllers have gone on strike in defiance of public opinion.
(B) The Globe is the only periodical covering the strike.
(C) The Globe is as likely to print letters from supporters of the strike as it is to print those from opponents.
(D) The Globe has fully informed its readers about the issues in the strike.
(E) Any comments by the editorial staff of the Globe have been neutral in their position on the strike.

4. The Jones's, who are enthusiastic sailors, have a child who will never be able to go sailing with them because he cannot swim.

Which of the following assumptions must be made before the conclusion above can be drawn?

I. The Jones's child will never learn to swim.
II. The Jones's child will never learn to sail.
III. People who go sailing must be able to swim.

(A) II only
(B) III only
(C) I and III only
(D) II and III only
(E) I, II, and III

GO ON TO THE NEXT PAGE

5. Every American has the basic right to participate in the political process. But many Americans do not have any money. The middle and upper classes can contribute large amounts of money to and spend money attending dinners and rallies for the candidate of their choice. Those without money are reduced to watching the political process on television. Clearly some of the money belonging to the rich should be transferred to the poor, so that the poor will be able to exercise this basic right.

The author's conclusion depends on which of the following assumptions?

(A) It is impossible to participate in the political process without money.
(B) The nation's wealth should be distributed equally among those Americans who are of voting age.
(C) A country must be Socialist for all its citizens to participate in the political process.
(D) Those without money always vote for the Republican candidate.
(E) It is possible for a country that is just in every respect to exist.

6. A supreme court judge only works four hours a day, five days a week for nine months of the year. A lower court judge works five hours a day, five days a week, for eleven months of the year. The salary of a lower court judge is only one half of the salary of a supreme court judge. This discrepancy in salary is quite reasonable because the job of a supreme court judge requires that extra time be spent doing research and writing opinions.

The explanation above assumes that:

(A) Lower court judges are not required to spend extra time researching and writing opinions.
(B) A judge's income should be a function of his status in the judicial hierarchy.
(C) Equal work should not necessarily receive equal compensation.
(D) the job of a supreme court judge is more mentally exhausting than the job of a lower court judge.
(E) making decisions at the supreme court level is more important than making decisions at the lower court level.

GO ON TO THE NEXT PAGE

7. If John were admitted to the bar after 1972, he
    must have passed the Multi-State Bar Examination
    (MBE).

    The statement above can be deduced logically from
    which of the following statements?

    (A) All persons admitted to the bar after 1972
         must have passed the MBE.
    (B) Only if a person were admitted to the bar
         after 1972 would he have passed the MBE.
    (C) Prior to 1972 it was not a requirement that
         candidates pass the MBE.
    (D) No person admitted to the bar before 1972
         would have passed the MBE.
    (E) At least one candidate admitted to the bar
         prior to 1972 would have passed the MBE.

8. The manager of a publishing company explained
    why all the company's books had one vertical
    column with fifty rows rather than two vertical
    columns, each with fifty rows.

    "When a typesetting machine gets to the end of a
    row there is a ten second interval until it can start
    the next row. The machine operator does not work
    for this ten second interval. One vertical column
    means that each row is longer which keeps the
    machine operator working more minutes per
    hour!"

    Which of the following can be most reliably
    inferred from the passage above about the way the
    typesetting machine operator's wages are
    determined?

    (A) The operator is paid by the number of words
         he typesets.
    (B) The operator is paid by the number of rows of
         words that he typesets.
    (C) The operator is paid in accordance with the
         speed that he typesets a page.
    (D) The operator is paid by the hour.
    (E) The operator gets a percentage of the sales
         from each book that he typesets.

GO ON TO THE NEXT PAGE

9. Each member of the President's cabinet, appointed by the President to serve during his term, must have had political experience in Washington.

The only way to have had political experience in Washington is to have been a Congressman or Senator.

The new President was a member of the Senate and is known for his bias toward Senators.

On the basis of the evidence stated above, which of the following conclusions is most likely to be true?

(A) The new President was a Senator all of his political career.
(B) All members of the cabinet have usually come from the branch of government from which the current President has come.
(C) The new President's cabinet will have some former Senators appointed to serve during the President's term.
(D) Both the Senate and House recommend persons to serve in the President's cabinet.
(E) The President's cabinet is not composed of any former Senators.

Missing Premise
Tip : These are often conditional statement questions. The answer must be a choice, which if added to the argument, will allow the conclusion to follow.

10. Bishop Desmond Tutu concluded that all apartheid laws are illegal. He stated this to be true because apartheid laws degrade human beings.

Which of the following is the missing premise that makes Tutu's conclusion valid?

(A) All illegal laws degrade human beings.
(B) All practices that integrate human beings are legal.
(C) All laws that degrade human beings are illegal.
(D) Only laws that degrade human beings are illegal.
(E) Apartheid laws are unjust and unfair.

11. None of the people on the tour had ever been to China. The Korean government allowed no one who had ever been to China to visit Seoul. So all those who went on the tour were allowed to visit Seoul.

The argument above requires the additional premise that:

(A) The Chinese are hated in Seoul.
(B) None of the people on the tour have ever been to Seoul.
(C) The only qualification to visit Seoul is that one has never been to China.
(D) The Korean government allows most people who have never been to China to visit Seoul.
(E) All passports have previous trips to China documented in them.

GO ON TO THE NEXT PAGE

<table>
<tr><td>

Detecting Misinterpretations

Tip : Although these appear in many formats, they are to test if you can understand how one person interpreted what another was saying. ·

</td><td>

Parallel Reasoning

Tip : You will be asked to select the choice that in structure or principle is most analogous to the argument. For many questions it is helpful to mentally set them up in conditional statement format.

</td></tr>
</table>

12. Tom: If I swim every Wednesday, I will build up my strength.

    Harry: No, swimming every Thursday will be just as good for building up your strength.

Harry's response shows that he has interpreted Tom's remark to mean which of the following?

(A) Only swimming and nothing else will build up Tom's strength.
(B) If Tom swims on Wednesdays he will not also swim on Thursdays.
(C) Wednesday is the only day Tom can swim.
(D) Swimming Wednesdays will build Tom's strength and nothing else.
(E) Swimming will build Tom's strength only if it is done on Wednesdays.

13. Every Neil Simon play that I have seen has been funny. Hence, the Neil Simon play that I am going to see tonight will be funny.

Which of the following most closely parallels the kind of reasoning used in the argument above?

(A) The Boston Celtics won the NBA championship in 1986. Therefore, they will win it in 1987.
(B) I have never passed a math test. Hence, based on the law of averages I should pass my next test.
(C) Russia is a Communist country. Hence, Gary Kasparov (Russian chess player) is a Communist.
(D) Each of my previous marriages has ended in a divorce. Hence, my present marriage will end in a divorce.
(E) I love money. My wife doesn't. Hence, I love money more that my wife.

GO ON TO THE NEXT PAGE

14. Interest rate increases become more likely if people expect interest rates to increase. When people expect interest rates to increase to fifteen percent, they become willing to pay interest rates of fifteen percent for mortgages and other loans, thus driving interest rates to fifteen percent. In this way, expectations of interest rate increases become a self-fulfilling prophecy.

In terms of its logical features, the argument above most closely resembles which of the following?

(A) When people expect a movie to be good, they notice its good aspects more than its bad aspects.

(B) When man acts on the belief that he cannot live on the moon, for all practical purposes man cannot live on the moon.

(C) If citizens expect government to be incompetent, competent people will not enter the public service resulting in an incompetent government.

(D) If a person's earning power is lower than he thinks, then he will have to lower his expectations of an endlessly rising standard of living.

(E) If a person really believes that he is the Messiah, then that might as well be the case.

15. Since Superman would die if he were exposed to kryptonite, and this person did not die when he was exposed to kryptonite just now, this person is not Superman.

Which of the following has a logical structure most like the logical structure of the argument above?

(A) Since all Japanese persons drive Nissans or Toyotas, and Mayumi is Japanese, Mayumi cannot drive a Ford.

(B) Since no chickens have four legs, and Sam is a chicken, Sam does not have four legs.

(C) Since students are never responsible, and this person is not responsible, this person is not a student.

(D) Since this house is made of wood, and houses not made of wood are better than wood houses, this wood house is not as good as a house not made of wood.

(E) Since all law students study only from Monday to Thursday, the student studying now during the weekend is not a law student.

GO ON TO THE NEXT PAGE

16. All students in this school have learning disabilities; therefore, it must be true that this school is only for those with learning disabilities.

Which of the following is most like the argument above?

(A) All constables on the Detroit police force are over six feet tall; therefore being over six feet tall must be one of the requirements to be a constable on the Detroit police force.

(B) All new Tylenol containers have safety locks; therefore this kind of lock must be the safest on the market.

(C) All the inmates in this prison have been convicted of "white collar" crimes; therefore judges sentence all the "white collar" criminals to this prison.

(D) No doctor I have seen has been able to cure my headaches; therefore my headaches cannot be cured.

(E) All students in this school are required to participate in sports; therefore all the students in this school are physically fit.

Method - The General Principles
Tip : You are asked to select the choice which objectively describes the method the author uses in advancing the argument. Be sensitive to the vocabulary in the answer choices. Impose a strict test. Ask, is this really being done?

17. Every Neil Simon play that I have seen has been funny. Hence, the Neil Simon play that I am going to see tonight will be funny.

The author uses a method in reasoning that may be best described as:

(A) circular reasoning
(B) generalizing from specific instances
(C) hearsay
(D) haphazard guessing
(E) appealing to emotion

18. How can this lawyer contend that the fact that Jones assaulted his wife five times before killing her on the sixth try is evidence that he intended to kill her? I could just as reasonably contend that evidence that Jones assaulted his wife five times before killing her is evidence that he didn't intend to kill her. After all, he already had five chances to kill her and never did. It seems to me that this is evidence that he didn't intend to kill her.

The author's method of questioning the claim of the lawyer is to:

(A) deny the intelligence of the lawyer
(B) cast doubt on the integrity of the lawyer
(C) present evidence contradicting the evidence offered by the lawyer
(D) show that he is more witty than the lawyer
(E) suggest an alternative interpretation of the evidence offered by the lawyer

GO ON TO THE NEXT PAGE

19. In concluding that Reagan's economic policies have been successful, economists have pointed to the decrease in the rate of inflation since 1980. However, one must note that this decrease in the rate of inflation did not come about because of an increase in production in the U.S., but because unemployment was so high that consumers did not have money to purchase goods and services. This caused a decrease in demand for goods and services. Under these circumstances the decrease in the rate of inflation since 1980 is at best a mixed blessing.

The passage criticizes the economists position by:

(A) showing that their conclusions merely repeat their assumptions.
(B) attacking the proponent of the argument rather than the argument.
(C) alleging that they have confused effect with cause.
(D) showing that the meaning of the word "inflation" is ambiguous.
(E) reinterpreting the evidence that they have used.

Questions 20 and 21

Speaker : The vast majority of Americans have the benefit of the finest public school system in the world.

Heckler : There are hundreds of Americans throughout the country who graduate from high school without being able to read.

20. Which of the following is true of the heckler's objection?

(A) It is not inconsistent with the speaker's statement.
(B) By citing specific information it confirms the speaker's statement.
(C) It attacks the speaker rather than his statement.
(D) It makes a hasty generalization from a small number of unconfirmed cases.
(E) It assumes that the cause and effect are the same.

21. A logical objection to the speaker's statement would point to the existence of:

(A) the existence of some rural families that do not have schools available to them.
(B) a higher percentage of high school graduates in other countries.
(C) a country in which the vast majority of people have access to a finer school system than the vast majority of Americans have access to.
(D) a higher percentage of private schools in America than in other countries.
(E) lower educational cost in countries other than America.

GO ON TO THE NEXT PAGE

Method - Some Well Used Question Types

Circular Reasoning

Let me repeat:

What Law Services refers to as "circular reasoning" is what many logic books refer to as the fallacy of "begging the question." In circular reasoning the conclusion assumes the truth of the premise and vice versa.

Example: To allow every man unbounded freedom of speech must always be, on the whole, advantageous to the state; for it is highly conducive to the interests of the community that each individual should enjoy a liberty, perfectly unlimited, of expressing his sentiments.

Attacking The Proponent Of The Claim Rather Than The Claim

What Law Services refers to as "attacking the proponent of the claim rather than the claim" is what logic books refer to as being an "ad hominem" argument. Imagine that person A advances an argument which contains a conclusion supported by premises. Imagine that person B responds to this argument not by addressing the substance of person A's argument but by saying that person A's position is wrong because of:

who person A is or because of the specific circumstances in person B's life. (Person A would make the claim that he is making anyway!)

Questions 22 - 24 refer to the following arguments.

(A) The committee studying the possible implementation of the new rules of civil procedure has repudiated the claim that implementation of the proposed rules will improve the administration of justice. But several members of the committee are lawyers whose practices will suffer if the proposed rules are implemented, so their objectivity is suspect.

(B) When Chrysler was on the verge of bankruptcy the federal government "bailed Chrysler out" by offering it financial assistance. Today Chrysler is a profitable company. Hence, it is clear that after receiving government assistance any company on the verge of bankruptcy will be a profitable company.

(C) Anyone who deliberately hits another person should be punished. Therefore, Mike Tyson, the current heavyweight boxing champion should be punished because he strikes all his opponents.

(D) Since the regulation of telecommunications is one of the most crucial and significant aspects of modern society, its regulation can be justly considered a matter of major social importance.

(E) More young people are attending university than at any time in the history of our nation. But more young people are using narcotics than ever before. Therefore, in order to eliminate the use of narcotics by young people we must eliminate universities.

GO ON TO THE NEXT PAGE

22. Which one of the arguments above is an example of circular reasoning?

 (A) A   (B) B   (C) C   (D) D   (E) E

23. Which one of the arguments above is directed against the proponent of the claim rather than the claim itself?

 (A) A   (B) B   (C) C   (D) D   (E) E

24. Which one of the above arguments is an example of reasoning from the general to the particular?

 (A) A   (B) B   (C) C   (D) D   (E) E

Questions 25 - 27 refer to the following arguments.

(A) Isn't it true that students who get all A's study hard? So if you want me to study hard, Professor, the best way to do it is to give me A's in all my courses.

(B) My client is the sole support of his aged parents. If he is sent to prison it will break their hearts, and they will be left homeless and penniless. You surely cannot find it in your hearts to reach any other verdict than "not guilty."

(C) Oil company executives claim that high profits are necessary for investment in exploration. But of course the basic purpose of an oil company is to make money, so that company spokesmen will defend their profits no matter how high they are. It is safe to conclude that oil profits are in fact excessive.

(D) There is no proof that Mr. X stole the car so he can't have done it.

(E) On Friday evening I ate a Big Mac. On Saturday morning I woke up sick. Hence, all Big Macs make people sick.

25. Which one of the above arguments contains circular reasoning?

 (A) A   (B) B   (C) C   (D) D   (E) E

26. Which one of the above arguments is directed against the proponent of the claim rather than the claim itself?

 (A) A   (B) B   (C) C   (D) D   (E) E

27. Which one of the arguments above is an example of reasoning from the specific to the general?

 (A) A   (B) B   (C) C   (D) D   (E) E

GO ON TO THE NEXT PAGE

GO ON TO THE NEXT PAGE

Identification Of Resolutions To Conflicts

28. Ounce for ounce, ABC astronaut food contains more protein and more vitamin D than a glass of milk does.

A serving of ABC astronaut food contains less protein than this glass of milk does.

Which of the following, if true, explains how the statements above can both be true at once?

(A) The glass of milk contains more ounces than the serving of ABC astronaut food does.

(B) The glass of milk contains more vitamin D than the serving of ABC astronaut food does.

(C) The serving of ABC astronaut food contains more vitamin D than the glass of milk does.

(D) The glass of milk has fewer calories than the ABC astronaut food does.

(E) The serving of ABC astronaut food weighs less than the glass of milk does.

Assessing Reasonableness

The Best Attack!

Tip : Look for answer choices that weaken the premise, conclusion, or linkage between them.

Many of you have studied logic and in the course of that study have developed a technical language to examine arguments. Some examples of this language are the words "valid" and "sound." Since the "Argument Analysis" section of the test does not presuppose formal knowledge of logic, this book will avoid "technical language." A good argument is one that seems "reasonable" from the perspective of our day-to-day experience.

**In this book we will use the word "reasonable"
to describe an argument that we think
makes sense and is convincing!**

What then is required for an argument to qualify as "reasonable?" For an argument to be reasonable we would expect that:

1. the conclusion is true;

2. the premises are true;

3. the truth of the premises does compel the truth of the conclusion. (linkage)

Since these are the three things that are required for an argument to be reasonable, an appropriate attack on an argument would point out that:

1. the conclusion is false;

2. the premises are false;

3. there is nothing about the truth of the premises that compels the truth of the conclusion. (linkage)

When you are asked to "weaken" or "attack" arguments on the test, simply ask:

1. Is the conclusion true?

2. Are the premises true?

3. Is there something about the truth of the premises that compels the truth of the conclusion? (linkage)

Anything that asks one of these three questions is an appropriate attack on the argument. Something that fails to ask one of these three questions is an inappropriate attack and is called a fallacy.

Questions 29 and 30

If it is wrong to kill a one-month-old infant but not a six- month fetus, there has to be a difference between them — not just some difference or other, but a morally relevant difference: there has to be something true of the six-month fetus but not of the one-month-old infant that makes it permissible to kill the former. Surely, though, there is no significant developmental difference, somatic or psychological. True, the six-month fetus is dependent on its mother for its life. But so, normally, is the one-month-old infant — in a different way, of course, but to no less a degree. Apparently there is no morally relevant difference. Therefore, if it is not wrong to kill a six-month fetus, it is not wrong to kill a one-month-old infant. But the latter is wrong. Hence, so is the former.

29. All of the following would be an appropriate attack on the above argument EXCEPT

(A) A one-month-old infant is not completely dependent on its mother, but can be taken care of by its father.
(B) It is not wrong to kill a one-month-old infant.
(C) There are morally relevant differences between a one-month-old infant and a six-month-old fetus, other than dependence and developmental differences.
(D) It is not wrong to kill a six-month-old fetus.
(E) The termination of pregnancies is most prevalent in urban areas.

30. Which of the following statements, if true, would most seriously weaken the above argument?

(A) The state can regulate abortion in the third trimester of pregnancy.
(B) Many one-month-old infants are fed in day care centers while their mothers work.
(C) Five percent of six-month-old fetuses are either born defective or die during birth.
(D) In many cases abortion is necessary to save the life of the mother.
(E) There are many morally relevant differences between a six-month-old fetus and a one-month-old infant which make it permissible to kill the fetus.

31. One cannot say that the New York Yankees have won more pennants than any other major league team, because no two Yankee pennant winning teams have had the same group of players.

Which of the following if true is the best rebuttal of the above argument?

(A) The Yankees do not always change from one season to the next
(B) The Yankee team is not identical with the players who are the members of it.
(C) When player changes occur, not all of the players are changed.
(D) The Baltimore Orioles won the pennant for two straight years without changing a player.
(E) Many of the Yankees have long term contracts which prevent them from being traded.

GO ON TO THE NEXT PAGE

Questions 32 and 33

If you are like most people and fear social rejection you need worry no more! We have determined how the socially acceptable act. All socially acceptable people are natural, honest and therefore, if they smoke, smoke an "honest" cigarette. "Dolphin Filter" is an honest cigarette. So, if you want to avoid social rejection smoke "Dolphin Filter!" Dolphin Filter "They're not for everybody (but they could be for you)."

32. Which of the following would be an appropriate criticism of the advertisement above?

  I.   Smoking is hazardous to your health.
  II. There are many non-smokers who are not social rejects.
  III. Dishonesty is a perfectly acceptable social characteristic.
  IV. You can be socially acceptable if you smoke any kind of cigarettes.

  (A) I and II only
  (B) I and III only
  (C) II, III and IV only
  (D) III and IV only
  (E) I, II, III and IV

33. If someone were to attack the advertisement by saying, "some of the most socially acceptable people I know are non-smokers" the author of the ad could best counter this objection by saying:

  (A) I never said that all socially acceptable people smoke.
  (B) If you don't smoke then you are a social reject.
  (C) If you are socially acceptable then you smoke.
  (D) The question of whether a person is socially acceptable is not a function of your perception of the issue!
  (E) How would you know, you are a social reject yourself!

34. Many people argue that cheating on taxes is all right because so many people do it. This is like suggesting that senility is all right because so many people become senile.

The analogy above would be strengthened if it were true that:

  (A) if something is done by the majority then it is morally right.
  (B) moral principles can be codified.
  (C) few people become senile
  (D) people have control over whether they become senile.
  (E) the words "all right" mean socially acceptable.

35. The top five percent of students who enter the Euclid math contest win "Euclid Scholarships." Last year fifty percent of the graduating class of Pythagoras High School won "Euclid Scholarships." This shows that the students at Pythagoras High are ten times as mathematically inclined as students in schools in the rest of the country.

Which of the following statements most weakens the argument above?

  (A) The mathematical inclinations of individuals in a student body is not proportional to the percentage who do well in the Euclid math contest.
  (B) The strength of the argument can be evaluated only by considering the percentage difference between the two groups.
  (C) It is very difficult to be accepted to Pythagoras High, and ninety percent of its graduates go on to careers in math.
  (D) The Euclid Math Contest is open only to students who have exhibited an aptitude in math.
  (E) The class that graduated from Pythagoras High last year was the smallest graduating class in the history of the school.

GO ON TO THE NEXT PAGE

36. Citizens of democratic societies continually face the prospect of change. Whether or not citizens will be able to cope with change will depend on whether they are able to learn new skills. Hence, the state must provide generous funding for public education. The greater the funding, the better the educational system, and the better the educational system, the better citizens can learn the new skills that are required for them to cope with change.

   Which of the following, if true, makes the strongest objection to the argument above?

   (A) Citizens of non-democratic societies are better able to cope with change than citizens of democratic societies.
   (B) Many people are motivated to learn the skills required to cope with change when the state does not provide generous funding to education.
   (C) Some citizens in a democratic society may fear change and refuse to take what steps are necessary to cope.
   (D) For those with vast financial resources private education is available to retrain people.
   (E) The extent to which citizens are able to cope with change is a function of only a person's motivation and not the availability of education.

ANSWERS AND EXPLANATIONS TO FOLLOW

ANSWERS AND COMMENTARY

What follows is a discussion of the topical exercises in this chapter. For some questions I have placed more emphasis on an analysis of the premises and conclusion. For others, I have placed more emphasis on the content and style of the answer choices. For the most part you will find heavy analysis of the wrong answer choices. I have noted when the wrong answer choice falls into a specific category of "wrong answer choice."

It is my intention to keep the analysis of the questions consistent with the method in the chapter itself. Therefore, when I discuss a conclusion **it will be boldfaced.** When I discuss a premise *it will be italicized.*

**Remember that you are looking for the "best" answer
and not for an "objectively correct" answer.**

1. The author would "LEAST agree" with the opposite of what he would most agree with. In this case the conclusion is that **truth is objective.** There are some things that are true whether anybody knows about them or cares about them. The author would least agree with a general statement that what something is, is purely a function of an individual's perception.

   (E) is wrong. Answer opposite. It is what the author would most agree with!
   (D) is wrong. Answer opposite. The focus is on objective truth (there is no such thing as an honest president). This is the opposite of what you want.
   (C) is a possible answer. It makes the claim that reality is a function of perception.
   (B) is also a possible answer. It makes the claim that reality is a function of perception.

   (A) is the best answer and is correct. It is a general statement that what something is from time to time is only a function of what that thing is perceived to be.

2. This question requires you to identify the main point that each of George and Vince is making. Vince says that the single most important consideration is whether one wins. George says winning is less important than overall performance.

   (B) is wrong. It is your typical "ambiguous term" wrong answer choice.
   (C) is wrong. Answer opposite. George does not take the position that it is necessary to win at all cost.
   (D) is wrong. Answer neutral. Neither party mentions the necessity of using best efforts.
   (A) is wrong. Although Vince says that winning is important, George does not.

   (E) is the best answer. For Vince winning is everything. For George it is less important than other considerations.

3. The conclusion is: **the letters published reflect public opinion.** The premise is: *ninety percent of the letters published assert that the controllers don't have the right to strike.*

   (A), (D), and (E) are all wrong because they are irrelevant.
   (B) is wrong. It is irrelevant, but note the word "only" as well.

   (C) is the best and only possible answer.

4. The conclusion is: **the child will never be able to go swimming with the Jones**. The premise is: *he cannot swim*. This is multiple option. **We do one thing at a time.**

1.　Eliminate II. It is a restatement of the conclusion. Hence, (A), (D) and (E) are wrong.

2.　Look at (B) and (C). Each includes "III." Therefore, "III" is in the answer.

3.　Ask is "I" an assumption. Yes! Remember the conclusion is that the child will **never** be able to go sailing.

(C)　is the best answer.

5. The conclusion is: **that money should be transferred from the rich to the poor so that the poor are able to participate in the political process**. The premise is: *the poor because of a lack of money are reduced to watching the political process on television.* Clearly, this assumes that one cannot participate in the political process without money.

(A)　is correct. Not only does it capture this idea, but it is the only one that is close.

6. The conclusion is: **salary discrepancies between the judges are reasonable**. The premise is: *supreme court judges must spend extra time writing opinions.* This assumes that lower court judges are not required to spend extra time writing opinions.

(B)　and (E) are both wrong. They are both "value judgment" type choices.
(C)　is wrong. It is irrelevant. It seems to contradict the claim that the judges are not engaged in equal work.
(D)　is wrong. Although it might justify the conclusion, it is irrelevant to the specific justification given in the argument.

(A)　is the best answer. It is a clear statement of the assumption.

7. The operative words are "deduced logically from." This is a strong inference. It means **must follow from**. The question should be interpreted to mean: from which of the five choices can one definitely infer that: If John were admitted to the bar after 1972, that he must have passed the MBE?

(C)　is wrong. This denies the antecedent. The statement "if you were admitted to the bar prior to 1972 you need not have passed the MBE" does not imply that "if you were admitted to the bar after 1972 that you must have passed the MBE!"
(B)　is wrong. Note the word "only." If we rewrite this conditional it would read: If he passed the MBE then he would have been admitted to the bar after 1972.
(D)　and (E) are both wrong. They talk about being admitted to the bar prior to 1972.

(A)　is correct. It is a general statement. The general statement would apply to John - the individual.

8. The operative words are "most reliably inferred." This does **not mean must follow from."** A weak inference is possible. The key part of the manager's statement is that one column keeps the operator working more minutes per hour. The implication is that the time spent actually working is what is important to the manager.

(A), (B), (C), and (E) are all wrong. None of them focuses on the time spent actually working.

(D) is the best answer because it focuses on the amount of time spent actually working.

9. The operative words are "most likely to be true." This does **not mean must follow from.** A weak inference is possible. The most important part of the statement is: "The new president was a member of the Senate and is know for his bias toward senators."

(A), (B) and (D) are wrong. There is no basis for inferring any of them.
(E) is wrong. It is the opposite of what the answer should be.

(C) is the best and only possible answer.

10. Conclusion: **All apartheid laws are illegal.**

Premise: *Apartheid laws degrade human beings.*

The issue is, which of the five answer choices if coupled with the claim that *"Apartheid laws degrade human beings"* will allow the conclusion that **"All apartheid laws are illegal."**

Each of (A), (B), (D), and (E) is wrong. Note the value laden language in (E), and the word "only" in (D). (D) actually means: "If a law is illegal then it is a law that degrades human beings." If you selected (D) then you are affirming the consequent.

(C) is correct. If it is added as a premise, we have:

1. *All laws that degrade human beings are illegal.*

2. *Apartheid laws degrade human beings.*

Therefore, Apartheid laws are illegal.

11. Conclusion: **All those on the tour were allowed to visit Seoul.**

Premise 1: *None on the tour had been to China.*

Premise 2: *None who had been to China were allowed to visit Seoul.*

The issue is: which of these five answer choices if coupled with the premise(s) would allow the conclusion that all those on the tour were allowed to visit Seoul?

Each of (A), (B), (D) and (E) is wrong.

(C)   is the best answer.

If the only qualification to visit Seoul is that one has never been to China, this means that once it is established that one has not been to China, it would follow that one is allowed to visit Seoul. The second premise becomes irrelevant. With (C) added as a premise the argument becomes:

1.   *None on the tour had been to China.*

2.   *All that is required to be allowed to visit Seoul is that one has not been to China.*

Therefore, all on the tour were allowed to visit Seoul.

12. These have been common question types over the years. Note that the only subject of the "verbal exchange" is swimming. Harry is interpreting Tom to mean that swimming will build his strength **only** if it is done on Wednesdays.

   (A)   is wrong. Tom talks about swimming only. He doesn't suggest that there are not alternative forms of exercise.
   (B), (C), and (D) are wrong for the same reason that **(E) is right.** They don't focus on Harry's interpreting Tom to mean that swimming will build his strength **only** if it is done on Wednesdays.

   (E)   is correct.

13. The reasoning takes the form of a statement about every member of a class (Neil Simon plays) that the person has experienced to a statement about a specific member of the class (the play that he is going to see tonight). You must select the answer choice that comes closest to satisfying this requirement.

   (E)   is wrong.
   (B)   is wrong. For it to be a possible answer the person's conclusion should be that he **will not pass his next test**.
   (C)   is wrong. To make it a possible answer it would have to read: *Every Russian I have met has been a Communist*. Hence, **Gary Kasparov is a Communist**.
   (A)   is wrong. For it to be a possible answer it would have to read: *The Boston Celtics have won the N.B.A. championship every year they have been in it*. Hence, **they will win it next time they play in it**.

   (D)   is correct. It is a statement about the person's experience about each of his/her past marriages. It then goes on to a projection about the fate of his/her current marriage.

14. The expectation of high interest rates **actually results** in the high interest rates. Hence, you want the choice where the expectation comes closest to actually producing the result.

(A) is wrong. The expectation of a good movie is not claimed to **actually** make the movie good.

(B) is wrong. It doesn't say that the person **actually** cannot live on the moon.

(D) is wrong. It doesn't talk about expectations. In addition, the conclusion should be that the person's earning power **is actually** low.

(E) is wrong. It doesn't talk about expectations. In addition, the conclusion should be that the person **is actually** the Messiah.

(C) **is correct. We have the expectation of incompetent government actually resulting in incompetent government.**

15. The form of the argument is:

1. *If a person is Superman then he would die if exposed to kryptonite.* (If A then B)

2. *This person did not die when exposed to kryptonite. (Not B)*

Therefore, **this person is not Superman**. (Not A)

We must identify the choice that has the same pattern.

(A), (B), and (D) are wrong. None of them is even close to this pattern.

(C) is wrong. The pattern is:
If student then not responsible. (If A then B)
This person is not responsible. (B)
Therefore, **this person is not a student.** (Not A)

(E) **is correct. The pattern is:**

If law student then does not study weekends. (If A then B)
This person is studying weekends. (Not B)
Therefore, this person is not a law student. (Not A)

16. The form of the reasoning is:

If student in this school then learning disability. (If A then B)
Therefore, **this school is only for students with learning disabilities**. (Only if B then A.)

(B) and (D) are wrong. Neither is even close.

(E) is wrong. The pattern is: If A then B. Therefore, If A then C.

(C) is wrong. The pattern is: If A then B. Therefore, If B then A.

(A) is correct. The pattern is:

If constable on Detroit police force then over six feet tall. (If A then B.)
Therefore, only those over six feet tall can be on the Detroit police force. (Only if B then A.)

17. This is the Neil Simon question in the form of objective description.

(A)   is wrong. We will look at circular reasoning separately. (See the discussion of the answers to questions 22 and 25.)

(C)   is wrong. This is not descriptive of hearsay.

(D)   and (E) are both wrong. Not even close.

(B)   **is the only choice that is close and it is more or less correct.**
The author is really saying: *Every Neil Simon play that I have experienced has been funny.* **Therefore, the class of Neil Simon plays is funny and by inference the one I am going to tonight will be funny.**

18. Look for the key word in each answer choice.

(A)   is wrong. The key language is "deny the intelligence." Not done.

(B)   is wrong. The key language is "cast doubt on the integrity." (As you know, lawyers have no integrity to cast doubt on.) But, this is certainly not done.

(C)   Is wrong. No evidence is presented. Not done.

(D)   is wrong. This is not the method of questioning the claim.

(E)   **is correct. It is the only possible answer.**

19. This question causes problems for people.

(A)   is wrong. Not done. This choice is descriptive of circular reasoning.

(B)   is wrong. We will see "attacks on the person" in other questions.

(D)   is wrong. It is an example of the "ambiguous term" wrong answer choice.

(C)   is wrong. This is not done. It is true that the passage does talk about an effect and it does talk about a cause. But there is no specific allegation of confusing that cause and that effect. Also, the "confusion of cause and effect" answer choice is often wrong.

(E)   **is correct. The evidence used for the success of Reagen's economic policies is the "decrease in the rate of inflation." But, the allegation is that the "decrease in the rate of inflation" is not indicative of the success of the policies but, of the failure in the area of employment.**

20. We have another verbal exchange. When you encounter this form of question make sure that you are clear which speaker the question refers you to. This question refers you to the **heckler's** objection.

(B)   is wrong. Although the heckler cites specific information there is no confirmation of the speaker's statement.

(C)   is wrong. There is no attack on the speaker, only on the claim.

(E)   is wrong. There is no basis for any inference of confusing cause and effect.

(D)   is wrong. For this to be a generalization the heckler would have to say: there are hundreds of Americans who graduate from high school without being able to read and therefore the vast majority (if not all) Americans graduate from high school without being able to read. Note also the word "hasty."

(A)   **is correct. The speaker never said that all Americans graduate from high school knowing how to read.**

21. This question refers you to the **speaker's** statement. The speaker speaks of the "vast majority" of Americans and the public school system in general. Therefore, the best objection would focus on these two things.

(A), (B), (D), and (E) are all wrong. None of them comes close.

(C) **is correct. It points to specific facts that are inconsistent with the speaker's specific claim.**

22. Look for a situation where the conclusion assumes the premise or vice versa.

(D) **is correct. The words "crucial and significant aspects of modern society" mean the same as "major social importance."**

23. Look for a situation where one attacks the person rather than the claim. The answer is usually institutional bias.

(A) **is correct. The claim of the committee is not attacked. Rather, what is attacked is the objectivity of members of the committee. This is an attack based on institutional bias.**

24. You are looking for reasoning from a claim about a group to a claim about a member of the group.

(B) is wrong. Answer opposite. It reasons from a claim about a member of a group to a claim about the group.

(C) **is correct. It reasons from a claim about "a group" to a claim about a specific member (Mike Tyson).**

25. Circular reasoning again.

People often confuse weak reasoning with circular reasoning. For reasoning to be circular it must assume the truth of the conclusion or vice versa.

(A) **is correct.**

26. Look for the choice that attacks the person rather than the claim.

(B) is wrong. It is an appeal to pity.

(C) **is correct. Once again, the claim is one of institutional bias.**

27. You must reason from a claim about a member of a group to a claim about a group.

(E) **is correct. The reasoning is from a claim about one Big Mac to a claim about the whole group of Big Macs.**

28. A specific serving of ABC can contain less protein than a specific glass of milk only if the serving of ABC is smaller in terms of liquid volume. So, look for an answer choice that **focuses on volume.**

    (D) is wrong. Totally irrelevant.
    (B) and (C) are both wrong. At a minimum neither of them addresses the issue of protein.
    (E) is wrong. Weight is not the same thing as liquid volume.

    (A) is correct. It is the choice that focuses on liquid volume.

29. Eliminate any choice that is an attack on the premises, conclusion or linkage.

    (A) is wrong. Attack on a premise.
    (B) is wrong. Attack on a premise.
    (C) is wrong. Attack on a premise.
    (D) is wrong. Attack on a conclusion.

    (E) is correct. It is outside the structure of the argument and is not an attack on the premise, conclusion or linkage. It is irrelevant and therefore neither strengthens nor weakens the argument.

30. The operative words are "most seriously weaken."

    (A) is wrong. It is irrelevant.
    (C) is wrong. It is irrelevant.
    (D) is wrong. It is a value judgment outside the structure of the argument.
    (B) is wrong. Although it does the attack the premise that the one month old is dependent on the mother, it is not as strong an attack as choice (E).

    (E) is correct. It is a strong attack on the linkage between the premises and the conclusion. It is saying that the conclusion simply does not follow from your premises.

31. The premise is: *the Yankees is not a distinct entity from the players that make it up at any given time.* The conclusion is: **The Yankees have not won more pennants than any other major league team.**

    (A), (C), (D), and (E) are wrong. None is an attack on the premise, conclusion or the linkage between them. People often select (A) or (C). Neither of these choices attacks the claim that the team is not distinct from the players.

    (B) is correct. It is a direct attack on that main premise.

32. This is multiple option. Do one thing at a time.

    1. "I" is not in the answer. It is a value judgment. Hence, we eliminate (A), (B), and (E). We are left with (C) and (D).
    2. The difference between (C) and (D) is that (C) contains "II."
    3. Ask, is "II" an attack. No, the ad is directed to smokers and not to non-smokers. Eliminate (C).

    (D) is the answer. ("III" is an attack on a premise. "IV" is an attack on the linkage between the premises and the conclusion.)

33. Reread the analysis of the previous question.

> (B), (C), (D), and (E) are wrong. None of them is a relevant response to the statement "some of the most socially acceptable people I know are non-smokers."

> **(A)** **is the answer. The ad talks about smokers. It does not talk about non-smokers. An attack on an argument must be directed to the class of persons that the argument talks about. It should not be directed to what the argument does NOT talk about.**

34. This question asks you to identify what would strengthen the claim rather than weaken the claim. The difference between becoming senile and cheating on taxes is the issue of control.

> (A) is wrong. People often choose it as an answer. The statement in choice (A) would provide some support for the claim that it is okay to cheat on taxes. But, that is not what the question is asking about. The "operative words" direct us to what would strengthen the analogy between cheating on taxes and becoming senile. One chooses to cheat on taxes and one does not choose to become senile. This is why the analogy is weak. But if one did choose to become senile, then the analogy would be stronger.

> **(D) is the only possible answer. It focuses on control and choice.**

35. This is a good example of a linkage attack. The conclusion is: **Students at Pythagoras High are ten times as mathematically inclined as students in the rest of the country.** The premises are the first two sentences.

> (E)   is wrong. It is irrelevant.
> (B)   is wrong. It is irrelevant, and if true is in no way directed toward weakening the claim.
> (C)   and (D) are wrong. Answer opposite. They each strengthen the claim.

> **(A)** **is correct. It is a strong linkage attack. It is a clear statement that the conclusion of the argument does not follow from the premises.**

36. Note that the argument talks about citizens of democratic countries. The operative words are "strongest objection."

> (A)   is wrong. The argument doesn't talk about citizens of non-democratic countries. Reread the explanation for question 33. To object to an argument the objection must be directed to the class of persons the argument talks about.
> (B), (C) and (D) are wrong. Each of them is, at best, a very weak objection.

> **(E)** **is a strong objection. Once again, (see questions 30 and 35) it is an excellent example of what a linkage attack looks like. It says, the conclusion does not follow from the premises.**

Chapter Seven

Logic Games - Analytical Reasoning Mastery

Law Services calls this section "Analytical Reasoning."

Format

You will get one thirty-five minute section consisting of four sets of conditions. Each set of conditions will be followed by approximately six questions.

Timing Considerations

Time Isn't Everything - It's The Only Thing!

The issue is how to get the largest number of right answers in the thirty-five minutes. You must decide whether to interact with three of the four sets of conditions (spending twelve minutes on each) or four of the four sets of conditions (spending nine minutes on each).

Remember to guess on any questions that you do not interact with!

Determine this only by practicing with actual LSAT exams!

Directions

Directions : "Each group of questions in this section is based on a set of conditions. In answering some of the questions, it may be useful to draw a rough diagram. Choose the response that most accurately and completely answers each question and blacken the corresponding space on the answer sheet."

Purpose

Law Services describes the purpose of the analytical reasoning section in the following way:

"Analytical reasoning items are designed to measure the ability to understand the structure of relationships and to draw conclusions about the structure."

Relevance To Law School

In commenting on the conditions in Analytical Reasoning Law Services states:

> "They simulate the kinds of detailed analyses of relationships that a law student must perform in solving legal problems. For example, a passage might describe four diplomats sitting around a table, following certain rules of protocol as to who can sit where. The test taker must answer questions about the implications of the given information, for example, who is sitting between diplomats X and Y."

The problem is time. Law students have time to analyze the problems. LSAT test takers have very little time. Therefore, I suggest that this section does not meet its goal!

The Correct Order To Do The Sets Of Conditions

There are different kinds of conditions. Through practice you will learn where your strengths and weaknesses lie. When you open your test book scan the sets of conditions. Quickly decide which you are most and least comfortable with. Do the sets of conditions in the order that you like them best. Your goal should be to:

Run out of time when you are doing the set of conditions that gives you the most trouble.

Do the sets of conditions in order of difficulty saving the most difficult for last!

Categories Of Games

Analytical Reasoning first appeared in 1982. Since that time there have been a number of different question types. Some types that appeared in the early years (for example, family relationships) are now obsolete. Others (for example, ordering questions) have appeared consistently since 1982. In commenting on the types of conditions that appear Law Services states:

"The passages used for each group of questions describe relationships that are common ones such as the following:

Assignment problems: Two parents, P and O, and their children, R and S, must go the dentist on four consecutive days, designated 1, 2, 3, and 4 ...;

Ordering problems: X arrived before Y but after Z;

Grouping: A basketball coach is trying to form a lineup from seven players - R, S, T, U, V, W, and X ... and each player has a particular strength - shooting, jumping, or guarding;

Spatial relationship problems: Country X contains six cities and each city is connected to at least one other city by a system of roads, some of which are one-way."

Although, these may be common relationships the list is by no means exclusive!

Characteristics Of The Answer

In analytical reasoning the response that most accurately answers the question is objectively correct. As a result, you need not read every choice before selecting an answer. This stands in stark contrast to the reading comprehension and the logical reasoning questions.

Emotional Difficulties

The Bad News

To put simply: this section terrifies test takers. The tenser one is the harder it is to do the questions and the harder it is to do the questions the tenser one gets! The "feel" of the section can be quite upsetting. This is particularly true for "high achievers" who are accustomed to feeling in control of every test situation.

The Good News

The good news is that the "bad news" applies to everybody. All test takers feel uncomfortable with Analytical Reasoning. If you are a test taker then you will feel uncomfortable too. Remember that your score on the LSAT is a reflection of how you perform relative to all test takers.

How To Read The Conditions - Factual Considerations

Taken individually the conditions are simple. But, when they are added together they can become quite complex. When you read the conditions the first time do not try to integrate them.

Read for factual context only.

How To Read The Conditions - Language Considerations

The single most important consideration when you read the conditions is to pay attention to language. In the words of Law Services:

"It is essential to pay particular attention to words that describe or limit relationships, such as "only," "exactly," "never," "always," "must be," "cannot be," and the like."

Be on the lookout for restrictive language as you read the conditions.

Therefore when you read the conditions you should:

1. Read for factual content; and
2. Identify the words that "limit relationships." When you encounter a word like "only," ask what significance it has for your interpretation of the conditions!

What To Look For In The Operative Words

The operative words are always the same as, or functionally equivalent to one of the following:

1. must be true

   You eliminate any choice that either could be false or must be false.

2. must be false

   You eliminate any choice that either could be true or must be true.

3. could be true

   You eliminate any choice that could never be true. (must be false)

4. could be false

   You eliminate any choice that could never be false. (must be true)

How To Read The Questions

First, it is important to remember that each question is independent from every other.

Second, it is important to recognize that some questions will add additional information to a question. This additional information should simply be added to the original conditions. It is not to be carried to any other question. For the purposes of this book we will call this additional information "variable information."

Third, some questions add additional information which has the effect not of adding to the original conditions, but rather of changing the original conditions. This kind of question is generally more difficult and should be answered last!

Law Services summarizes these ideas in the following way:

"Each question should be considered separately from the other questions in its group; no information, except what is given in the original conditions, should be carried over from one question to another. In some cases a question will simply ask for conclusions to be drawn from the conditions as originally given. Some questions may, however, add information to the original conditions or temporarily suspend one of the original conditions for the purpose of that question only. For example, if Question 1 adds the information "if P is sitting at table 2 ...," this information should NOT be carried over to any other question in the group."

Are The Questions In Any Order Of Difficulty?

Neither the questions nor the sets of conditions are in any order of difficulty. Hence, you must not become sidetracked by anything that is overly difficult for you. Simply, find something that is easier for you to do!

Don't Worry! There is something for everybody on the LSAT!

Is It Important To Diagram?

Yes! I have yet to see a test taker who does not diagram for at least some of the questions. You should know that there is no one right or wrong diagram. There are, however, some right and some wrong ways to go about the problem of constructing a diagram!

Before we go further in this discussion you would do well to remember that the only purpose of a diagram is to help you identify the answer more quickly and more accurately. A diagram has no value by itself!

The Requirements Of A Workable Diagram

For a diagram to help you identify the answer a diagram must be:

1. Focused - It has to be drawn to find the answer to a specific question! Many test takers spend lots of time at the beginning simply trying to draw a picture! Remember: You can't hand your test book in to get extra credit for the art.

2. Used only as long as is necessary to find the answer - Many test takers simply do not keep their eyes on the answer choices. They typically will try to complete the diagram when an incomplete diagram is all that is needed to identify the answer.

Don't overwork the questions!

The Single Biggest Diagraming Mistake One Can Make!

It is a mistake to read the conditions and try to draw a diagram without reference to the questions. Many test takers do the following:

1. Read the conditions.

2. Fail to understand the conditions

3. Attempt to draw a diagram based on conditions they don't understand. All of this results in "drawing the wrong diagram." Have you ever heard of anybody saying "I drew the wrong diagram"?

You should:

1. Read the conditions.

2. Decide which question to start with. (Pick the question that you think will be easiest.)

3. Draw a diagram in relation to that question and for the purpose of answering only that question.

If you do it this way you will have lost nothing and have guaranteed a focus to your work which will help you avoid the wrong diagram.

The Nuts And Bolts Of Good Diagraming

Ten General Principles Of Good Diagraming

Some of these are extensions of our general principles of multiple choice.

Principle 1 : Think down! Determine the most simple thing that is true. This is usually the most specific information in terms of where one thing is by itself or in terms of where one thing is in relation to another.

Principle 2 : Focus on the most rigid condition (the troublemaker). Generally every other condition will revolve around this one.

Principle 3 : Just diagram the conditions that are definitely true. Diagram what could be true only if you see that it will be a definite help to you. Resist the temptation to list too many possibilities.

Principle 4 : Less is better than more. Don't put too much into the diagram. Too much information will obscure the important relationships thereby making the diagram harder to use.

Principle 5 : Do one thing at a time. After each conclusion, you should try to identify the condition that will allow you to build on that conclusion.

Principle 6 : Keep your diagrams small and neat. Ensure that you have space left over to draw additional diagrams.

Principle 7 : Be visual!! The diagram is to help you "see" the situation. If your focus is not on being "visual" you are involved in something that is not workable.

Principle 8 : Ensure that your diagram distinguishes between "fixed information" and "variable information." "Fixed information" is information that is based solely on the initial conditions. "Variable information" is information that is added to the question for the purposes of that question only.

 Principle 9 : Diagram in reference to a specific question. This will keep you focused on the question and answer choices and minimize your chances of "drawing the wrong diagram."

 Principle 10 : While diagraming keep your eyes focused on the answer choices. Don't diagram further than is required to identify the answer to the question asked.

Remember that the value of a diagram depends upon only its usefulness in answer identification. Don't overdo it. You won't get extra credit for drawing a more complete diagram.

Draw the minimum diagram that is required to identify the answer!

Warning!! A number of LSAT preparation books have suggested that test takers draw part of the diagram in pen! Although this may have been permissible in past years PENS ARE NOT ALLOWED!

In the words of Law Services:

"You may use only an HB (soft lead) or N. 2 pencil or highlighter pen to underline passages in the test book. Ink or ballpoint pens are not permitted."

Some Specific Diagraming Exercises

These exercises are to give you some practice in organizing information visually. While doing these you should remember your conditional statement rules. Diagraming is highly personalized. There is no absolutely correct or incorrect way to do these.

EXERCISE : Take the following sentences and organize the information visually.

Condition Representation

1. B is further right than position 4.

2. C and D are both further left than E.

3. D is next to E.

4. C is immediately to the right of D.

5. B lies between A and C.

6. There are eight seats numbered consecutively from 1 to 8. A can sit anywhere but on either end.

7. Tom will go to a party only if Nora goes to the party.

8. A, B, and C are men and D, E, and F are women.

9. Some students play golf.

10. B is further left than A.
    C is further left than B.
    D is further left then E.
    E is further left than A.

11. C is two seats from D.

12. W and Z are each taller than V and Y.

13. M is heavier than Q, and is lighter than R.
    S is heavier than Q, and is heavier than R.
    U is heavier than Q, and is heavier than R.

14. At least one instructor must accompany each student.

GO ON TO THE NEXT PAGE

15. Assume a swimming pool with ten lanes
    which are numbered consecutively from 1
    to 10 with 1 at the left.

    There are 10 swimmers - 3 from the U.S.,
      1 from Japan, 4 from Mexico, and 2 from
      Cuba.
    One swimmer is in each lane.
    No U.S. swimmers are in adjacent lanes.
    The Japanese swimmer is exactly between
      the Cuban swimmers.
    Each Mexican swimmer is adjacent to at
      least one other Mexican.

16. City H is 40 miles along a straight road
      from City J.
    City I is 20 miles along a straight road
      from City J.
    City K is 10 miles along a straight road
      from City I.

Answers to questions 1 - 16

1. 4 B

2. C D E   ⌢ = can be reversed

3. D I E   I = directly adjacent

4. D I C

5. A B C

6. 1 2 3 4 5 6 7 8

7. T ⟶ N   ⟶ = if...then

8. a,b,c D,E,F   You can designate category
                   by putting some in lower case
                   and some in upper case.

9. Stu ---> Golf   ---> = some

10. C B A
     D E

11. 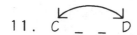 C _ _ D

12. ^W Z^ ┊ ^W Z^
     V ┊   Y

Use the symbol "^" to indicate that something can move up in direction of the arrow. We don't know if W is above, below or equal to Z.

13. S U^
   R
   M
   Q

We don't know where U is relative to S. U could be above, below or equal to S.

14. Stu ⟶ Instructor   ⟶ = If then

15. 3 U.S. + 1 Japan + 4 Mexico + 2 Cuba = 10

  1 2 3 4 5 6 7 8 9 10

  | M ┃ M | | C * J * C | | ⊠ U┃U ⊠ |

┃ = directly adjacent

* = equally spaced but not necessarily directly adjacent.

16.
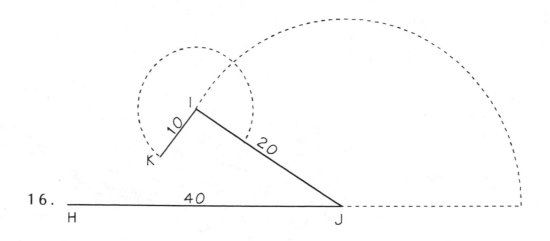

━━━▶ EXERCISE : Organize the information visually and use the diagram to
determine the correct answer for the following questions
which appear in LSAT format.

Questions 17 - 18

An airport has ten intersecting runways.

> Five of the runways run north-south, and are
> numbered consecutively from 1 to 5, with
> runway number 1 farthest west.
> The other five runways run east-west, and are
> numbered consecutively from 6 to 10, with
> runway 6 farthest south.
> FAA regulations permit only northerly
> movement on runways 1, 3 and 5 and only
> westerly movement on runways 6, 8 and 10.

17. A plane lands on runway 8 and must taxi to the
intersection of runways 1 and 6. The fastest
legal way for him to get there is to:

(A) make a left turn on to runway 3, followed
by a right turn on to runway 6
(B) make a left turn on to runway 1
(C) make a left turn on to runway 2 followed
by a right turn on to runway 6
(D) make a right turn on to runway 3 followed
by a right turn on to runway 6
(E) change his flight plan to land on the corner
of runways 1 and 6

18. A plane taxiing east on a runway could make a
right turn at each of the following intersections
except:

(A) runways 9 and 2
(B) runways 7 and 4
(C) runways 9 and 4
(D) runways 8 and 2
(E) runways 7 and 2

19. There are five people standing on the rungs of a
ladder with no more than one person on each
rung.

B is two rungs above A.
D is one rung above C.
A is on the rung which is exactly between the
rungs that B and C are on.
A is one rung below E.

From top to bottom the order of the people is:

(A) E, A, B, C, D
(B) B, E, A, D, C
(C) C, D, B, E, A
(D) D, E, A, B, C
(E) D, B, A, E, C

GO ON TO NEXT PAGE

Questions 20 - 21

All students are subsidized from public funds.
All people who get subsidies from public funds
are public charges.
All people on welfare are public charges.
Most students are Democrats.
Some people who are permanently employed are
students.
Some public charges are Democrats.
All Democrats are believers in subsidized
medicare.

20. On the basis of the above information it must
    be concluded that:

    (A) Some people who are permanently
        employed are Democrats.
    (B) Some Students are on welfare.
    (C) Some permanently employed people are
        public charges.
    (D) All believers in subsidized medicare are
        students.
    (E) The class of persons who are students is
        identical to the class of persons on welfare.

21. On the basis of the above information it must be
    concluded that:

    (A) All people on welfare believe in subsidized
        medicare.
    (B) Some public charges believe in subsidized
        medicare.
    (C) All permanently employed people are public
        charges.
    (D) Some people who are permanently
        employed are on welfare.
    (E) None of the above.

Questions 22 - 24

Six persons A, B, C, D, E, and F walk into a restaurant.

The restaurant has a smoking area and a non-smoking
area with a square table with four seats (one on each
side) in each of the two sections.
No smoker will sit in the non-smokers area and vice
versa.
One and only one of A and B smoke.
Both C and E smoke and there is a seat between them.

22. If E and F are seated side by side at the same
    table, and if A and D are seated side by side at the
    same table then it must be true that:

    I.   B is a smoker
    II. There is an empty seat across from A
    III. There is an empty seat across from F

    (A) I only
    (B) I and II only
    (C) II only
    (D) II and III only
    (E) I, II and III

23. If the waiter, W, sat down at one of the two tables
    and sat beside B of B's table, then it must be
    concluded that:

    (A) B smokes.
    (B) A is sitting between C and E at their table.
    (C) D is a smoker.
    (D) E is a non-smoker.
    (E) W is sitting across from F.

24. If B and E are seated at the same table, with E to
    the immediate right of B, and if D and F are
    seated at the same table, with F to the right of D,
    then it must be true that

    (A) A is sitting at the same table as E.
    (B) A is sitting to the immediate right of F.
    (C) A is sitting to the immediate left of D.
    (D) A is sitting to the immediate left of C.
    (E) There is an empty seat between C and E.

ANSWERS ON NEXT PAGE

Answers to questions 17 - 18

17. (C)
18. (D)

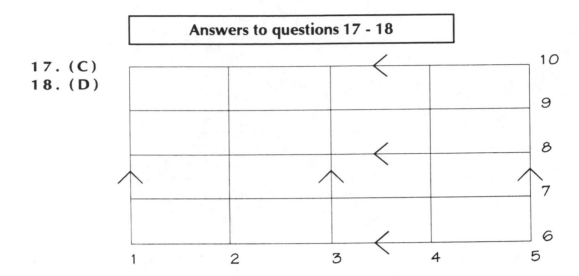

Answer to question 19

19. (B)   Step 1 = working with condition 1

- B
-
- A
-
-

Step 2 = step 1 + condition 3

- B
-
- A
-
- C

Step 3 = step 2 + condition 2

- B
-
- A
- D
- C

Step 4 = step 3 + condition 4

- B
- E
- A
- D
- C

Answers to questions 20 - 21

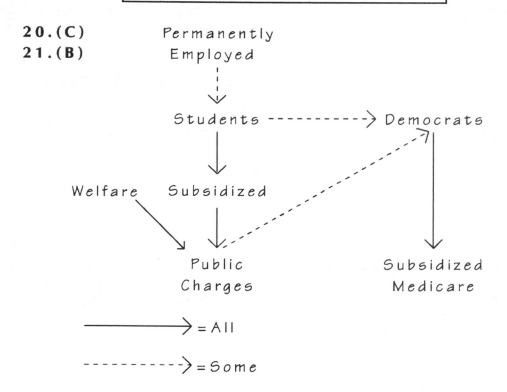

20.(C)
21.(B)

Permanently Employed

Students - - - - - - - - > Democrats

Welfare   Subsidized

Public Charges

Subsidized Medicare

———————> = All

- - - - - - - - -> = Some

Answers to questions 22 - 24

General Fixed Information

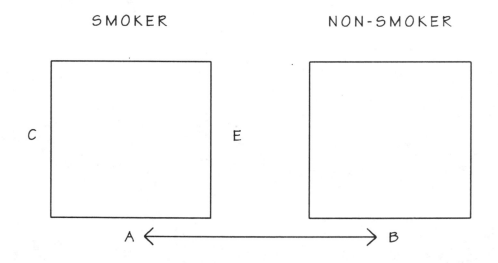

SMOKER

NON-SMOKER

C

E

A <———————————> B

22.(B) SMOKER   NON-SMOKER

B   A

C   E   D

F

23.(B) SMOKER   NON-SMOKER

C   E   B

A   W

24.(E) SMOKER   NON-SMOKER

C   E   F

A

B   D

SUMMARY TEST - TOPICAL EXERCISES

Examples Of Specific Types Of Patterns

Assignment Problems

Questions 1 - 4

An airline administrator is scheduling flight attendants to fly for one seven-day period beginning on a Monday and ending on a Sunday. The administrator must assign exactly two flight attendants to fly on exactly one plane for each of the seven days. The administrator can choose from a total of six flight attendants.

> There are three senior flight attendants - K, L, and M.
> There are three junior flight attendants - P, Q, and R.
> At least one senior flight attendant must fly on each of the seven days.
> Each flight attendant flies at least two of the seven days.
> L flies exactly three of the seven days and they are consecutive.
> K always flies on Friday.
> P never flies on Thursday.
> M never flies on Saturday.
> M and Q never fly together.

1. Which of the following is an acceptable schedule, beginning with Monday and ending with Sunday?

   (A) KR; LR; LQ; LQ; KM; KP; MP
   (B) KR; LR; LQ; LQ; KP; KP; MR
   (C) LQ; LQ; LR; KR; KP; MP; MP
   (D) LQ; LQ; LQ; KP; KR; MP; MP
   (E) LR; QR; LP; LP; LR; KQ; MQ

2. Which of the following must be true?

   (A) M flies only two of the seven days.
   (B) Q flies only two of the seven days.
   (C) P, Q, and R fly an equal number of days.
   (D) No flight attendant flies more than three of the seven days.
   (E) Three flight attendants fly three of the seven days.

3. If M, R, and P are scheduled to fly on Friday, Saturday, and Sunday, respectively, which of the following must be true?

   (A) M flies on Sunday.
   (B) Q flies on Tuesday.
   (C) L and Q fly together at least one day.
   (D) L and P fly together at least one day.
   (E) M and R fly together at least one day.

4. If there are no days on which L and Q are scheduled to fly together, which of the following must be true?

   (A) L flies on Thursday.
   (B) Q flies on Monday.
   (C) R flies on Thursday.
   (D) K flies with Q two of the seven days.
   (E) M flies with R two of the seven days.

Author's Note On Variable Information

The "variable information" has been italicized in questions 3 and 4. This will not be done on the the actual LSAT. I have done this to assist those of you who have difficulty identifying the "variable information." This is necessary for understanding the explanations.

GO ON TO NEXT PAGE

Questions 5 - 10

On Saturday, Sunday, and Monday of every Victoria Day weekend, a small charter plane company uses each of its three planes, plane 1, plane 2, and plane 3, for separate all-day trips. The flying assignments for Victoria Day weekends are distributed among four pilots, K, L, M, and N, in accordance with the following restrictions:

K does not fly plane 2.
M flies plane 3 only.
N must not be given more flying assignments than L on any Victoria Day weekend.
Each of the pilots must be given at least one flying assignment on a Victoria Day weekend.

5. If on a particular Victoria Day weekend N's only assignment is to fly plane 3 on Saturday, all of the following must be true EXCEPT:

(A) K is assigned to fly plane 1 on Sunday.
(B) L is assigned to fly plane 2 on Monday.
(C) Plane 1 has the same pilot throughout the weekend.
(D) Plane 2 has two different pilots in the course of the weekend.
(E) The flying assignments for Sunday and for Monday are identical.

6. Which of the following must be true of L's flying assignment for any Victoria Day weekend?

(A) L flies plane 1 only once, if at all.
(B) L does not fly plane 3.
(C) L is given at least two flying assignments.
(D) L flies on all the days that M flies.
(E) L flies on all the days that N flies.

7. If on a particular Victoria Day weekend N's entire flying assignment is to fly plane 1 on Saturday and again on Monday, which of the following must be among the flying assignments for that weekend?

(A) M flies plane 3 on Saturday.
(B) M flies plane 3 on Sunday.
(C) K flies plane 3 on Monday.
(D) L flies plane 1 on Sunday.
(E) L flies plane 3 on Monday.

8. If K and M are given an equal number of flying assignments for a particular Victoria Day weekend, which of the following could also be true of that weekend's flying assignments?

(A) K and L have an equal number of flying assignments.
(B) L and N have an equal number of flying assignments.
(C) M and N have an equal number of flying assignments.
(D) K's assignments are all for different days than M's assignments.
(E) L's assignments are all for the same days as N's assignments.

9. If N is assigned to fly a different plane on each of the three days of a particular Victoria Day weekend, which of the following could be true of that weekend?

(A) On one of the three days, K flies plane 3.
(B) On one of the three days, K and M both fly a plane.
(C) On one of the three days, L flies none of the planes.
(D) K and M have an equal number of flying assignments.
(E) M and N have an equal number of flying assignments.

10. If exactly three of the four pilots are given equal numbers of flying assignments for a particular Victoria Day weekend, which of the following must be true of that weekend's flying assignments?

(A) K flies plane 1 only.
(B) L flies plane 2 only.
(C) N flies plane 3 on at least one of the three days.
(D) L is the pilot who has a different number of flying assignments from the other three.
(E) N is one of the three who have equal numbers of flying assignments.

GO ON TO THE NEXT PAGE

Grouping

Questions 11 - 16

A five-member group of doctors composed of two men and three women is to be selected. The male applicant pool consists of Kevin, Bill, Gil, and Steve. The female applicant pool consists of Marie, Roma, Alice, Clara, and Jane.

Marie and Alice will not serve together.
Bill and Gil will not serve together.
Kevin and Clara will not serve together.
Only Kevin, Gil, Alice, and Jane have clinical experience.
At least three people with clinical experience must be selected.

11. If the four applicants with clinical experience are selected to serve in the group, which of the following applicants will also be selected?

   (A) Clara
   (B) Marie
   (C) Roma
   (D) Bill
   (E) Steve

12. If Kevin is not selected to serve in the group the only other decision to be made is whether to select:

   (A) Marie or Alice
   (B) Marie or Roma
   (C) Roma or Clara
   (D) Bill or Gil
   (E) Bill or Steve

13. Which of the following pairs of women CANNOT serve together in the group?

   (A) Marie and Roma
   (B) Marie and Clara
   (C) Roma and Alice
   (D) Roma and Jane
   (E) Alice and Clara

14. Which of the following pairs of men CANNOT serve together in the group?

   (A) Kevin and Bill
   (B) Kevin and Gil
   (C) Kevin and Steve
   (D) Steve and Bill
   (E) Steve and Gil

15. If Steve is not selected, which of the following statements must be FALSE?

   (A) Jane is selected.
   (B) Roma is selected.
   (C) Alice is selected.
   (D) Clara is not selected.
   (E) Kevin is not selected.

16. Which of the following persons must be selected to serve in the group?

   (A) Gil
   (B) Kevin
   (C) Steve
   (D) Jane
   (E) Roma

GO ON TO THE NEXT PAGE

Questions 17 - 22

A stockbroker has nine blocks of stock which have been allocated to the portfolios of three different clients.

> One block of stock consists of 100 shares of the stock in question. There are two blocks of stock L, two blocks of stock M, and one block each of types N, O, P, Q, and R.
> Each portfolio consists of at least two different kinds of stock.
> The two blocks of stock L are in different portfolios.
> The two blocks of stock M are in different portfolios.
> Blocks L and N are in different portfolios.
> Blocks Q and R are in the same portfolio.
> Block O is in a portfolio with one of the blocks of M.

17. If blocks P, Q, and R are in the same portfolio, which of the following must be true?

   (A) Blocks N and O are in the same portfolio.
   (B) Blocks P, Q, and R and one block of L are in the same portfolio.
   (C) Blocks P, Q, R, and N are in the same portfolio.
   (D) No block of L is in the same portfolio as block O.
   (E) No block of M is in the same portfolio as P.

18. If one portfolio contains exactly five blocks of stock, which of the following must be true?

   (A) Block Q is in a portfolio with a block of M.
   (B) Block N is in a portfolio that contains exactly five blocks.
   (C) One portfolio contains only a block of L and a block of M.
   (D) One portfolio contains only the N and the P.
   (E) One portfolio contains only P and a block of L.

19. If there are three blocks of stock in each portfolio, which of the following must be true?

   (A) Blocks N and O are in the same portfolio.
   (B) Block P and a block of L are in the same portfolio.
   (C) If blocks N and P are in the same portfolio, a block of M is with them.

(D) If blocks N and P are in the same portfolio, blocks Q, R, and a block of M are together in another portfolio.
(E) If blocks Q and L are in the same portfolio, blocks N, P, and a block of M are together in another portfolio.

20. If block N is not in the same portfolio as a block of M, which of the following are groups of stock that can be together in a portfolio?

   I.   Blocks O, Q, R, a block of L, and a block of M.
   II. Blocks P, Q, R, a block of L, a block of M.
   III. Blocks N, P, Q, R.

   (A) I only
   (B) I and II only
   (C) I and III only
   (D) II and III only
   (E) I, II and III

21. If there are three blocks in each portfolio and block N is not in a portfolio with either blocks of M, which of the following is a group of blocks that must be together in a portfolio?

   (A) P, Q, and R
   (B) N, Q, and R
   (C) O, P, and one block of M
   (D) Q, R, and a block of L
   (E) Q, R, and a block of M

22. If block P and a block of M are in the same portfolio, which of the following must be true?

   (A) Blocks N, O, and a block of M are in the same portfolio.
   (B) Blocks N, P and a block of M are in the same portfolio.
   (C) If block N is in a portfolio with block P and a block of M, then block O is in another portfolio.
   (D) If block N is in a portfolio with block P and a block of M, then blocks Q, R, and a block of L are together in another portfolio.
   (E) If block P, L, and one of blocks M are in the same portfolio, then blocks Q, R and one of blocks L are together in another portfolio.

GO ON TO NEXT PAGE

Ordering

Questions 23 - 28

Carie, Gerry, Jim, Nancy, Ron, and Steve are members of a dance class. The talents of the members vary greatly. Although other participants join and leave the class at different times , the following information is always true.

Gerry is more talented than Carie.
Gerry is less talented than Jim.
Ron is less talented than Nancy.
Ron is more talented than Steve.

It is possible for some members to have the same ability.

23. If Ron is less talented than Gerry, which of the following statements must be true?

    (A) Nancy is less talented than Gerry.
    (B) Nancy is less talented than Carie.
    (C) Ron is more talented than Carie.
    (D) Jim is more talented than Steve.
    (E) Carie is more talented than Steve.

24. If Gerry and Ron have equal talents, which of the following must be true?

    I. Steve is less talented than Jim.
    II. Jim is more talented than Nancy.
    III. Nancy is more talented than Carie.

    (A) I only
    (B) II only
    (C) III only
    (D) I and II only
    (E) I and III only

25. Additional information about class members Paul, Kev, and Al reveals that Paul and Kev are more talented than Steve and Al is less talented than Carie. If Steve is more talented than Gerry, each of the following could be the most talented EXCEPT:

    (A) Jim
    (B) Kev
    (C) Nancy
    (D) Paul
    (E) Ron

26. Assume that Larry and Martin join the class. If Larry is less talented than Nancy, if Martin is more talented than Jim, and if Jim is less talented than Larry, which of the following must be true?

    I. Nancy is the most talented.
    II. Ron is less talented than Martin.
    III. Larry is more talented than Carie.

    (A) I only
    (B) II only
    (C) III only
    (D) I and III only
    (E) II and III only

27. Assume that Bert and Will join the class. If Bert is less talented than Carie, if Will is more talented than Nancy, and if Bert is more talented than Will, which of the following must be true?

    (A) Ron is less talented than Gerry.
    (B) Ron is more talented than Bert.
    (C) Steve is more talented than Will.
    (D) Bert is more talented than Jim.
    (E) Will is more talented than Carie.

28. Assume that Fred and Travis join the class. If Fred is more talented than Steve, if Travis is more talented than Gerry, and if Gerry and Ron have equal talents, each of the following can be true EXCEPT:

    (A) Gerry is more talented than Fred.
    (B) Fred is more talented than Nancy.
    (C) Travis is less talented than Carie.
    (D) Jim is less talented than Travis.
    (E) Nancy is less talented than Jim.

GO ON TO NEXT PAGE

Questions 29 - 35

Seven patients addicted to chemicals arrived, one at a time, to attend a meeting of only those patients.

The first patient to arrive had the same addiction as the last.
The number of patients who arrived between the two alcoholics is one more than the number who arrived after the Valium addict.
The caffeine addict arrived before the marijuana addict.
Two patients were cocaine addicts.
No patient has more than one addiction.

29. If the second patient to arrive was an alcoholic, which of the following must be true?

   I. The sixth patient to arrive was the Valium addict.
   II. The third patient to arrive was the caffeine addict.
   III. The fifth patient to arrive was either an alcoholic or the Valium addict.

   (A) I only
   (B) II only
   (C) I and II only
   (D) II and III only
   (E) I, II, and III

30. Each of the following describes a possible order of arrival EXCEPT:

   (A) both alcoholics arrived before the Valium addict.
   (B) both cocaine addicts arrived before the Valium addict.
   (C) both cocaine addicts arrived after the marijuana addict.
   (D) at least one alcoholic arrived after the caffeine addict.
   (E) the marijuana addict arrived between the caffeine addict and the Valium addict.

31. If the first three patients to arrive at the meeting were women, which of the following statements must be true?

   (A) The last patient to arrive was a man.
   (B) Only three patients at the meeting were women.

(C) At least one alcoholic was a woman.
(D) At least one cocaine addict was a woman.
(E) The Valium addict was a man.

32. If the marijuana addict arrived immediately after the caffeine addict and the Valium addict arrived before the caffeine addict, which of the following must be true?

   I. The second patient to arrive was a cocaine addict.
   II. The last patient to arrive was an alcoholic.
   III. The third patient to arrive was the Valium addict.

   (A) I only
   (B) II only
   (C) III only
   (D) I and II only
   (E) I, II, and III

33. If no one arrived between the cocaine addicts, the second patient to arrive was:

   (A) the Valium addict.
   (B) the caffeine addict.
   (C) the marijuana addict.
   (D) one of the cocaine addicts.
   (E) one of the alcoholics.

34. Assume that one of the cocaine addicts was from California and the other was from Florida and that the Florida addict arrived after the California addict and immediately after one of the alcoholics. How many orders of arrival would satisfy these, as well as the original conditions?

   (A) 1
   (B) 2
   (C) 3
   (D) 4
   (E) 5

GO ON TO NEXT PAGE

35. If the first patient to arrive was the caffeine addict, which of the following original conditions could NOT be true?

(A) Seven patients attended a meeting.
(B) The first patient to arrive had the same addiction as the last.
(C) The number of patients who arrived between the two alcoholics is one more than the number who arrived after the Valium addict.
(D) The caffeine addict arrived before the marijuana addict.
(E) Two of the patients were cocaine addicts.

Spatial Relationships

Questions 36 - 41

The City of Markville has exactly seven schools. Markville has only one high school and six elementary schools.

A, B, C, D, E, and F are the only elementary schools.
G is the only high school.
The high school is in the center of Markville and the elementary schools are positioned around it.
A, B, and D are north of G.
C, E, and F are south of G.
F is due south of A.
D is due north of E.
There are one half the number of schools west of G as there are east of G.
Those who travel exactly northeast from C first encounter G, then A, and then D.

36. School B lies in which direction from School G?

(A) Due north
(B) Due south
(C) Northeast
(D) Northwest
(E) Southwest

37. Which of the following directions could be taken in going directly from School B to School C?

I. Due south
II. Exactly southwest
III. Southeast

(A) I only
(B) II only
(C) III only
(D) I and II only
(E) I and III only

38. If someone were to travel directly east from school C, what is the maximum number of schools that person could encounter?

(A) 0
(B) 1
(C) 2
(D) 3
(E) 4

39. Which of the following statements must be true?

(A) School D is south of School A.
(B) School B is south of School D.
(C) School C is east of School B.
(D) School E is east of School G.
(E) School E is west of School F.

40. How many of the schools must be north of B?

(A) 4
(B) 3
(C) 2
(D) 1
(E) 0

41. What is the maximum number of schools that can be west of School A?

(A) 0
(B) 1
(C) 2
(D) 3
(E) 4

GO ON TO NEXT PAGE

Questions 42 - 47

Six cars are to be placed on a revolving circular display stand. There are exactly six spaces for cars on the stand. Each space faces the center of the display stand and is directly opposite another space on this stand.

The six cars that must be placed on the stand are a Ford, Chrysler, Jaguar, Mercedes, Toyota, and Nissan. These cars must be placed on the stand subject to the following constraints:

The Ford cannot be placed next to the Toyota.
The Chrysler cannot be placed next to the Nissan.
The Jaguar must be placed next to the Toyota.

42. If the Ford is placed next to the Jaguar, and if the Chrysler is placed next to the Toyota, which cars must be placed on either side of the Mercedes?

    (A) Ford and Chrysler
    (B) Ford and Toyota
    (C) Ford and Nissan
    (D) Chrysler and Jaguar
    (E) Chrysler and Nissan

43. If the Chrysler is placed next to the Jaguar, and the Mercedes is placed next to the Toyota, which car must be placed directly across the display stand from the Toyota?

    (A) Ford
    (B) Chrysler
    (C) Jaguar
    (D) Mercedes
    (E) Nissan

44. If the Jaguar is placed beside the Mercedes, which of the following is a complete and accurate list of the cars that can be placed on the other side of and beside the Mercedes?

    (A) Ford
    (B) Chrysler
    (C) Nissan
    (D) Ford, Chrysler
    (E) Chrysler, Nissan

45. If the Jaguar is placed to the immediate right of the Toyota, and the Chrysler is placed to the immediate left of the Toyota, which of the following is the total number of arrangements in which the other cars can be placed in relation to one another?

    (A) 1
    (B) 2
    (C) 3
    (D) 4
    (E) 5

46. If the Chrysler is placed directly across from the Mercedes, on the stand, which cars must be placed beside and on either side of the Nissan?

    (A) Ford and Mercedes
    (B) Ford and Toyota
    (C) Chrysler and Jaguar
    (D) Jaguar and Mercedes
    (E) Mercedes and Toyota

47. If the Ford is placed directly across from the Toyota on the stand, which of the following could NOT be true?

    (A) The Chrysler is placed directly across from the Mercedes.
    (B) The Jaguar is placed directly across from the Nissan.
    (C) The Chrysler is placed beside the Mercedes.
    (D) The Jaguar is placed beside the Mercedes.
    (E) The Nissan is placed beside the Mercedes.

ANSWERS AND COMMENTARY

Introduction

There are many generalized principles of approach that apply to logic games. I encourage you to be as flexible as possible when you do this question type. In order to understand my explanations you must understand what I mean by the words "variable information." Therefore, I want to remind you of this.

"Variable information" is information that is **added to an individual question to be used in that question only.** It is not to be carried to another question. **It is extremely common for "variable information" to begin with the word "if."**

Questions 1 - 4

Preliminary Discussion - This is a good starter set of questions. The conditions talk about senior flight attendants and junior flight attendants. In order to keep them distinct, you could designate the senior attendants in upper case ("K, L, M") and the junior flight attendants in lower case ("p, q, r"). Secondly, let's use this set of questions as an exercise in reading and interpreting language.

We are told that **exactly** two attendants are on each day. We are told that **at least one** must be senior. It would be a mistake to interpret this to mean that one must be a senior and one must be a junior. In fact, it is possible to have two senior flight attendants. Make sure that you have all occurrences of restrictive language underlined. (at least, exactly, etc.)

1. The operative words are "is an acceptable schedule." Your job is to eliminate any choice that is not acceptable. A choice will not be acceptable if it conflicts with one or more of the conditions. Remember that we eliminate from condition to answer choice.

Let's start with the condition that says that M never flies on Saturday.
(C) and (D) are wrong because they violate that condition.

Now let's look at the condition that says that M and Q never fly together.
(E) is wrong because it violates that condition.

Finally, let's consider the condition that says that each attendant must fly at least two days.
(B) is wrong because M works only one day.

(A) is the correct answer. It is the only one that cannot be eliminated.

2. The operative words are "must be true." This question focuses on the numerical distribution. Remember that there is no requirement that there be both a senior and junior flight attendant each day. On some days it is possible to have two senior flight attendants. But, we must have at least one senior flight attendant on each of the seven days. This leaves seven additional openings. There are three junior attendants and each must fly at least two days. This accounts for six of the remaining seven openings. There is **one left. This extra day could be flown by either a senior or a junior flight attendant.**

(A) is wrong. M is a senior attendant and could fly the extra day giving M three days.

(B) is wrong. You will recall that Q is a junior attendant and could fly the extra day giving Q three days.

(C) is wrong for the same reason that (B) is wrong. If it is possible for Q to fly the extra day, this would mean that Q would fly three days and each of P and R would fly two days.

(E) is wrong. There are fourteen slots in total. There are six attendants and each must get at least two. If three attendants filled three slots, this would leave five slots. But there are three remaining attendants. Each of the three must get at least two slots. Therefore, we would need a total of six slots for the three remaining attendants. But, we would only have five left. Hence, three attendants cannot fly for three days filling nine of the fourteen slots.

For another way to eliminate (E) consider the following. We identified (A) as the answer to the previous question. This is to say that **the combination depicted in that choice is possible.** In that choice there is no case of three of the attendants getting three days of work. **Therefore, it does not have to be the case that three attendants work three days.**

(D) is correct. It is the remaining and only possible choice.

3. The operative words are "must be true." Your job is to eliminate any choice that does not have to be true. We are told that M, R, and P are scheduled to fly on Friday Saturday and Sunday. **What is the effect of this variable information?** There are two basic diagrams. The first has the three Ls on Monday, Tuesday, and Wednesday. The second has the Ls on Tuesday, Wednesday, and Thursday.

Diagram #1

M	T	W	T	F	S	S
L	L	L		K		
		q	q	M	r	p

Diagram #2

M	T	W	T	F	S	S
	L	L	L	K		
	q	q		M	r	p

(A) is wrong. M could fly on Monday. See diagram 2.

(B) is wrong. Q could fly on Wednesday and Thursday. See diagram 1.

(D) is wrong. See diagram 2. P could fly on Monday avoiding L.

(E) is wrong. In either diagram M could fly on Sunday and R could fly on another day.

(C) is correct. In either diagram Q must fly with L at least one day.

4. The operative words are "must be true." Your job is to eliminate any choice that does not have to be true. We are told that there are no days in which L and Q are scheduled to fly together. **What is the effect of this variable information?** Each senior flight attendant must fly at least two days and on each day there must be at least one senior flight attendant. Therefore, if L flies three days, K must fly at least two days, and M must fly at least two days. We are told in the initial conditions that M and Q never fly together. We are now told that L and Q never fly together. This means that the only senior flight attendant left for Q to fly with is K. Therefore, Q must fly with K on the two days that K is the senior flight attendant. See the following two diagrams.

Diagram #1

M	T	W	T	F	S	S
L	L	L	M	K	K	M
				q	q	

Diagram #2

M	T	W	T	F	S	S
M	L	L	L	K	K	M
				q	q	

(D) is the correct answer.

Questions 5 - 10

Preliminary Discussion - There is no way to read these conditions and know exactly what is going on. You must use the questions to learn how the conditions operate. You should not necessarily do the questions in the order given. Search for the easiest ones first. Questions 5 and 7 look like they might be the easiest to start with. The reason is that each of these questions contains variable information which places specific pilots in specific planes on specific days. Although the questions are discussed in numerical order, I think that you should look first at questions 5, 7 and 9.

5. The operative words are "must be true EXCEPT." Your job is to eliminate the answer choices that must be true. **What is the effect of the variable information?**

   First, if N's only assignment is to fly plane 3 on Saturday that means that K, L, and M fly on Sunday and Monday. M flies only plane 3 and K will not fly plane 2. This means that K, L, and M will fly planes 1, 2, and 3 on Sunday and Monday.

   Second, for Saturday, the fact that M will fly only plane 3 and that N is already flying plane 3 on Saturday means that M will not fly on Saturday. This leaves K and L. But, K will not fly plane 2. For Saturday, this means that K will fly 1, L will fly 2, and N will fly 3. See the following diagram.

	Sat	Sun	Mon
1	K	K	K
2	L	L	L
3	N	M	M

   (A), (B), (C), and (E) are wrong. They are consistent with the diagram.

   (D) is correct. It is the only choice that is not consistent with the diagram. Therefore, it must not be true.

6. The operative words are "must be true." Your job is to eliminate any choice that does not have to be true. These questions are generally among the most difficult. **But, often some additional information can be learned by doing them.**

   (A) is wrong. Why not put L in plane 1 and N in plane 2 for all three days? Then put K in plane 3 on Saturday and M in plane 3 on Sunday and Monday.
   (B) is wrong. This does not have to be true. There is nothing to prevent a situation where L is in 3, K is in 1, and N is in 2.
   (D) is wrong. You can have M without L. Why not, L in 3, K in 1 and N in 2?
   (E) is wrong. You can have N without L. Why not M in 3, K in 1 and L in 2?

   (C) is correct. L must have at least two assignments. If L does not have at least two, then N would have more assignments than L. This is forbidden by the rules.

7. The operative words are "must be among." Your job is to eliminate the choices that need not be among the flying assignments for the weekend. **What is the effect of the variable information?**

If N's entire assignment is to fly plane 1 on Saturday and on Monday, that means that N does not fly on Sunday. This means that K, L, and M fly on Sunday. K flies 1, L flies 2, and M flies 3. This is illustrated in the following diagram.

	Sat	Sun	Mon
1	N	K	N
2		L	
3		M	

(A), (C), (D), and (E) are wrong because they don't have to be true.

(B) is correct. You can see the answer in the diagram.

8. The operative words are "could also be true." Your job is to eliminate the choices that could not be true. We are told that K and M are given an equal number of assignments. **What is the effect of the variable information?**

The question focuses on numerical distribution. We have a total of 9 flying assignments to be allocated among 4 pilots. **Remember that N cannot be given more assignments than L.** The following chart reveals the following possibilities for numerical distribution.

K	L	M	N
2	3	2	2
3	2	3	1

(A) and (B) are wrong. See the chart.

(D) is wrong. Since K and M each fly at least two days, they must fly on the same day at least once.

(E) is wrong. The chart reveals that L flies more days than N. Hence, L will not always fly on the same day as N.

(C) is correct. Our diagram reveals that it is possible for M and N to each have two flying assignments.

9. The operative words are "could be true." Your job is to eliminate any choices that could not be true. **What is the effect of the variable information?**

Since N flies a different plane on each of the three days, N flies each day. Since N cannot be given more assignments than L, L must also fly on each of the three days. This leaves three slots left for K and M. One and only one of them will fly on each of the three days. This is illustrated in the following diagram.

	Sat	Sun	Mon
1	N	L	
2	L	N	L
3			N

(B) is wrong. You can't have K and M together on the same day.
(C) is wrong. L flies on each day.
(D) is wrong. There are only three slots left to be divided between K and M.
(E) is wrong. N has more assignments than M.

(A) is correct. Our diagram shows that it is possible for K to fly plane 3 on one of the days.

10. The operative words are "must be true." Your job is to eliminate choices that must not be true. We are told that exactly three of the four pilots are given an equal number of assignments. **What is the effect of the variable information?**

The question focuses on numerical distribution. The effect of exactly three of the four pilots being given equal numbers of flying assignments is that three of the pilots have two assignments and one has three. N can never be the pilot who gets three flying assignments. (N would then have more than L.) This is illustrated in the following chart.

	K	L	M	N
Scenario 1	2	3	2	2
Scenario 2	3	2	2	2
Scenario 3	2	2	3	2

(A), (B), and (C) are wrong. Although they could be true, they don't qualify as must be true.
(D) is wrong. See the second and third scenarios. In each of these L has the same number as two others.

(E) is correct. N can never be the pilot that has three assignments. Remember, N cannot have more assignments than L.

Questions 11 - 16

Preliminary Discussion - Grouping questions are difficult to diagram. They have been heavily tested over the years. It is important to be clear on how many people you are dealing with.

Fixed Information

2 Men + 3 Women = 5 Total

11. The operative words are "will also." Your job is to eliminate the choices containing people who will not be selected. **What is the effect of the variable information?** We know that the two men have been accounted for. Therefore, the final person must be a woman. See the following diagram.

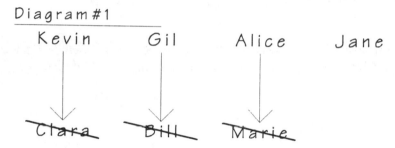

Diagram #1

(D) and (E) are wrong because they are men. The third person must be a women. This leaves us with (A), (B), (C).

(A) is wrong. If we have Kevin we cannot have Clara.

(B) is wrong. If we have Alice we cannot have Marie.

(C) is correct. It is the only choice left. This means that Roma is the final person. The group of five now appears as follows.

Diagram #2

Kevin, Gil, Alice, Jane, Roma

12. The operative words are "is whether to select." **What is the effect of the variable information?** If Kevin is not selected it means that the other three with clinical experience are selected. See the following diagram.

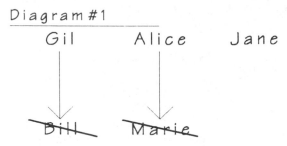

Diagram #1

(D) and (E) are wrong because each contains Bill. Once we have Gil we cannot have Bill.

(A) and (B) are wrong because we cannot have Marie. Once we have Alice we cannot have Marie.

(C) is the answer. It is the only choice left. The choice is whether to select Roma or Clara. This question gives us two possible groups of five.

Diagram #2

13. The operative words are "CANNOT serve together." Your job is to eliminate the pairs that can serve together. An easy way of knowing that something can be true is if we have it drawn in one of our diagrams. Let's look at diagram #2 from question 12.

(C), (D) and (E) are all wrong. Note that each of these combinations is depicted in diagram #2 for question 12.

(A) is wrong. It is a possible combination.

(B) is correct. You cannot have both Marie and Clara. If you have Marie you cannot have Alice. If you have Clara you cannot have Kevin. If you cannot have Alice and Kevin you have lost two of the four with clinical experience. You must have at least three of the four with clinical experience.

14. The operative words are "CANNOT serve together." You must eliminate the pairs that can serve together. An easy way of knowing that something can be true is if we have drawn it in one of our previous diagrams. Let's look at both diagrams #2 from questions 11 and 12.

(B) and (E) are both wrong. They are depicted in the above diagrams. This leaves us with (A), (C), and (D).

(A) and (C) are both wrong. Each is possible.

(D) is correct. Steve and Bill are not possible. It will make it impossible for us to have a group of two men and three women, where at least three out of five must have clinical experience. Let's try to construct a group with Steve and Bill.

Remember that:
1. We need 3 women and 2 men. If we have Steve and Bill the remaining 3 must be women.
2. We must have 3 out of 4 with clinical experience. If we have Bill we can't have Gil. Without Gil we must have Kevin, Alice and Jane. But "Kevin, Alice and Jane" is **not** a group of 3 women. Therefore, we can't have both Steve and Bill.

15. The operative words are "must be FALSE." Our job is to eliminate every choice that is or could be true. We know that something can be true if it appears in a diagram to one of our previous questions. The variable information tells us that Steve is not selected. Let's look at a diagram #2 for question 11. This is a diagram where Steve had not been selected.

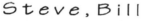

(A), (B), (C), and (D) are selected are wrong. As the above diagram illustrates each of these can be true if Steve is not selected.

(E) is the correct answer. It is false that Kevin was not selected. Kevin is in the above diagram.

16. The operative words are "must be selected." Eliminate any choice that does not have to be selected.

(B) is wrong. The variable information in question 12 tells us that Kevin need not be selected.

(C) is wrong. The variable information in question 15 tells us that Steve need not be selected.

(E) is wrong. The answer to question 12 tells us that the remaining decision is whether to select Roma or Clara. That means that one need not select Roma.

(A) is wrong. If you have Bill then you cannot have Gil. Since it is possible to have Bill, it is possible not to have Gil.

(D) is the correct answer. It is all that is left. Note that Jane is in every one of our previous diagrams.

Questions 17 - 22

Preliminary Discussion - Most students find this to be a very difficult set of questions. It is an excellent teaching tool to demonstrate how one possible arrangement in the form of a diagram can be used to eliminate wrong answers and identify the correct answer. **Therefore, let's make the use of diagrams to eliminate wrong answers, the theme of this discussion.** As always it is a good idea to begin by identifying the **total number** of blocks of stocks and what that total consists of.

$$2 - L + 2 - M + 1 - N + 1 - O + 1 - P + 1 - Q + 1 - R = 9$$

When we are concerned with numerical distribution, we should recognize that there are three portfolios. Each portfolio consists of at least **two** different **kinds** of stock. The possibilities for numerical distribution of each group are:

1	2	3
5	2	2
4	3	2
3	3	3

As always you should note any items that **must be grouped together** and note those items that **cannot be grouped together.**

Items That Must Be Together		Items That Cannot Be Together
Q	O	No M and M
R	M	No L and L
		No L and N

Since the two Ls are in different portfolios and block N cannot be with a block of L:

The 2 Ls and 1 N must be in different potfolios.

17. The operative words are "must be true." Your job is to eliminate any choice that need not always be true. We are told that "P, Q, and R" are in the same portfolio. **What is the effect of this variable information?** What follows is one possible diagram which is consistent with the variable information and the fixed conditions. You will note that by allowing for the possible reversal of N and L, this diagram has really given us two possibilities.

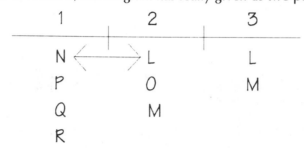

How To Use A *Possible Diagram* To Eliminate Wrong Answers

> **Rule:** No answer choice that describes a situation that is inconsistent with a possible diagram can ever qualify as must be true!

(A) is wrong. The diagram shows that it is possible for N and O to be in different portfolios.

(B) is wrong. The diagram shows that it is possible that P, Q, R, and one block of L need **not** be in the same portfolio.

(C) is wrong. The diagram shows that it is possible that P, Q, R, and N, need not be in the same portfolio. (Reverse N and L).

(D) is wrong. The diagram shows that it is possible for a block of L and a block of O to be together.

(E) **is correct. The other choices have been eliminated and choice (E) is consistent with our diagram.**

18. The operative words are "must be true." Your job is to eliminate any choice that does not have to be true. We are told that one portfolio contains exactly five blocks of stock. **What is the effect of this variable information?** The following diagram is consistent with the variable information and the fixed conditions. You will note that the possible reversal of M and P gives us two possibilities from this one diagram.

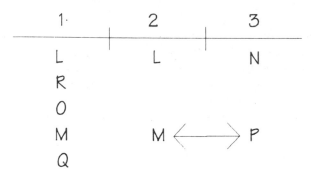

We are now going to use this diagram to eliminate wrong answers. **Remember, no answer choice that describes a scenario inconsistent with this diagram can ever qualify as "must be true."**

(B) is wrong. In our diagram, N is **not** in a portfolio that contains exactly five stocks.

(C) is wrong. In our diagram, it is possible that one portfolio does **not** contain only a block of L and a block of M. (Reverse M and P).

(D) is wrong. In our diagram, it is possible that one portfolio does **not** contain only N and P. (Reverse M and P).

(E) is wrong. In our diagram, it is possible that one portfolio does **not** contain only P and L.

(A) is correct. It is the only choice remaining and is consistent with our diagram.

19. The operative words are "must be true." Your job is to eliminate any answer choice that does not have to be true. We are told that there are three blocks of stock in each portfolio. **What is the effect of this variable information?** Let's remind ourselves of the following pieces of information.

1. L, L, and N are in three different portfolios.

2. The variable information tells us that there are exactly three blocks of stock in each portfolio.

3. "O and M" must be together and must be paired with one of L, L, or N.

4. "Q and R" must be together and must be paired with one of L, L, or N.

See the diagram #1 top of next page.

Diagram #1

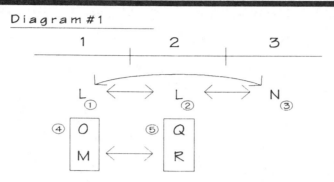

Since there are exactly three in each group "P and M" must be together in the third group. Hence, our diagram now looks like this.

Diagram #2

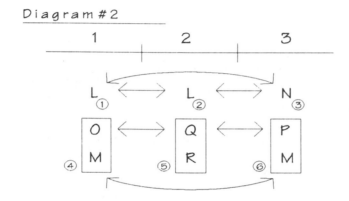

(A) is wrong. N and O do not have to be in the same portfolio.
(B) is wrong. P and L do not have to be in the same portfolio.
(D) is wrong. The diagram reveals that Q, R, and M can never be together.
(E) is wrong. The diagram reveals that is possible for Q and L to be together, and for N, P, and M to **not** be together. (Reverse 6 and 4.)

(C) is correct. P and M are always together. Hence, if N is with P, then N must be with M.

20. The operative words are "can be together." Your job is to eliminate choices with combinations that cannot be together. This is a multiple option question. Do one thing at a time. The variable information is that "N cannot be with M." **What is the effect of this variable information?** If N cannot be with M, then each block of M must be with a block of L. See the following diagram.

Diagram #1

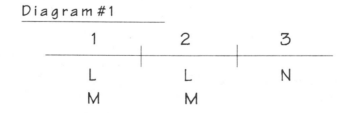

QUESTION 20 CONTINUES ON NEXT PAGE

We know also that O must be with M. Let's incorporate that into the diagram.

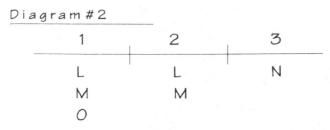

Diagram #2

1	2	3
L	L	N
M	M	
O		

1. Focus on "II." Let's try to put "P, Q, and R" with "L and M." It is impossible because it won't leave us with enough stocks so that the third portfolio has at least two. Look at the following diagram.

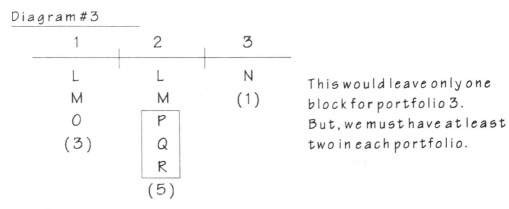

Diagram #3

1	2	3
L	L	N
M	M	(1)
O	[P	
(3)	Q	
	R]	
	(5)	

This would leave only one block for portfolio 3. But, we must have at least two in each portfolio.

Since "II" is not in the answer, eliminate (B), (D), and (E). We are left with (A) and (C).

2. Don't consider "I." It is in both (A) and (C). The only issue is whether "III" is part of the answer. It is possible to have N, P, Q, and R in one portfolio. See the following diagram.

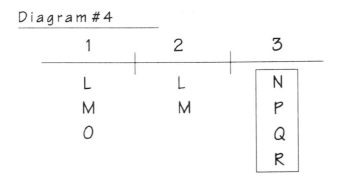

Diagram #4

1	2	3
L	L	[N
M	M	P
O		Q
		R]

"III" is possible.

(C) is the correct answer.

21. The operative words are "must be together." Your job is to eliminate any choices that do not always have to be together. We are told that there are three blocks in each portfolio and that N is not with M. **What is the effect of the variable information?** Groups "O and M" and Groups "Q and R" must be separate. This means that "M and P" must be together. What follows is one diagram that is consistent with this information and with the fixed conditions.

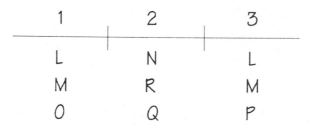

We will eliminate any answer choices that are inconsistent with the possible diagram.

(A), (C), (D) and (E) are all inconsistent with the above diagram. Hence, no one of them qualifies as "must be true."

(B) is the correct answer. It is the one remaining choice and it is consistent with the above diagram.

22. The operative words are "must be true." Your job is to eliminate any answer choice that does not have to be true. The variable information is that "P and M" are together. **What is the effect of the variable information?** Let's look at the following diagram.

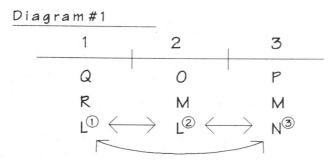

(A) is wrong. It is inconsistent with the diagram.
(B) is wrong. If you reverse N and L (③ and ②) you will see "N, P, and M" need not be in the same portfolio.
(E) is wrong. First reverse the positions of N and L (③ and ②). Then reverse the positions of N and L (③ and ①). You can see that Q, R, and N are in the first portfolio.

We are now left with (C) and (D). Let me remind you that there is nothing wrong with guessing! Notice that each is a conditional statement.

QUESTION 22 CONTINUES ON NEXT PAGE

(C) is wrong. It does not have to be true. Note the following diagram where we have N, P, M, and O together.

Diagram #2

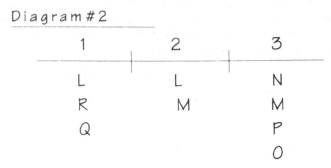

(D) is correct. **It is the remaining choice and it is consistent with both diagrams.**

Questions 23 - 28

Preliminary discussion - This is a "relative ordering" set of questions. The issue will be where one person is relative to another. The initial conditions give us the following fixed information.

Fixed Information

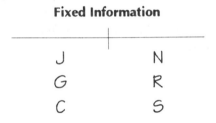

Note that we don't know where J is relative to N, or where G is relative to R, etc. This question type is difficult because there is rarely one diagram. Rather, your diagrams should be interpreted to depict one of a number of possibilities.

23. The operative words are "must be true." Your job is to eliminate any choice that does not have to be true. **What is the effect of the variable information?** We know that "G" is above "R" and therefore above "S." See the following diagram **which is one of a number of possible diagrams.**

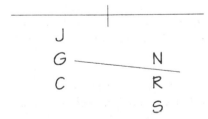

(A) is wrong. Gerry may or may not be above Nancy.
(B) is wrong. Nancy is more talented than Carie.
(C) is wrong. Carie may or may not be above Ron.
(E) is wrong. Steve may or may not be above Carie.

(D) is correct. Since, Steve is below Gerry and Gerry is below Jim, Steve is below Jim.

24. The operative words are "must be true." Your job is to eliminate any choice that does not have to be true. **What is the effect of the variable information?** See the following diagram. This is a multiple option question. Do one thing at time.

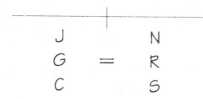

1. Jim is definitely above Steve. Hence, "I" is in the answer. Eliminate choices (B), and (C).
2. We don't know where Nancy is relative to Jim. Hence, "II" is not in the answer. Eliminate choice (D). We are left with (A) and (E).
3. **Must** it be the case that Carie is below Nancy? Yes. Hence, "III" is in the answer.

(E) is the correct answer.

25. The operative words are "could be ... EXCEPT." Your job is to eliminate any choice that can be true. **What is the effect of the variable information?** See the following diagram. Note that we don't know where "P" and "K" are relative to each other or to "R" or "N."

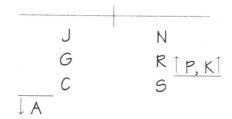

The question is really asking you to identify which of the five choices could never be at the top.

(A), (B), (C), and (D) are wrong. Each of them could be at the top.

(E) is correct. Under no circumstances could Ron ever be at the top. Ron is always less talented than Nancy.

26. The operative words are "must be true." Your job is to eliminate any choice that does not have to be true. **What is the effect of the variable information?** See the following two diagrams. This is a multiple option question. Do one thing at a time.

1. See diagram #2. Nancy does not have to be at the top. Hence, eliminate choices (A) and (D). We are left with (B), (C) and (E).

2. See diagram #1. It is possible for Ron to be above Martin. Hence, "II" is not in the answer. Eliminate (B) and (E).

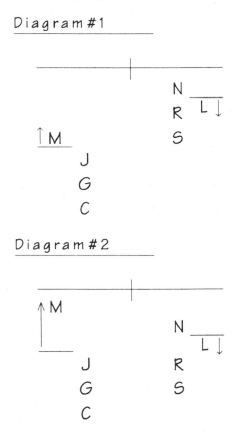

Diagram #1

Diagram #2

(C) is the correct answer. If Jim is below Larry and Carie is below Jim, then Carie is below Larry.

27. The operative words are "must be true." Your job is to eliminate any choice that does not have to be true. **What is the effect of the variable information?** See the following two diagrams. We start off with the first diagram, but the fact that Bert is above Will means that we can determine the exact order. The exact order is depicted in the second diagram. Once we have diagram #2, the question is easy.

Diagram #1

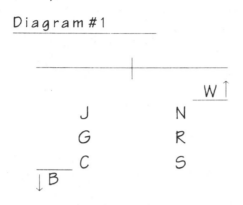

Diagram #2

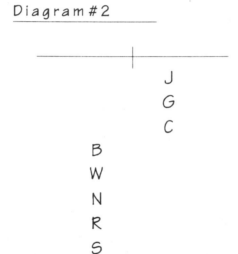

(A) is the correct answer.

28. The operative words are "can be true EXCEPT." Your job is to eliminate any choices that can be true. **What is the effect of the variable information?** See the following diagram.

(A), (B), (D), and (E) all can be true and are wrong.

(C) is the correct answer. Carie is always below Travis.

Questions 29 - 35

Preliminary Discussion - This is an ordering question. The ordering is not based on the specific identity of the addict. Rather, it is based on what kind of addict the person is. In other words, the ordering is based on membership in a particular group and is not based on specific identity. It is always important to remember the total number of people and how many people are in each category. Here is our fixed information.

Fixed Information

$$2\text{-Coc} + 2\text{-Al} + 1\text{-M} + 1\text{-V} + 1\text{-Cf} = 7$$

29. The operative words are "must be true." Your job is to eliminate any choice that does not have to be true. This is a multiple option question. Do one thing at a time. **What is the effect of the variable information?** Remember that the first patient to arrive has the same addiction as the last. This would mean that the first and last patient are either both cocaine addicts or alcoholics. If the second patient to arrive was an alcoholic this would mean that the first and last patient were cocaine addicts.

Diagram #1

```
1 - Coc
2 - Al
3
4
5
6
7 - Coc
```

Now, we must work with the condition that says that the number who arrived between the two alcoholics is one more than the number who arrived after the Valium addict. Bearing in mind that the caffeine addict arrived before the marijuana addict, we are able to generate two possibilities.

Diagram #2	Diagram #3
1 - Coc	1 - Coc
2 - Al	2 - Al
3 - Cf	3 - Cf
4 - M	4 - M
5 - Al	5 - V
6 - V	6 - Al
7 - Coc	7 - Coc

1. The sixth patient to arrive does not have to be the Valium addict. "I" is not in the answer. Eliminate (A), (C) and (E).
2. Clearly "II" is in the answer. Let's just consider "III."
3. **Must** it be the case that "III" is in the answer? Must the fifth patient to arrive be an alcoholic or valium addict? Yes. See the above two diagrams.

(D) is the answer.

30. The operative words are "describes a possible order EXCEPT." Your job is to eliminate any choice that describes a possible order. One of the best ways of knowing that something can be true is if we have already drawn it in one of our diagrams.

(C) and (D) are wrong. Both describe possible orders of arrival.

(A) and (E) are both wrong. They both describe possible orders of arrival. Look at diagram #2 for our work with question 29.

(B) is correct.

31. The operative words are "must be true." Your job is to eliminate any answer choice that does not have to be true. **What is the effect of the variable information?** You cannot assume that there are only three women. We know that either the alcoholics are arriving 1st and 7th or the cocaine addicts are arriving 1st and 7th. If the alcoholics are 1st and 7th we know that the Valium addict must be 3rd. If the cocaine addicts arrive 1st and 7th we know it is possible for:

1. the alcoholics to be in 2 and 6 and the Valium addict to be in 5; and

2. the alcoholics to be in 2 and 5 and the Valium addict to be in 6.

All three of these possibilities may be seen in the following diagrams.

Diagram #1	Diagram #2	Diagram #3
1 - Al	1 - Coc	1 - Coc
2	2 - Al	2 - Al
3 - V	3	3
4	4	4
5	5 - V	5 - Al
6	6 - Al	6 - V
7 - Al	7 - Coc	7 - Coc

(A) is wrong. There is no basis for concluding this.

(B) is wrong. The key word is "only."

(D) is wrong. See diagram #1. There is no reason why a cocaine addict must arrive in the first 3 or why there should be only 3 women.

(E) is wrong. There is no basis for inferring this one way or theother.

(C) is correct. An alcoholic always arrives in the first 3 and we are told that the first 3 to arrive were women.

32. The operative words are "must be true." Your job is to eliminate any choice that does not have to be true. This is a multiple option question. Do one thing at a time. **What is the effect of the variable information?** Given the variable information it is impossible for the cocaine addicts to arrive 1st and 7th. Try it and see. Therefore, the alcoholics must arrive 1st and 7th. If the alcoholics arrive 1st and 7th there will be 5 people arriving between the alcoholics. This means that there have to be 4 arriving after the Valium addict. This would put the Valium addict in position 3. Caffeine and marijuana arrive either in 4 and 5 or in 5 and 6. This implies that one of the cocaine addicts must arrive in position 2. See the following two possibilities.

Diagram #1

1 - Al
2 - Coc
3 - V
4 - Cf
5 - M
6 - Coc
7 - Al

Diagram #2

1 - Al
2 - Coc
3 - V
4 - Coc
5 - Cf
6 - M
7 - Al

1. "I" is in the answer. Hence, eliminate (B) and (C).
2. "III" is in the answer. Hence, the answer must be (E). There is no need to consider "II." This is an advantage of the multiple option question format. (I realize in this particular case it is easy for us to know that "II" is in the answer. In other cases it might not be so easy.)

(E) is the answer.

33. The operative words are "second patient to arrive was." This is functionally equivalent to "must be true." Your job is to eliminate any choice that does not have to be true. **What is the effect of the variable information?** If nobody arrived between the cocaine addicts it means that the alcoholics arrived 1st and 7th. This means that the Valium addict arrived 3rd. The cocaine addicts must then have arrived either 5th and 6th or 4th and 5th. Because the caffeine addict arrived before the marijuana addict, the caffeine addict must have arrived 2nd. This means that the marijuana addict arrived either 4th or 6th. Here are the two possibilities in the form of two diagrams.

Diagram #1

1 - Al
2 - Cf
3 - V
4 - M
5 - Coc
6 - Coc
7 - Al

Diagram #2

1 - Al
2 - Cf
3 - V
4 - Coc
5 - Coc
6 - M
7 - Al

(B) is the answer. See the above two diagrams.

34. The operative words are "how many would satisfy." **What is the effect of the variable information?** We are told that the Florida addict arrives **both**:

after the California addict; and

immediately after one of the alcoholics.

This would be impossible if the alcoholics arrived 1st and 7th. Hence, the cocaine addicts arrived 1st and 7th and the Florida addict arrived 7th. Because the Florida addict arrived immediately after one of the alcoholics, one of the alcoholics arrived 6th. Since the latest the Valium addict could arrive is 5th, at least two **must** arrive after the Valium addict. But for two to arrive after the Valium addict, three **must** arrive between the two alcoholics. For three to arrive between the two alcoholics, the other alcoholic **must** arrive 2nd. (This would put three between the two alcoholics.) Caffeine and marijuana must be 3rd and 4th. Hence, the **only possibility is shown in the following diagram.**

$$1 - Coc \ (California)$$
$$2 - Al$$
$$3 - Cf$$
$$4 - M$$
$$5 - V$$
$$6 - Al$$
$$7 - Coc \ (Florida)$$

(A) is the correct answer.

35. The operative words are "could NOT be true." Your job is to eliminate anything that could be true. This question is by far the easiest question of the group.

(B) is the only possible answer. There is only one caffeine addict. Hence, if the caffeine addict arrives first, another kind of addict must arrive last.

Questions 36 - 41

Preliminary Discussion - This is a fairly easy spatial relationship question. It is an unusual set of questions because the complete diagram may be drawn from the fixed conditions. There are no variable information questions. This is not a question type that has been tested heavily in recent years. A diagram will be helpful for all the questions. In constructing the diagram you should begin with the condition:

"Those who travel exactly northeast from C first encounter G, then A, and then D."

The rest of the diagram will fall into place from here. Here, is what the diagram looks like.

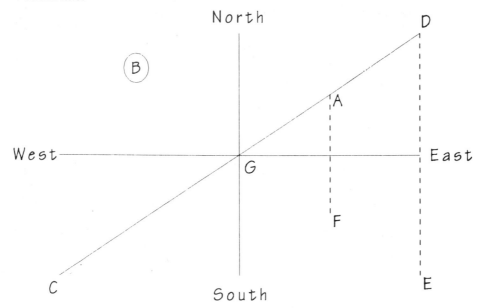

36. The operative words are "in which direction."

(A), (B), (C), and (E) are wrong. They are inconsistent with the diagram.

(D) is the only possible answer.

37. The operative words are "could be taken." This is multiple option. Do one thing at a time.

1. "I" is possible. C could be due south of B. Eliminate (B) and (C).
2. "III" is possible. One could travel in a southeasterly direction from B to C. Hence, "III" is in the answer. Hence, the answer must be (E). (E) is the only choice that has both "I and III" in it.

Note that we need not even consider "II."

(E) is the correct answer.

38. The operative words are "directly east" and "could encounter." A look at the diagram reveals that the person could encounter F and E.

(C) is the correct answer.

39. The operative words are "must be true." Your job is to eliminate anything that does not have to be true.

(A), (B), (C), and (E) are wrong. No one of them has to be true.

(D) is the correct answer.

40. The operative words are "must be north." A look at the diagram reveals that there is no school that has to be north of B.

(E) is the correct answer.

41. The operative words are "maximum" and "can be west of A." A look at the diagram reveals that only schools B, C, and G can be west of school A.

(D) is the correct answer.

Questions 42 - 47

Preliminary Discussion - This is a very basic circular seating arrangement. There have been a large number of seating arrangements. Look for the words "facing the center." It is critical that you know whether the objects are facing the center so that you will understand what is left or what is right. When you read the conditions you will find little definite information telling which car is definitely beside which car. All that we know with certainty is that the Jaguar is next to the Toyota. This is what our fixed information looks like.

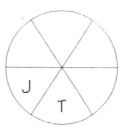

42. The operative words are "must be placed." Your job is to eliminate answer choices that describe cars that do not have to be placed beside the Mercedes. We are told that the Ford is next to the Jaguar and that the Chrysler is next to the Toyota. **What is the effect of this variable information?** Since, the Chrysler cannot be next to the Nissan, the Nissan must go next to the Ford. The Mercedes will then go between the Nissan and the Chrysler. Here is what it all looks like in the diagram.

(E) is the correct answer. You can just read it off the diagram.

43. The operative words are "must be placed directly across." Your job is to eliminate any choices that need not be placed directly across from the Toyota. We are told that the Chrysler is placed next to the Jaguar and that the Mercedes is placed next to the Toyota. **What is the effect of this variable information?** Since the Nissan cannot be next to the Chrysler, the Nissan must be next to the Mercedes. This means that the Ford must be placed between the Chrysler and the Nissan. Here is what it all looks like in the form of a diagram.

(A) is the correct answer. You can just read it off the diagram.

44. The operative words are "complete and accurate list." We are told that the Jaguar is placed beside the Mercedes. **What is the effect of this variable information?** To place the Ford beside the Mercedes would mean that the Chrysler and Nissan would have to be placed beside each other. This would violate the conditions. Therefore, the Ford cannot be beside the Mercedes. Hence, we must eliminate choices (A) and (D). Either the Chrysler or the Nissan can be placed beside the Mercedes. Here is what the possibilities look like in the form of a diagram.

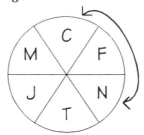

(E) is the correct answer. See the diagram.

45. The operative words are "total number of arrangements." We are told that the Jaguar is placed to the **immediate right** of the Toyota and that the Chrysler is placed to the **immediate left** of the Toyota. **What is the effect of this variable information?** Remember that the Nissan cannot be placed beside the Chrysler. This means that only the Ford or Mercedes can be placed beside the Chrysler. Here is what this looks like in the form of a diagram.

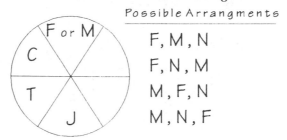

The very fact that either Ford or Mercedes can be placed beside the Chrysler means that there is more than one possible combination. Hence, eliminate choice (A).

There are four possible combinations and they are listed along with the diagram.

(D) is the correct answer.

46. The operative words are "must be placed beside and on either side." We are told that the Chrysler is placed **directly across from the Mercedes**. **What is the effect of this variable information?** The Nissan cannot be beside the Chrysler. Hence, the Nissan must be placed beside the Mercedes and the Ford must be placed across from the Toyota. Let's see what this looks like in the form of a diagram.

(A) is the correct answer. You can read it off the diagram.

47. The operative words are "could NOT be true." Your job is to eliminate any choices that can or must be true. We are told that the Ford is placed directly across from the Toyota. **What is the effect of this variable information?** Let's look at the following diagram.

Diagram #1

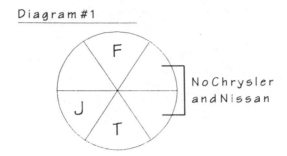

Because the Chrysler and Nissan cannot be beside each other, those two cars **cannot take up the two spaces between the Ford and the Toyota**. We could not have any situation from which it would follow that the Chrysler and Nissan would take up those two spaces. If the Mercedes were placed between the Ford and Jaguar, then the only places left for the Chrysler and Nissan would be those two spaces between the Ford and Toyota. See the following diagram.

Diagram #2

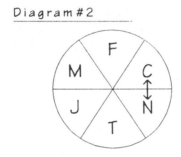

Hence, the Mercedes cannot be between the Jaguar and the Ford.

(D) is the correct answer.

Chapter Eight

Reading Comprehension Mastery

Format

The current format has four passages to do in 35 minutes. Each of the four passages will contain six to eight questions. There will be approximately twenty-eight questions in total. It makes sense to think of the reading comprehension section as containing four 9 minute tests. You may of course choose to do only three of the four tests and guess on the last.

**Think of the reading comprehension section
as being a series of four tests!**

Timing considerations

Once again, the issue is whether you should answer three of the tests, spending 12 minutes on each passage, or four of the tests spending 9 minutes on each. This should be determined by your performance on actual tests.

The Correct Order To Attack The Passages

Your ability to read the passages will be influenced by your response to the topic. If you dislike a topic or find it difficult you will find it harder to read. Hence, it is critical that you read the passages in the order that you like them best. **This will ensure that you will run out of time when you are reaching the passage that is most difficult for you!**

Do the passages in the order of difficulty saving the most difficult for last!

Directions

Directions: "Each passage in this section is followed by a group of questions to be answered on the basis of what is **stated** or **implied** in the passage. For some questions, more than one of the choices could conceivably answer the question. However, you are to choose the **best** answer; that is the response that most accurately and completely answers the question, and blacken the corresponding space on your answer sheet."

Definition Of Best Answer

In reading comprehension "best answer" does not mean objectively correct. It means "better than the other choices." Use the approach of compare and contrast.

Does The Reading Comprehension Section Test Your Ability To Read?

Definitely not! In my years of working with students I have seen students who could barely read English score higher than graduate students in the humanities. I have seen students answer over ninety-five percent of the questions correctly **without even reading the passages!**

Answer identification in the reading section has little to do with reading comprehension!

The Job Of The Test Maker

The job of the test maker is to:

1. Use the **passage**;

2. To provide stimulus for the **questions**; and

3. To **disguise the answer.**

The Job Of The Test Taker

The test maker makes the game. Their job is to use the passage to provide stimulus for the questions and disguise the answer. Our job is to identify the answer within the context of this mess. It will be helpful to consider the characteristics of the passage, the questions, and the manner in which Law Services attempts to hide the answer.

The Predictable Kinds Of Reading Questions

The only purpose of the passage is to provide stimulus for the questions. Law Services has indicated that there are six different kinds of questions. Each of the six question types belongs to one of the following three categories of questions: Main Idea, Specific Detail, and Inference/Extension.

Main Idea

These are general questions. In general absorbing specific details is irrelevant to answer identification for this question type. The wrong answers are descriptive of things that are overly broad, overly narrow, or simply not done.

1. Main Idea Or Primary Purpose

Which one of the following best expresses the main idea of the passage?

The most appropriate title for the passage would be ...

Specific Detail

The answer to this question type will always be found in the text. It will generally be a paraphrase. Be careful that the answer you select is an answer to the question asked and not simply something stated in the passage.

2. Specific Information Stated In The Passage

According to the passage, ...

The author states which one of the following ...

Inference/Extension

These are questions which involve the evaluation of text. Answer identification for this question type will involve making inferences from the text or applying information in the text to a new situation outside of the text.

3. Meaning Or Purpose Of Words In The Passage

In the context of the passage, the word _____ in line _ refers to...

4. Information Or Ideas That Can Be Inferred

The passage suggests that _____ would likely agree on which of the following?

Which of the following situations is most analogous to the history of ____ as it is described in the passage?

5. Method The Author Uses In Making His Or Her Points

The primary function of the first paragraph in the passage is to...

The author mentions the _____ in order to provide an example of...

6. The Attitude Or Tone Used By The Author

The author would be most likely to agree with which of the following about ___?

Remember these are the only kinds of questions you will get!

The Source Of LSAT Passages

Many of the passages have their origins in law review articles. They are, however, drawn from a number of sources and offer a wide variety of topics. These topics include the humanities, social sciences, ethics, philosophy, and the law. They have been heavily edited to ensure that they have the appropriate characteristics.

Please note that the passages must be heavily edited so that they conform to the requirements of LSAT passages!

The Consistency Requirement Of LSAT Passages

Remember that every edition of the LSAT must test the same things in the same ways. It follows from this that **all LSAT passages must have common characteristics**. To put it another way: LSAT passages are selected because of their characteristics and **not** because of their specific subject matter.

The Design Requirement Of LSAT Passages

Must Provide Stimulus For The Six Specific Question Types

The six question types are used to test the basic reasoning skills that the LSAT is designed to test. The questions refer to the reading passages. Therefore, the passages must be selected and edited so that they contain characteristics that are relevant to the six question types. Since there are:

1. **Main idea or primary purpose questions** - each passage must have a main point or purpose.

2. **Specific information questions** - each passage must have specific details and examples.

3. **Meaning or purpose of words in the passage questions** - many passages will have unconventional words and phrases that can be determined only in context.

4. **Information-or-ideas-that-can-be-inferred questions** - each passage must suggest further inferences.

5. **Method-the-author-uses-in-making-his-or-her-points questions** - each passage must have a specific logical structure.

6. **Attitude or tone questions** - each passage must contain competing points of view one of which will be preferred by the author. Frequently one point of view will be that of "authorities" in the field. The author will often disagree with that point of view.

**The passages must have these characteristics.
Otherwise, they will not be suitable
for the specific question types that are asked.**

As you can see there must be a basic structure to each passage.

The Wrong Way To Read The Passages!

Don't focus too much on the content. The topic of the passage is unimportant (except to the extent that it makes you more or less comfortable with the passage). The passages are heavy in specific detail. You will never be able to absorb all the specific details. If you try to absorb everything you will find that you have absorbed nothing!

Read for main ideas and don't worry about the specific details.

The Correct Speed To Read

Don't slow down for the purpose of trying to absorb more. Don't speed up because you fear the quantity of reading.

**Read the passage at your normal reading speed.
Don't slow down. Don't speed up.**

The Right Way To Read Passages

Focus on the main idea and the general characteristics of the passage. If you don't you will be overwhelmed by the specific details. For the most part the specific details are irrelevant to the main idea and the general structure. Read for the purpose of getting the "big picture." Don't be overly concerned about missing small details.

**Assign the priority to main ideas!
Feel free to skim over the specific details!**

So, What Is The Big Picture?

The passage will contain from three to five paragraphs. Each paragraph will have a main idea and the passage as a whole will have a main idea. Concentrate on these.

Concentrate on the main idea of the passage as a whole
and the main idea of each paragraph!

Will You Have Time To Read The Passage More Than Once?

Not in its entirety! You may have time to return to certain parts of the passage to locate specific information.

You will be forced to select many responses
feeling that you have missed a good part of the passage!
This will be uncomfortable. Get used to it!

The Answer Choices - Basic Rule Of Design

Remember that Law Services wants the test to be hard! A hard test is one where the test taker has difficulty in identifying the answers. Hence, Law Services will do its best to disguise the best answer. In other words, it must make one or more of the other four answer choices seem attractive to the test taker. Hence, the job of Law Services is:

1. To attract test takers to an answer choice if it is wrong; and

2. Repel test takers from an answer choice if it is right.

Law Services will do its best
to keep you away from the best answer!

How Does Law Services Attract You To The Wrong Answer?

Law Services will play on you emotionally in two important ways.

First, by playing on your emotional need for something familiar. This is accomplished in two primary ways.

1. The answer choices will use language that is identical to the language in the passage. Let's call this the "same language" choice.

**Warning!! This does not mean that answer choices
that use the same language as the language in the passage
are always wrong!
But, be careful with them.**

2. The answer choice will contain a true statement or something clearly stated in the passage. The trap is that the choice won't qualify as an answer to the specific question asked.

**In any unfamiliar situation you will be attracted
to something that you recognize!**

Second, they will encourage you to decide that a choice is correct before having completely read the choice and each of the other choices. Many answer choices are long and involve compound thoughts. Often the first part of the choice has been designed to attract you to the answer when the second part of the choice clearly disqualifies it! Consider the following compound statement.

In 1992 Bill Clinton was elected president of the
United States *and* in 1993 Pierre Trudeau became the
Prime Minister of Canada.

Clearly the first part of this statement is correct and the second part is incorrect. This makes the complete statement incorrect. For the statement as a whole to be correct both parts of the statement must be correct. Many test takers will read only the first part of the statement and select it before reading the rest!

**Rule!! Read and consider the meaning of every word
in an answer choice!**

The Necessity Of *Comparing* Answer Choices!

The "best answer" may not be objectively correct. It is only better than the other choices. **Never ask if an answer choice is correct! Ask only, how it compares to the other choices!** This means that in addition to reading every word of a single choice you must read every word of every choice.

Rule!! Never select an answer choice until you have read every word of every choice!

You will find it much easier to eliminate answer choices if you use the approach of comparing them. It is easier to know if one choice is better than another; than it is to know if a choice, viewed in isolation, is the best choice.

Rule!! Compare the answer choices until you have eliminated all the choices except one!

The Importance Of Giving Meaning To Every Word In Every Choice

Students who are unable to distinguish one answer choice from another are generally not reading the choices carefully enough. Although it is not important to pay attention to every word in the passage, it is critical to pay attention to every word in the answer choices. "Reading comprehension" is much more important in the answer choices than it is in the passages.

Rule!! Give meaning to every word of every answer choice!

The Characteristics Of The "Best Answer"

In general the "best answer" will:

■ answer what is asked

■ not be inconsistent with the main idea of the passage

■ not contain language or ideas that are susceptible to criticism

■ probably be a paraphrase

Some Examples Of LSAT Paraphrases

The answer choices often contain language that is a paraphrase of language in the passage. Here are some examples.

Language In Passage	Language In Answer Choice
"limited sovereign rights over coastal waters"	"few controls or restrictions applied to ocean areas"
"careless"	"typical lack of foresight"
"careless introduction of fish"	"human-engineered changes in the ..."
"destruction of forests"	"deforestation"

Possible Approaches To Each Passage

Reading is the most complex skill on the LSAT. Test takers read differently and were taught to read differently. Some like reading. Others don't. Hence,

it is important that you do what works best for you!

Nevertheless, almost all test takers spend far too much time poring over the passage and not enough on the questions and the answer choices.

**The real test of reading comprehension
is in the questions and answer choices.**

Practice spending more time on the answer choices themselves. At the beginning I encourage you to:

1. Read the passage one time only; and

2. Force yourself to select an answer to each question without even once looking back at the passage.

This will help you focus on the questions and answer choices and not on the passage!

The Importance Of Flexibility

Should you read the questions first? Should you read the passage first? Should you look for answers to specific questions as you read the passages? You should experiment with different approaches deciding which one works best for you. You may find that different approaches work differently for different kinds of passages. For example, it may be that with an applied science passage it could be helpful to read the questions first. Do what works best for you. Keep your attitude and approach flexible! You may find that you wish to respond to different kinds of passages in different ways.

Five "Safe Suggestions" - They Can Only Help!

First "Safe" Suggestion

As you know every five lines the reading passages are numbered. There are often questions which ask you to determine the meaning of a word in context. Many test takers find it helpful to:

underline the word that the question refers to
prior to reading the passage.

This will ensure that you pay more attention to it at the time that you read the passage.

Second "Safe" Suggestion

Be conscious of the "main idea" of the passage and each paragraph.

Third "Safe" Suggestion

Be sensitive to words that indicate the transition from one idea to the next. These words are usually called "trigger words." A trigger word is a word that indicates a transition from one idea to the next. Here are some samples:

But,   Nevertheless,   However,   Correspondingly.

Underline these words as you read the passage. At the very least they indicate a change in the direction of ideas. They are often useful in determining the author's attitude toward a topic and the way in which the author's views differ from those of other commentators, authorities, or conventional wisdom.

Fourth "Safe" Suggestion

Don't worry about absorbing the specific details. Just concentrate on the big picture.

Fifth "Safe" Suggestion

Answer all the questions of a certain type together. For example, do all the "main idea" questions at the same time. Do all the "specific detail" questions at the same time. Do all the "inference/extension" questions at the same time.

Now Let's Try It All Out

Exercise : What follows is a passage and questions that are similar in design requirement to the actual LSAT. Begin by spending 9 minutes on both the passage and answer choices. After the 9 minutes has expired make a notation of how far you have gone and what your answer choices are. Then spend another 3 minutes to see if you can finish more or otherwise improve your performance.

Use the following procedure.

1. Read the first and last paragraph of the passage.

2. Read the passage in its entirety focusing on characteristics and structure. Do not worry about absorbing all the specific details.

3. Peruse the questions. Decide which are the "main idea", "specific detail", and "inference/extension" questions.

4. Use the approach of "compare and contrast" to isolate the best answer to each question.

It has been widely believed that the common law, that is, the law made by judges, always favored freedom of trade. The common law should be contrasted to statutes enacted by

(5) legislative bodies which clearly do not and have not always favored freedom of trade. When English and American judges during the eighteenth and nineteenth centuries decided cases on common law principles against monopolists,

(10) engrossers, or restrainers of trade, they thought they were continuing a tradition that reached back into "time of which no man hath memory." Similarly, the congressmen who drafted and passed the Sherman Antitrust law, a statute which

(15) made concerted action in restraint of trade illegal, thought that they were merely declaring illegal, offenses that the common law had always prohibited.

Those judges and legislators, like other lawyers,

(20) must have known, or at least would not have doubted, that the common law rules on these subjects had changed in the course of time, for it is taken as axiomatic that the common law "grows." But it is not always recognized that the

(25) common law can change its direction, and without much warning begin to prohibit practices it had formerly endorsed, or to protect arrangements it had earlier condemned. Lawyers do not so readily see that the common law at any

(30) given time reflects the economic theories and policies then favored by the community, and may change as radically as those theories and policies. As a result they have too easily accepted the mistaken view that the attitude of the common

(35) law toward freedom of trade was essentially the same throughout its history.

But the common law did not always defend freedom of trade and abhor monopoly. For a long time it did quite the opposite: it supported an

(40) economic order in which the individual's getting and spending were closely controlled by kings, parliaments, and mayors, statutes and customs, and his opportunities limited by the exclusive powers of guilds, chartered companies, and

(45) patentees. The common law first began to oppose this system of regulation and privilege at the end of the sixteenth century; it did not do so wholeheartedly until the publication of Adam Smith's **The Wealth Of Nations** during the

(50) eighteenth century; and by the middle of the nineteenth century, it had again lost its enthusiasm for the task.

It would have been surprising if the pattern of development had been different. Changes in the

(55) common law are changes in the attitudes of judges and of lawyers; it would have been remarkable if they had persistently opposed monopoly when the rest of the community did not know the word and considered the

(60) phenomenon natural or desirable. It would have been strange if lawyers had upheld laissez-faire policies centuries before any statesman or economist had advocated or stated them, or had continued following them long after they had

(65) been abandoned or denied by the rest of the community. In fact, the common law governing monopoly and policies for the economic organization of society changed together with changes in community attitudes toward freedom

(70) of trade, except for minor differences in timing.

These changes in the common law reflect changes in the policy for the economic organization of society that show a development from an active support of monopolies in the

(75) earliest period, to a recognition of the benefits of opposition to monopolies during an interlude of less than two centuries, to the leniency and indifference that characterized them in 1890.

1. The primary purpose of the passage is

(A) to show that the common law, when contrasted to the statutes of legislative bodies, is dynamic and subject to change.

(B) to show that the congressmen responsible for the Sherman Act were mistaken with respect to their view that the common law had always prohibited restraints against trade.

(C) to show that judges who made law have historically been inconsistent in their judicial pronouncements concerning the law of freedom of trade.

(D) to argue that laws promoting freedom of trade are necessary to restrain monopolists and engrossers.

(E) to show that the attitudes of judges and lawyers are influenced by and mirror prevailing community opinion.

GO ON TO THE NEXT PAGE

2. It may be inferred that an economist who advocated freedom of trade and who was able to influence the economic organization of society was most influential during which of the following time periods

(A) 1550 - 1650
(B) 1650 - 1700
(C) 1700 - 1800
(D) 1850 - 1900
(E) 1900 - 1950

3. According to the passage, each of the following statements is true about the common law except:

(A) The attitude of the common law towards freedom of trade has not been the same throughout history.
(B) Although the common law continually progresses, its progression may take the form of a reversal.
(C) The common law has recognized the power of guilds to restrict individual initiative and opportunity.
(D) The common law is influenced by and is ultimately determined by the views of society.
(E) The common law principles governing freedom of trade have continued a tradition reaching back into time of which no man hath memory.

4. The author mentions the enactment of the Sherman Antitrust Act (end of first paragraph) primarily in order to

(A) illustrate the difficulty that Congressmen have in ensuring that legislation is passed into law.
(B) emphasize that the Sherman Antitrust Law was required to combat monopolies and other restraints on freedom of trade.
(C) illustrate that the congressmen were attempting to give legislative sanction to principles that had a long history of judicial sanction.
(D) affirm that the common law had always prohibited restraints on trade.
(E) demonstrate that prior to the enactment of the Sherman Act there was a strong lobby to make monopolies the norm in American industry.

5. The tone and content of the passage suggest that the author of the passage is most probably

(A) a legislator in favor of the further enactment of statutes favoring freedom of trade.
(B) a historian interested in the benefits of freedom of trade and the relationship between community values and the views of judges.
(C) a lawyer who approves of the Sherman Antitrust law.
(D) a legal researcher writing a law review article about patents.
(E) a journalist writing an article for a community paper who is neutral on the benefits of freedom of trade.

6. Which of the following would be the most appropriate title for the passage?

(A) The Reasons For The Enactment Of The Sherman Antitrust Act
(B) The Common Law Concerning Free Trade
(C) Freedom Of Trade - A Necessary Condition For Future Economic Growth
(D) The Influence of Adam Smith on the Common Law
(E) Has the Conduct of Engrossers always been Illegal?

7. According to information provided in the passage, each of the following has detrimentally affected freedom of trade EXCEPT:

(A) industries with restrictions to entry
(B) legislative bodies
(C) those who dominate markets
(D) laws restricting the minimum workers may be paid
(E) companies with charters limiting their activity.

Analysis Of The Passage

What follows is the main idea of each paragraph italicized.

Main Ideas are italicized. Most of the rest of the text contains specific details.

It has been widely believed that the common law, that is, the law made by judges, always favored freedom of trade. The common law should be contrasted to statutes enacted by
(5) legislative bodies which clearly do not and have not always favored freedom of trade. When English and American judges during the eighteenth and nineteenth centuries decided cases on common law principles against monopolists, (10) engrossers, or restrainers of trade, they thought they were continuing a tradition that reached back into "time of which no man hath memory." Similarly, the congressmen who drafted and passed the Sherman Antitrust law, a statute which
(15) made concerted action in restraint of trade illegal, thought that they were merely declaring illegal, offenses that the common law had always prohibited.

Those judges and legislators, like other lawyers,
(20) must have known, or at least would not have doubted, that the common law rules on these subjects had changed in the course of time, for it is taken as axiomatic that the common law "grows." But it is not always recognized that the
(25) common law can change its direction, and without much warning begin to prohibit practices it had formerly endorsed, or to protect arrangements it had earlier condemned. Lawyers do not so readily see that the common law at any
(30) given time reflects the economic theories and policies then favored by the community, and may change as radically as those theories and policies. *As a result they have too easily accepted the mistaken view that the attitude of the common* (35) *law toward freedom of trade was essentially the same throughout its history.*

But the common law did not always defend freedom of trade and abhor monopoly. For a long time it did quite the opposite: it supported an
(40) economic order in which the individual's getting and spending were closely controlled by kings, parliaments, and mayors, statutes and customs, and his opportunities limited by the exclusive powers of guilds, chartered companies, and

(45) patentees. The common law first began to oppose this system of regulation and privilege at the end of the sixteenth century; it did not do so wholeheartedly until the publication of Adam Smith's **The Wealth Of Nations** during the
(50) eighteenth century; and by the middle of the nineteenth century, it had again lost its enthusiasm for the task.

It would have been surprising if the pattern of development had been different. Changes in the
(55) common law are changes in the attitudes of judges and of lawyers; it would have been remarkable if they had persistently opposed monopoly when the rest of the community did not know the word and considered the
(60) phenomenon natural or desirable. It would have been strange if lawyers had upheld laissez-faire policies centuries before any statesman or economist had advocated or stated them, or had continued following them long after they had
(65) been abandoned or denied by the rest of the community. *In fact, the common law governing monopoly and policies for the economic organization of society changed together with changes in community attitudes toward freedom* (70) *of trade, except for minor differences in timing.*

These changes in the common law reflect changes in the policy for the economic organization of society that show a development from an active support of monopolies in the
(75) earliest period, to a recognition of the benefits of opposition to monopolies during an interlude of less than two centuries, to the leniency and indifference that characterized them in 1890.

Analysis And Discussion

There are three important points that should be made before we begin.

First, what matters is that you are able to **identify the answer.** By using the approach of compare and contrast you will be able to eliminate most of the answer choices. You need not be overly analytical. Your sense that the answer is wrong is sufficient.

Second, as the author of this book I am forced to analyze the answer choices in a way that anticipates a wide variety of problems with the choices. As a result, there may be times when I seem overly analytical. You should not infer that you should attempt the same degree of analysis. You won't have time.

Third, I am going to discuss the questions by category. You should experiment by doing them by category as well. The grouping is as follows:

1. Main Idea Questions - Questions 1 and 6;

2. Inference/Extension Questions - Questions 2, 4 and 5; and

3. Specific Detail Questions - Questions 3 and 7.

You will recall that we are attempting to identify the "best answer" and not the objectively correct answer. **We must try to give meaning to every word of every choice!**

Let's begin.

Main Idea Questions

The wrong answers to main idea questions are generally:

■ overly broad

■ overly narrow

■ not done

Question 1 - The "primary purpose" of a passage is always to convey the main idea.

(D) is wrong. It is simply not done. Note the use of the word "necessary" in the answer choice. The author is not arguing that laws promoting freedom of trade are necessary for anything.

(B) is wrong. It is too narrow. Although the author does show that the "congressmen were mistaken with respect to their view" this is a minor part of the passage.

(E) is wrong. It is too narrow. Although the passage does show that the attitudes of judges and lawyers are influenced by community opinion, this is done for the purpose of explaining why the common law has not always supported freedom of trade.

(A) is wrong. You must give meaning to the words "when contrasted to the statutes of legislative bodies." In context this implies that statutes are not subject to change. The passage implies the opposite.

(C) is the remaining choice and is best.

Question 6 - The most "appropriate title" is asking for a main idea.

One reason why the passages are difficult to read is that they appear out of context. The lack of a title increases the confusion and makes the passages harder to read.

(A) is wrong. First, the "Reasons" for the enactment of the Sherman Antitrust Act are not given. Second, even if they were, the discussion of the Sherman Act is a small detail, making choice (A) far too narrow to be the answer.

(E) is wrong. It is too narrow. The focus of the passage is on freedom of trade in general and not on engrossers.

(D) is wrong. It is too narrow. The passage is about the common law of freedom of trade in general.

(C) is wrong. Note the word "Necessary." There is no suggestion in the passage that freedom of trade is a necessary condition for economic growth.

(B) is the remaining choice and is best.

Inference/Extension Questions

These questions will require you to evaluate the text. Examples of evaluation of text include recognizing inferences, applying information in the passage to a new situation, identifying the role that a fact plays in the development of the argument, recognizing the author's tone, or recognizing what kind of text the passage was excerpted from.

Remember that the answer to this type of question will not be stated directly in the passage. Rather, the answer will be an inference.

Question 2 - This is a straight inference question. The third paragraph states that it was during the 18th century that the common law began to oppose regulation and privilege. The passage also states that the common law was a function of community opinion. From this we can infer that an economist who was influential and advocated freedom of trade and was most influential probably was influential during the 1700s.

(A) is wrong because it does not refer to the 1700s.
(B) is wrong because it does not refer to the 1700s.
(D) is wrong because it does not refer to the 1700s.
(E) is wrong because it does not refer to the 1700s.

(C) is the remaining choice and is best.

Question 4 - This is a question that asks about the role that a specific detail plays. Let's examine the context of the statement. Read the first paragraph paying particular attention to the last sentence. The word "Similarly" suggests that the author is using the enactment of the Sherman Act as an example of a general principle. This general principle is that during the 18th and 19th century the prevailing view was that the common law always favored "freedom of trade."

(A) is wrong. The Sherman Act is not mentioned for this reason. The key words are "illustrate the difficulty."
(B) is wrong. The Sherman Act is not mentioned for this reason. Note also the use of the word "required."
(D) is wrong. This is the direct opposite of the reason that the Sherman Act is mentioned.
(E) is wrong. First, the Sherman Act is not mentioned for this reason. Second, the passage does not mention any strong lobby to make monopolies the norm.

(C) is the remaining answer choice and is best.

Question 5 - This question directs us to focus on both the **tone** and the **content**.

Content - Questions 1 and 6 were "main idea" questions. Our answers to these two questions indicate that the test maker thinks that the passage is mainly about **"the common law and freedom of trade."**

Tone - The author's attitude toward freedom of trade is hidden until the last paragraph. By referring to the **"benefits"** of opposition to monopolies the author reveals that he or she has a positive attitude toward freedom of trade.

    (E) is wrong. First the journalist is neutral about freedom of trade. Second, it seems quite unlikely that this article would be found in a community paper.

    (D) is wrong. There is only one reference to patents in the passage.

This leaves us with (A), (B), and (C). Each of these choices is in favor of freedom of trade.

    (C) is wrong for two reasons. First, the passage is about the common law and freedom of trade. Second, the passage (see the second paragraph) is critical of lawyers.

    (A) is wrong. The focus of the passage is not to promote the enactment of more laws. It is clearly more historical in nature.

    (B) is the remaining and best answer.

Specific Detail Questions

The answer to a specific detail question must be explicitly stated in the passage. It will likely be a paraphrase. **Make sure that you select a choice that answers the question asked!**

**Beware of answer choices
that describe something stated in the passage
but are not an answer to the question asked.**

Question 3 - Notice that the final word of the question is "except" in lower case. In some questions the word "except" will be in lower case and in some cases in upper case. **Be careful!**

The four wrong answers are statements that are stated in the passage as being about the common law. The right answer is not stated in the passage.

(A) is wrong. It is in fact close to the main idea of the passage.
(B) is wrong. It is stated in the second paragraph.
(C) is wrong. It is stated in the third paragraph.
(D) is wrong. It is stated in the third paragraph.

(E) is the remaining and best answer. (This is a rare question where the "same language" answer choice is correct.)

Question 7 - Note that last word of the question is "EXCEPT." In this case it is in upper case. On the test it has been in both upper and lower case.

(A), (B), (C), and (E) are all paraphrases of things stated in the third paragraph. Hence, they are all wrong. Let's use this question to examine how the paraphrases work.

Choice	Language In Passage	Language In Answer Choice
(A)	guilds	industries with restrictions
(B)	parliaments	legislative bodies
(C)	engrossers	those who dominate markets
(E)	chartered companies	companies with charters limiting

(D) is the remaining and best answer.

Summary

Seventeen Basic Principles Of Approach
For The Reading Section

These principles work well for most test takers most of the time. But, reading is a complex skill. What works well for one person will not necessarily work well for another. So, if you don't like one of these principles, don't use it!

Principles For Reading The Passages

 Principle 1 :   Don't slow your reading down for the purpose of absorbing more information.

Commentary - The LSAT is not a good time to create a new reading style for yourself.

 Principle 2 :   Don't feel that you have to take a speed reading course in order to get through the material.

Commentary - LSAT passages are heavy in detail. You can't read faster than you can absorb the information and ideas. Speed reading will not help for this section of the test.

 Principle 3 :   Don't try to absorb all the specific details in the passage.

Commentary - There are just too may of them. The more you concentrate on the specific details the less you will understand the main idea. Have you heard the saying: You can't see the forest but for the trees?

 Principle 4 :   Read for the main idea of each paragraph and for the passage as a whole.

Commentary - Main ideas aren't everything. They are the only thing!

Principle 5 : The LSAT in general and reading comprehension in particular is not for the purpose of testing the acquisition of information.

Commentary - The LSAT is to test **reasoning skills** in the context of the reading comprehension, logical reasoning and analytical reasoning question types.

Principle 6 : First, skim the first and last paragraphs of the passage. Then read the complete passage.

Commentary - The passages are hard because they appear out of context. They do not come with titles. Reading the first and last paragraph will help provide some context.

Principle 7 : Assume that you will have time for only one complete reading of the passage.

Commentary - Talk to anyone who has done the real test.

Principles For Reading The Questions And Answer Choices

Principle 8 : Allow the "operative words" to define precisely what you must answer.

Commentary - There are many answer choices which describe things stated in the passage. The problem is that they are not an answer to the specific question asked.

Principle 9 : Read and give meaning to every word of every answer choice.

Commentary - A committee of test makers spends hours and hours attempting to hide the "credited response." Assume that the significance of every word in an answer choice must be considered.

Principle 10 : Use the approach of "compare and contrast" to isolate the "best answer."

Commentary - There are few objectively correct answers. You may be selecting the best of a number of bad answers. This can be done only by "compare and contrast."

Principles For What To Specifically Look For In The Answer Choices

 Principle 11 : Be distrustful of answer choices that contain direct quotations from the passage itself.

Commentary - They aren't always wrong. But, the use of paraphrases does accomplishes two things for the test maker. First, paraphrases allow the test maker to do a better job of hiding the answer. Second, paraphrases make the test a better test of reading comprehension.

 Principle 12 : Be careful with answer choices that contain compound thoughts.

Commentary - Frequently the first half of an answer choice sounds good and the second half disqualifies it. The problem is that the first half is so good that you may **want it to be the answer!**

 Principle 13 : As always be sensitive to language like "only," "requires," "sufficient," "never," "all," etc.

Commentary - This is true of every section of the test.

Principles For Effective Practice

 Principle 14 : Spend as little time as possible on the passage and as much time as possible on the questions and answer choices.

Commentary - Think of the LSAT and the reading section in particular as a game of:

"Find the hidden answer."

To find a hidden answer you must be looking at the answer choices.

 Principle 15 : Be flexible! Remember our "toolbox approach." What works well on one passage may not work on another.

Commentary - There is no one method for handling the reading section. If it works, it is the right way to do it!

Principles For Timing And Organization

 Principle 16 : Practice with actual LSAT exams to determine whether you will actively interact with three passages spending twelve minutes on each or four passages spending nine minutes on each.

Commentary - There is a saying that "life can be full of rude awakenings." It is said most frequently by test takers who do not practice with actual LSAT questions. Remember, the test is written to a formula.

 Principle 17 : Do the passages in the order that you like them best.

Commentary - If you hate economics, don't start with that passage. (This principle also applies to other topics and subjects.)

Chapter Nine

Writing
Sample Mastery

The writing sample is the one part of the LSAT that is not multiple choice. It is a thirty minute exercise which is administered either before or after the main LSAT. The question and scrap paper are distributed separately and collected separately. A copy of your writing sample is sent along with your LSAT score to every school that receives a copy of your score.

What Role Does The Writing Sample Play
In The Admissions Decision?

The writing sample is part of your application file. It is there to be read. Although all schools look at your LSAT score, not all schools look at your writing sample. Even the schools that do look at your writing sample do not do so in a consistent way.

**As long as even one school considers your writing sample
you should treat the exercise seriously!**

Why Is The Writing Sample Part Of The LSAT Experience?

The writing sample became part of the LSAT experience in June of 1982. The format of the topic was changed in June of 1985. It replaced a multiple choice test of English grammar. According to Law Services the writing sample has been designed to test:

■ how clearly you support the position you take

■ how skillfully you support that position

■ your writing mechanics

■ your organization

■ your vocabulary

As a practical matter, these things cannot be tested in a thirty minute writing sample.

Format

You will be asked to write an answer to one question in thirty minutes. Law Services will provide a lined "answer sheet" to write your answer. The number of lines has varied over the years, but is currently equal to approximately the space on one side of one 8 1/2 by 11 sheet of paper.

Timing Considerations

The principal timing issue is the amount of time to spend organizing the answer and the amount of time spent writing it. Spend approximately ten minutes organizing the answer and approximately fifteen minutes writing it. This will leave you with five minutes to proofread.

Key Elements Of Directions

You are required to:

■ write on the topic specified

■ confine your writing to the lined area of the page that is distributed

- write on every line

- ensure that your handwriting is legible

- write your answer in black ball point (a pen is provided to ensure a high quality photocopy)

How Should You Define Your Objectives For The Writing Sample?

Damage Control! Good writing is like good cooking. It takes time. It requires rewriting. The quality of your "writing sample" will be affected because there is no time to rewrite. As a result, it is unlikely that your "writing sample" will enhance the quality of your application. But, a poorly written answer could hurt!

Your job is to construct a writing sample that won't hurt your chances!

The Characteristics Of A Bad Writing Sample

A bad writing sample will be bad either because of **what you say** or because of **how you say it**.

What You Say

- a failure to answer the question - one of the two options must be clearly selected

- a failure to use the facts provided - your option must be justified by using the facts provided

How You Say It

- poor grammar

- poor punctuation

- long sentences

- poor handwriting

- poor organization

Is There A Right Or Wrong Answer To The Question?

In a word, No! The issue is whether you can clearly take a position and justify that position, using the facts provided, in a reasonably literary manner.

What Is The Format Of The Writing Sample Topic?

Part 1 - The Requirement That You Select One Of Two Alternatives.

Part 2 - General Criteria To Use To Select One Of The Alternatives.

Part 3 - Two Paragraphs Of Specific Facts Which Bear On The General Criteria.

Here is an example.

Part 1 - The Requirement

Read the following description of the choice open to Don Davidson, who has successfully worked for an eminent New York City Publishing company for six years. Then, in the space provided, write an argument for the career choice you would advise Don Davidson to make. Use the information in this description and assume that Don Davidson highly values the following:

Part 2 - The General Criteria

1. The well-being of his family and eventually owning his own business;

2. The "well-being" of his family includes quality of education for his children, quality of life and health care for his family, and his wife's career.

Part 3 - Two Paragraphs Of Specific Facts

Don Davidson has drawn on extensive editorial and marketing experience (with his father's weekly newspaper) and two years of post-graduate religious studies to revive the slumping performance of his publishing house's Religious Books Division, most of whose publications are directed to the general reader. He has received a sizable raise and has been promoted to manager of that division. He has been told that his chances of further advancement are very good. His wife, employed by a fast-growing book publishing firm, has been promoted to director of marketing. Although, their apartment is cramped and overpriced, both Don and his wife enjoy New York's cultural and intellectual life. Their two children, aged six and eight, attend excellent schools. The younger child's dyslexia was diagnosed early and the disability is being given state-of-the-art treatment.

One of the oldest and closest friends of Don Davidson's father recently contacted Don. This man owns a small publishing company specializing in academic books in the fields of religion, history, and anthropology. The profit margin has been chronically slim but the business has survived for a long time. Don has been invited to manage this business and then buy the business when the older man retires in several years. The company is located at a small town in the Midwest, a twenty minute drive from the state university which is a cultural center and major employer in the region. Spacious, inexpensive housing and good schools are available. Both children would enjoy playing more freely outdoors. The older child could finally have the dog she's longed for. Lower living expenses might compensate somewhat for an initially sharp drop in family income were Don to take the new job. In the long run, by owning his own business he might make more money than he could in New York. The older man's offer has made Don realize how much he would like to eventually own his own business and be his own boss, but he doesn't want to harm his wife's career or in any way jeopardize the well-being of his family.

All LSAT writing sample topics have this format.

We will take advantage of the predictability of the format to devise a strategy to answer the question.

The Importance Of A Strategy

It is important that you know **how to write and organize your answer** before the actual test. You will have enough to do dealing with the specific facts of the question. It would be imprudent to have to both construct your answer and think about how to construct your answer during the limited time that you have!

A Clear Plan Of Attack

Your plan of attack will be the result of a consideration of timing aspects, organizational aspects, and writing style aspects.

Timing Aspects Of Your Of Attack

Objective - Your objective is to finish while leaving time to proofread. You must feel comfortable and in control from beginning to end.

Allocation Of Time

1. Spend ten minutes reading the question and organizing your answer.

2. Spend fifteen minutes writing the answer in your best handwriting.

3. Spend the remaining five minutes proofreading.

Organizational Aspects Of Your Plan Of Attack

Objective - Your objective is to demonstrate that you are a person who follows directions and does so in an organized manner. The directions require you to take a position and to justify that position. You must do these two things - no more and no less.

What follows is one suggestion for how to organize your answer. It is not the only way. However, it does work nicely for most students most of the time.

1. State your position in the first paragraph and preferably in the first sentence.

2. Reiterate your position in the last paragraph.

3. Allow the general criteria to provide the organizing principle for the middle paragraphs.

4. Use the middle paragraphs to discuss the specific facts as they relate to the general criteria.

5. Discuss the facts pertaining to both options. Make it a comparative analysis.

Writing Style Aspects Of Your Plan Of Attack

Objective - Your objective is to ensure that you do not demonstrate that you are unfamiliar with the rules of grammar and punctuation. In addition, you must ensure that your handwriting is the very best that it can be! These objectives will be accomplished through the use of short, concise sentences.

1. Your handwriting will be difficult to read. Shorter sentences will minimize the effects of poor handwriting.

2. Your grammar and punctuation may not be what they should be. Shorter sentences will "mask" how little you may know about the rules of grammar and punctuation.

3. Don't write as though your pen is directly connected to your brain. Always ask:

    A. What do I want to say?

    B. How do I say it in the fewest number of words?

    Then say it. Repeat this process for every sentence.

Put Yourself In The Position Of The Reader

It is inconceivable that anybody could find it interesting to read writing sample answers. Therefore, **don't do anything that could irritate the reader!** Here are two quick ways to irritate the reader.

1. Irritate the reader by not following the directions. Examples of not following directions include:

    ■ not being clear on which option you are arguing for

    ■ not using the facts provided

    ■ inventing new facts

2. Irritate the reader with an illegible answer.

In addition to being difficult to read, poor handwriting conveys a negative image. To project a positive image in a job interview, you would dress nicely. The application file is your "interview" for law school. Good handwriting will help project a positive image.

Let's Apply This To Our Sample Topic

A Basic Outline

We can see that Don's career choices are to stay in New York or to move to the Midwest. This is to be decided in terms of how the specific facts bear on his main concerns - his family and owning his own business. Let's do a preliminary analysis based on how the specific facts relate to the general criteria. The questions are designed so that there is no right or wrong answer. It is easy to argue for either alternative.

This is my (and only my) interpretation of where the facts fall. I would argue that Don Davidson should go to the Midwest.

Criteria Specific Facts

	Favors New York	Approximately Equal	Favors Midwest
Owning Own Business			✓
Quality Of Education		✓	
Wife's Career	✓		
Quality Of Health Care	✓		
Quality Of Life			✓

What follows is a **skeletal outline** of how you should organize and develop your answer.

Development Of The First Paragraph

Let's assume that we choose to advise Don to leave New York and move to the Midwest. We will make our preference known in the first sentence.

Don Davidson's professional development and the well being of his family dictate that he should move to the Midwest. . . .

Development Of The Middle Paragraphs

Let The General Criteria Organize The Answer For You!

Be careful to use the facts as they are given to you. You should devote a separate paragraph to each of the main issues. The main criteria for Don Davidson are:

- owning his own business

- the quality of education for his children

- his wife's career

- quality of life and health care

We will organize our answer around these criteria by devoting a separate paragraph to each criterion. In addition, we will make it clear in each paragraph which criterion we are addressing.

First Criterion - Owning His Own Business

Don's present job has been good to him. It has equipped him with the tools that he needs to do what he really wants to do. That is to own his own business...

Second Criterion - Quality Of Education

A consideration of the schools available to Don's children reveals that...

Third Criterion - His Wife's Career

Don's wife has an excellent job in New York. It is important to her, and the move to the Midwest...

Fourth Criterion - Health Care

Fortunately the younger child's dyslexia has already been diagnosed. Although "state-of-the-art" treatment is available in New York,...

Fifth Criterion - Quality Of Life

By moving to the Midwest Don and his family would be trading the cultural and intellectual life of New York for the quality of life available in a small center. The Midwest will offer Don's family a living environment in which they can all flourish...

Development Of The Last Paragraph

The purpose of the last paragraph is to reiterate the preference expressed in the first paragraph. It is for the purpose of "wrapping the answer up."

Although it will be difficult to leave New York, the move to the Midwest will further Don's long term professional interests and further the "well being" of his family!

The Outline Has Been Completed - Now What?

Your job is to make use of the facts! Remember, the directions tell you to do two things.

1. Take a position.

2. Justify that position. Your position can be justified only by using the facts.

Now let's add our discussion of the specific facts. We will bring our chart back into the picture.

Criteria Specific Facts

	Favors New York	Approximately Equal	Favors Midwest
Owning Own Business			✓
Quality Of Education		✓	
Wife's Career	✓		
Quality Of Health Care	✓		
Quality Of Life			✓

In the answer that follows the criteria specific facts are boldfaced. The introductory sentences that are for the purpose of organizing the answer remain in italics.

Don Davidson's professional development and the well being of his family dictate that he should move to the Midwest.

Don's present job has been good to him. It has equipped him with the tools that he needs to do what he really wants to do. That is to own his own business. **Don cannot realize his dream of owning his own business** if he stays in New York. The time has come to put his lessons into practice. The move to the Midwest is a tremendous business opportunity for him.

A consideration of the schools available to Don's children reveals that good schools are available in the Midwest. They should compensate for the loss of the "excellent schools" that the children will be leaving behind in New York.

Don's wife has an excellent job in New York. It is important to her, and *the move to the Midwest* would mean that she would have to leave her present job in marketing. But, she could put her tremendous talents to work as marketing and advertising manager of Don's own business! In this way she could spend more time with her children. This would allow her to have more of the best of both worlds!

Fortunately the younger child's dyslexia has already been diagnosed. It was a blessing to have been in New York for the purpose of early diagnosis and prescription of "state-of-the-art" treatment. Although the treatment is "state-of-the-art," once prescribed it is available in other centers. Of course, in the event of an emergency, the child could be brought to New York for special treatment.

By moving to the Midwest Don and his family would be trading the cultural and intellectual life of New York for the quality of life available in a small center. The Midwest will offer Don's family a living environment in which they can all flourish. Although New York is rich in cultural activities, no New Yorker participates in these things every day. On the other hand, the benefits of spacious housing, the outdoors, and having a dog are benefits that may be enjoyed each day. Assuming that Don does eventually have a higher income the Davidson's will be able to make trips to New York to absorb the benefits of New York culture. The extra income will also help the Davidson's provide a better education for their children!

Although it will be difficult to leave New York, the move to the Midwest will further Don's long term professional interests and enhance the general "well being" of his family!

The preceding example has been for the purpose of showing you how to organize and develop a writing sample. The approach is firmly rooted in the structure of the topic. In addition, I am not suggesting that this is a particularly good answer. Some of you may think it is, and some of may not. But, it does meet the requirements of the section.

What About Grammar?

I suggest that you **not** go to the trouble of improving your grammar for the purpose of the writing sample. The use of short concise sentences will obviate the need for a firm command of the rules of grammar.

But, there is one small point that you should remember!

**When you are comparing two things
you use the words "better and worse,"
not the words "best and worst!"**

What About Punctuation?

Although punctuation is important for your writing in general, it is not worth reviewing for the LSAT. The use of short sentences will obviate the need for a firm command of the rules of punctuation. Simply restrict yourself to the use of the period, and comma.

What About Vocabulary?

Don't ever use a word unless you know what it means and how to spell it. Don't even consider learning a collection of new words for the purposes of the LSAT writing sample!

A Sample Answer

What follows is one sample answer to the Davidson question. It is included not because it is particularly good, but because it demonstrates organization and how to use of the facts.

Given Don Davidson's concern for the well-being of his family and his desire to have his own business, moving to the Midwest is the superior choice.

Don has been with the same publishing house for six years. If he stays with them, his opportunities for further advancement would be very good. But staying in New York will not bring him closer to owning his own business.

Don's wife has an excellent job in New York and holds a very high position. It is possible that moving could hurt her career. Clearly, she is very good at marketing. The publishing company in the Midwest has a small profit margin and would benefit from new and innovative marketing strategies. Don's wife could, therefore, use her talents to improve the business. Furthermore, she would be able to enjoy the benefits of being her own boss.

Moving to the Midwest would be better for the children. They would no longer have to live in a cramped New York apartment. Moreover, they would be able to play freely outdoors. There are good schools in the area. Consequently, the younger child's dyslexia would not be neglected.

Relocating a family is never an easy task, but for Don and his family moving to the Midwest is the better option. Moving will improve the quality of their life and will bring Don closer to fulfilling his dream of being his own boss.

Chapter Ten

Practice Testing Mastery

The purpose of this chapter is to outline some specific things that you should do when you "practice." Although most of these things are simple, it is important that you internalize them.

What you do in practice you will do on the test!

Therefore, it is essential that you practice your full length sections and full length tests according to our prescribed plan of attack.

The General Attitude

1. People get answers wrong on the LSAT.

2. Are you a person?

What is the correct inference?

Be A High Achieving Realist And Not A Perfectionist!!

Your goal is not to get everything right but to:

**Identify The Best Answer
To As Many Questions
As You Can!**

 ## General Principles Applicable To All Question Types

For any question type you should:

- ■ underline the operative words.

- ■ determine the relationship between the right and wrong answers.

- ■ keep your eyes on the answer choices.

- ■ aggressively eliminate any answer choices that are wrong.

- ■ do one thing at a time.

- ■ select an answer before moving on to another question.

- ■ be sensitive to key words that limit conditions.
  (only, exactly, at least, etc.)

- ■ focus on what is simple and obvious.

- ■ ensure that you have sufficient time to do the questions that are easiest for you.

- ■ ensure that you run out of time when you hit the questions that are hardest for you.

- ■ ensure that you enter an answer for every question.

General Principles Always Applicable To Logic Games

When you encounter the logic games section you should:

- know how many of the sets of conditions you wish to work with.

- decide the order in which you will attack the individual sets of conditions.

- read the conditions for factual content and key words.

- take the big jump! Begin! You will become more comfortable by doing the questions.

- diagram only in conjunction with answering a specific question.

- decide the question order within individual sets.

General Principles Applicable To Reading Comprehension

When you encounter the reading comprehension section you should:

- know how many of the passages you wish to work with.

- decide the order in which you will attack the individual passages.

- when you read the passages:
  1. Don't slow down and try to absorb all the specific details.
  2. Do pick up on the main idea and the structure of the passage.

- begin with the main idea questions so that you focus on that aspect of the passage.

- never select an answer choice until you have read every word of every choice.

- watch out for key words and compound statements in the answer choices.

- identify the "best answer" by using the approach of compare and contrast.

- develop a tolerance for imprecision. The "best answer" will rarely be objectively correct.

General Principles Applicable To Logical Reasoning

When you encounter the logical reasoning section you should:

- remember that most test takers score higher by working fewer questions.

- if a question seems too difficult then find an easier one.

- begin every question by reading the question and noting the "operative words."

- when reading the arguments zero in on the conclusion (bottom line).

- when reading the arguments eliminate irrelevant information.

- identify the best answer by using the approach of "compare and contrast."

- never select an answer choice until you have read every word of every choice.

- develop a tolerance for imprecision. The best answer will rarely be objectively correct.

- eliminate answer choices that are the opposite of what you want or are irrelevant.

Chapter Eleven

LSAT Training Period and Test Day Mastery

How To Take Control Before And During The Test!

Different things work for different people. If you like the suggestions in this chapter use them. If not, then don't use them!

This chapter should be used to give you suggestions.
If you like what you read do it.
If you don't then don't.

The LSAT Is The Main Event!

Training for the LSAT is like training for an athletic event. Stamina is important. A plan of attack is important. The confidence that you can execute that plan of attack is important. The "internalization" of that plan of attack is important.

On the day of the event (LSAT) you will have to wake up relatively early and perform at a high level for a major part of the day. You will want a minimum of stresses, strains and surprises. You want to be in a position to perform at the top of your abilities for a long period of time. In order to achieve this you should consider how to prepare yourself in terms of the content of the test and in terms of the content of your life.

The Content Of The Test

Ideally you should start your preparation a minimum of several weeks before the actual test. Remember that your preparation objective is to "internalize" a set of principles of approach. The process of internalization is best accomplished by doing small amounts most days for a longer period of time than by doing a larger amount on each of fewer days!

**You may be able to pull an "all nighter" on an essay.
This is not the best way to prepare for the LSAT.
Work a little bit every day!**

Remember that practice without a clear approach can be hazardous.

**When you practice you should be practicing
the specific application of a specific plan of attack!**

1. Work with the chapters in this book.

2. Work with actual past exams.

3. Work in the context of a quality LSAT training program.

The Content Of Your Life

Here are some suggestions for how to organize your life the week before the test, the night before the test, the morning of the test, and during the test. All of these things will be easier if you register for the test early.

Registration For The Test

Don't be one of those people who never does today what he or she can put off until tomorrow! Register for the LSAT early. This will ensure that you get your choice of test center. If you get your choice of test center (maybe a familiar room), you will be able to sleep at home in familiar surroundings (and of course save money).

**Register for the test before the official registration deadline!
This will ensure that you get your choice of test center!**

The Week Before The Test

Sleep

Many students have made the following comment about their LSAT experience.

*"I was doing quite well. Then after the break
I started to get tired and fell apart!"*

Test takers get tired. Those who get the most tired are those who feel that rising at 7:00 a.m. is the equivalent of rising in the middle of the night.

**If you are a nocturnal creature who habitually rises at 7:00 p.m.
instead of 7:00 a.m. - reorganize your schedule.
Get into the habit of going to bed at a reasonable hour
and rising at a reasonable hour.**

Your goal is to be rested when you wake up on LSAT day!

Diet

Food Science and nutrition are the trends of the 90s. The quality of your diet will in part influence the quality of your life. Eat a balanced diet. It will keep your energy level high and your mind sharp.

The Day Before The Test

You want LSAT day to be like staying in a Holiday Inn. **No surprises!** Check out the room that you will be taking the LSAT in. You should know:

- how to get there

- where to park

- what the room looks like

- where you might want to sit (assuming that you have a choice)

- where the restrooms are located

Get organized. You should have the following things laid out.

- pencils (they shouldn't be too sharp or they may puncture the answer sheet)

- erasers

- pencil sharpeners

- timing device

- highlighters if applicable

- LSAT admission ticket

- identification

- food (something that is quick and quiet)

- money

Learning

The day before the test is too late to consider learning anything new. It will cause you anxiety which will be counterproductive. For example, you should not try to learn brand new categories of logic games.

Don't try to learn anything new the day before the test!

Practice

Practice by doing "full length" exercises. Some people like to practice questions the day before the test and some don't. If practice causes you additional anxiety then don't! The most that you should do is one "full length" exercise of each of the three main question types. If you do more you will tire yourself out. In addition, the more you do the more likely you are to hit a set of questions that you cannot do. Again, this will result in unnecessary anxiety.

**The most you should practice the day before the test
is one full length section of each of
logic games, logical reasoning, and reading comprehension!**

The Evening Before The Test

The purpose of this evening is to relax, enjoy yourself, have a good dinner, and get to bed at a reasonable hour.

Under no circumstances should you look at LSAT questions!

Do what you enjoy doing. Go to a movie (not just anything but something you like). Go swimming (or if you don't swim try some other activity). Read a novel (but not one about people taking the LSAT). Have a good dinner. Go to bed neither too early nor too late. Spend the evening with friends (if you don't have any friends spend the evening with your mother or your dog).

The Morning Of The Test

Dress in layers. You may find the test room either too hot or too cold. For example, it would be nice to have a sweater to put on or to take off.

Dress Flexibly!

Have a decent breakfast. The test will neither start nor end on time. But, don't eat too much or too little. Don't drink too much coffee.

Eat Sensibly!

Leave early enough so that you don't have to rush.

Don't Get A Late Start!

Follow the directions of the test administrators. Assume that the process will take some time. Assume also that the environment will be tense and that there will be some angry people. The test administrators are not out to get you. In fact, they are probably frightened of you!

Try to picture yourself in the position of the test administrators.

Don't feel that you have to try any LSAT questions. However, if you feel that you must then follow this suggestion.

Don't try more than one set of conditions of games (6 questions), one reading passage (7 questions) and 6 logical reasoning questions.

If you do any questions don't check the answers to your work!

Avoid listening to or conversing with the other test takers. You will be feeling anxiety. Have you ever been soothed by a person who is stressed out?

Don't pay attention to the other test takers!

At some test centers you have a choice of where to sit. Try to sit in a place where you will be least likely to be distracted by other test takers.

Be smart about where to sit!

If you are required to sit in a specific seat and you find that it is unsatisfactory, find a proctor and insist that you be moved.

**Take as much control over where you sit
as the circumstances require!**

If the test administrators are using a clock on the wall then you should synchronize your watch with that clock. This will make life easier.

Synchronize your timing device with the official test timing device!

During The Test

Stick to your game plan. You developed it during your training period. For example, if you are accustomed to doing only three of four reading passages, don't change the day of the test.

The actual test is not a good time to experiment with new ideas!

Although everybody gets the same sections that count, not everybody gets them in the same order. For example, while you are working on games, your neighbor may be working on reading passages. His or her answers to reading will be of no use to you while doing games.

**Keep your eyes to yourself.
There is no benefit to looking at someone else's answer sheet!**

The test administrators are required to post the time remaining for each section. However, they are inconsistent in how they do this. There have been instances (few and far between) where they have made mistakes. It is imperative that you time yourself. Don't rely on the test administrators.

Take control of the timing of the test yourself!

Remember that there is one experimental section. It will not be announced and it will be a repeat of something you have already done. For example you might get an extra set of reading passages.

**If you do badly on a section
tell yourself that it was the experimental section!**

You will get a break half way through the test. Simply relax. Resist the temptation of talking to other test takers. It is more likely to upset you than to comfort you.

Be unsociable during the break!

If you start coming unglued during the test, simply ask permission to leave the room. You are free to leave at any time to use the restroom. Take a walk, take some slow deep breaths. Calm down. Return to the test room and start again.

If you get into trouble, take your own short break!

Don't lose sight of your goal. You will not get everything right. You can get many wrong answers and still perform well on the test. Your goal was never to get everything right. Stay focused on the answer choices eliminating those that are clearly wrong. Don't be a perfectionist! Be a realist! Stay in control emotionally.

Your goal is to identify the best answer to as many questions as you can.

The worst thing that can possibly happen is that you will have to do the test again. Remember that you don't have to have your test scored. If you are having a bad day, simply get the practice effect of doing the test, cancel your score and try again another day.

The worst case scenario is that you will do the test again!

Chapter Twelve

Post-LSAT Mastery

In this chapter we will explore the following three issues.

1. Should You Cancel Your Test Score?

2. What Do You Do About Adverse Test Conditions?

3. Should You Retake The LSAT After Receiving A First Score?

Issue 1 : Should You Cancel Your Score?

If you leave the LSAT **feeling certain that you did not perform up to your potential**, you have an opportunity to cancel your score.

**Take the LSAT early enough so that you know
you have time to cancel your score and do the test again!**

The procedure for canceling an LSAT score may be found in the **Law Services Information Book**. If you cancel your score, Law Services will report that you took the test but that the score was canceled. There is nothing that the admissions committees can infer from this.

When Should You Exercise The Option Of Canceling Your Score?

You can underperform for a variety of reasons. Some reasons are personal and some are related to the conditions under which the test was administered.

General Guidelines For Making Your Decision

This is a decision that you and only you can make. There are few test takers who leave and feel that they performed extremely well. The question should be:

**Do you honestly feel that you could score higher
if you took the LSAT again?**

If you are reasonably certain that you "bombed" then cancel your score.

**Make every effort to ensure that your first score
reflects the top end of your abilities!**

After every LSAT I receive telephone calls from students wondering whether they should cancel. I am personally aware of many instances of students canceling their first score and receiving an extremely high score on a subsequent attempt! In these instances the only reportable score was the subsequent high score.

Issue 2 : What Should You Do
About Adverse Testing Conditions?

This poses a special problem.

Provided that you register early you will have a choice of where to take the LSAT. Regrettably, not all LSAT test centers are the same. Law Services does not always do a good job of ensuring that the test conditions are adequate. There have been some instances of conditions being sufficiently bad to impact adversely on candidates' scores. Examples of adverse conditions can include:

- inadequate lighting

- background or other noise

- incorrect timing of sections by the proctors

- extreme room temperatures

If you find that the conditions at your test center were bad, **complain immediately!** A letter should go to Law Services outlining the nature of the complaint.

You will probably find Law Services to be sympathetic. There have been some instances of Law Services offering to let students retake the LSAT at no additional charge.

**Retain all correspondence that you send to
or receive from Law Services.
It is the only thing that can act as documented evidence
of adverse testing conditions.**

In the event that you allow your LSAT to be scored (which I would not recommend unless you have no choice) it is essential that you have **documented evidence** of the nature of the test conditions and the fact that you complained. The correspondence between you and Law Services should suffice as **documented evidence.** Use this evidence to argue to the law schools that your LSAT score was adversely affected by the difficult test conditions. The application form of many schools includes a section that invites applicants to explain any conditions which have adversely impacted on grades or LSAT scores.

There are two groups of people who have LSAT scores which were adversely affected by the test conditions. Members of the first group are applying with only that (adversely affected) LSAT score. Members of the second group have a subsequent LSAT score which is higher. What follows are some suggestions for "damage control" for each of the two groups.

Applicants With One (Adversely Affected) LSAT Score

Argue forcefully that your LSAT score should not be given the weight that it normally would. All schools require an LSAT score. It is unlikely that you will be able to persuade the committee to completely disregard the score.

**Your goal is to persuade the committee
to place less emphasis on that LSAT score!**

Applicants With A Subsequent Higher LSAT Score

It will be easier to argue that your LSAT score was adversely affected by the test conditions if you have a subsequent score that is higher. If you have a subsequent higher score ask the school to completely disregard the first score. (This will be of benefit to you if you are applying to a school that averages LSAT scores.)

**In this instance your goal should be
to persuade the committee to completely disregard your first score!**

Issue 3 : Should You Retake The LSAT After Receiving A First Score?

Law Services would like you to believe that it is next to impossible to increase one's LSAT score. This is patently false! Over the years I have observed hundreds of students increase their scores by retaking the test. **It is possible and common to increase one's LSAT score!** In fact students frequently score better on the second attempt than on the first attempt.

This reality should be tempered by three further thoughts.

1. Many law schools average multiple LSAT scores.
2. If you take the LSAT again and receive approximately the same score, the first score may be reinforced in the minds of the committe.
3. It is possible (but less common) to score lower on a subsequent attempt!

If Your Score Is Too Low Then You Must Retake The LSAT!!

Call the law schools and determine what is a competitive score for the category in which you are applying. If your score is too low, then take the LSAT again.

Continue to take the LSAT until you reach the point where you have more to lose than to gain.

If your score is comparable to the average LSAT score of first year law students then it is probably time to stop.

A Final Thought

You should get the LSAT out of your life
at the earliest possible moment.
There is no reason to become an LSAT Historian!

Chapter Thirteen

Application Process Mastery

Your goal in the application process is twofold.

1. You want to be accepted to the law school of your choice.

2. You want to be accepted in the spring! You do not want to be sitting on "pins and needles" throughout the summer waiting to hear from the law schools. For this reason it is important to ensure that your file is complete as early as possible.

The Application Is The Interview!

Many students approach law school applications in the same way as they approach constructing a resume. There is an important difference. A resume is used for the purpose of obtaining an interview. **The law school application and other components of the file are the interview!**

The Application Process Is A Big Job!

It will pay you to do a good job on the application process. Although grades and LSAT scores continue to be primary considerations for law admissions, the other components of your file are becoming increasingly important. Schools that require personal statements rely heavily on them. Law School applications are becoming increasingly lengthy. It will take a substantial amount of time to properly develop them.

Start Early

The completion of a law school application and personal statement should be thought of as the equivalent of writing a term paper. They will require:

- research

- focus

- editing

- rewriting

They should be carefully checked for spelling, grammar, punctuation, and visual appeal. You should begin as soon as the law school applications become available.

How Many Law Schools Should You Apply To?

Lots! If you want to attend law school you must be accepted. The more schools you apply to, the greater your chances of acceptance.

How To Determine Where To Apply

If you are applying to U.S. law schools you should obtain the **Official Guide To U.S. Law Schools** from Law Services. It will give you a strong indication of where (given your grades and LSAT scores) you will be accepted. Target your applications to those schools.

There are fifteen Canadian common law schools. If you want to attend law school in Canada there is no reason to not apply to all of them.

The Necessity Of Direct Marketing

Law schools spend a lot of money deciding who to admit to their first year classes. It is clear that they care who they admit. Law schools have their own objectives to meet when they fill their first year classes. Some schools want students with a social conscience. Others look more closely at extra-curricular activities. There is a trend in law admissions to the effect that the composition of law school classes should better reflect the composition of society as a whole. Some schools admit students in an attempt to meet this objective.

Different employers look for different things in selecting job applicants. Therefore, you would apply to different jobs differently. For the same reason you should apply to different law schools differently.

Direct Marketing - The Practical Consequences

You must not think in terms of one application and personal statement for all the schools to which you are applying. Rather, you must develop a different personal statement for each law school. Your application should emphasize different things about you for each law school. You may want to use different kinds of letters of recommendations for different law schools. For example, at some schools and for some categories of applicants, your employment history may be relevant and a letter from an employer might be relevant. At other schools these considerations may not be relevant.

How To Determine What Law Schools Look For

There are three sources of information.

1. The school's calendar.

2. The school's application form.

3. The **LSAT Registration Book** for Canadian schools and the **Official Guide To U.S. Law Schools** for U.S. schools.

As you peruse these sources of information look for a statement of a generalized policy on admission. You must then emphasize the specific facts about you which are most relevant to the school's criteria for admission. Look for special programs that the school offers which you are specifically interested in.

For example, if a school states that it will look favorably on applicants who are interested in a specific program, then make it clear that you are interested in that program! If a school indicates that it will look favorably on applicants who come from a background that would give the applicant a special perspective on law and society (assuming you qualify) make it clear that you qualify. Explain exactly **how** you qualify! These are two examples of obvious and necessary "direct marketing."

What Are The Components Of Your Application File?

Your file will consist of the following components:

1. Completed Application - Sent by you.

2. Transcript Of Grades - To be sent by your school.

3. Personal Statement If Applicable - Sent by you.

4. Letter(s) Of Reference If Applicable - To be sent by the referee.

5. LSAT score - To be sent by Law Services.

6. LSAT Writing Sample - Sent by Law Services with your LSAT score.

Your job is to ensure that each of these components is as good as it can be. Your application and personal statement are under your complete control. They should be worked and reworked until you are satisfied with their contents.

How To Obtain Law School Applications And Calendars

In the early fall call or write the law schools. Ask that they send you their current calendar and application form when they become available.

What To Do When You Get The Application Form

1. Make Photocopies Of It.
You must practice filling it out. It is important that it have visual appeal as well as content.

2. Determine What Category You Will Apply In.
Most schools have more than one category for admissions. Most students will find themselves applying in the "mainstream category." This category is for students who are just completing or who have recently completed their university prerequisites for law school. (Most students will have a Bachelors degree.) There is often a "residual category" for applicants who cannot meet the minimum academic requirements. Applicants in this category will often have been away from the academic world for number of years.

3. Determine What Date The Application Must Be In And What Date The File Must Be Complete.
The date that the application must be received may be different from the date that the file must be complete. Be careful! Sometimes schools have different dates for different categories of applicants.

4. Determine How The School Uses The LSAT.
Does it average scores or take the highest? How recent of a score is required? Does the test have to be taken no later than a certain date? (for example the December LSAT) Make certain that Law Services has been directed to send your score to the law schools. It is Law Services and not you who is responsible for sending your LSAT scores to the law schools.

5. Are Letters Of Reference Required? If So, How Many And What Kind?
It is important that you know well in advance how these letters are used. It will take you time to organize the people who will be sending you references.

6. Take immediate steps to ensure that your grades are sent to the law schools.
It is amazing how many people fail to do this on a timely basis. There is no reason to delay this vital step. If you don't receive an early acceptance you will also have to send transcripts of your final grades when they become available. It is not necessary that the school have received your application in order for the transcripts of your grades to be sent.

The Nuts And Bolts Of Completing The Application Form

Here are some simple steps for how to complete the application form.

1. Make copies of the blank form.

2. Acquaint yourself with the school's generalized policies on admission.

3. Complete a first draft of the application.

4. Put the first draft away for a few days.

5. Complete the second draft.

6. Give the completed second draft to others for comment.

7. Complete the third draft or as many additional drafts as you wish.

The Nuts And Bolts Of Constructing A Personal Statement

These should be crafted slowly and carefully. They should be carefully edited. You should think in terms of a different one for each school. Research the schools generalized policies on admissions.

Use the same procedure that was suggested for completing the application form itself.

It is impossible to do justice to the topic of personal statements in one chapter. You may wish to consult some of my other books.

Mastering The Personal Statement ISBN: 0-9696290-4-4 (1998)

Law School Bound ISBN: 0-9696290-0-1 (1992)

Law School Bound 2nd Edition ISBN: 0-9696290-2-8 (2000)

In addition, you may want to consider my internet based resources:

www.prep.com

"Law School Bound®" email newsletter. Request it at learn@prep.com

Letters Of Reference - Some Helpful Hints

Not all schools require letters of reference. Some require them only for certain categories of applicants. A law school will require a letter of reference to obtain third party comments about factors that are relevant to their admissions criteria. All law schools are interested in your academic ability to do law school work. For this reason most letters of reference are required to be academic. The referee should be a person who can comment on your academic ability. A professor is a logical choice.

How Not To Obtain Letters Of Reference

Don't simply ask a professor to write a letter of reference. The professor may write a poor one!

The Right Way To Obtain Letters Of Reference

There are two factors to keep in mind.

First, you must **qualify** the person to write the letter for you.

Second, you must **educate** the person about what to write.

The Qualification Issue

The appropriate question to ask is:

Do you feel that you could and would you be willing to write me a strong and positive letter of reference?

Notice that by answering in the affirmative the person is agreeing to write a good letter.

The Education Issue

A good letter must be focused and address issues that are relevant to admissions criteria. You must sit down with the person who is writing the letter and ensure that he or she understands how the letter is to be used and what issues the school is interested in. There is no reason why your professors should know anything about law admissions. They don't. It is up to you to teach them.

Some Specific Types Of Letters To Avoid

Many applicants attempt to obtain letters from people with some status in the community. (lawyers, judges, politicians, etc.) In general these letters are unlikely to be helpful. As a general rule, these people have not had the opportunity to observe your academic work.

Some Matters Of Common Courtesy

It takes a great deal of time to write good letters of reference. Make sure that you express your gratitude in the form of a "thank you" letter. In addition, you should offer to absorb any out of pocket costs.

A Final Comment

Obtain your information about specific law schools from that specific law school. Don't listen to your friends and associates. Although their advice may be well intended it is often dated and sometimes completely wrong.

You take control of your situation!

Chapter Fourteen

Career Choice Mastery

With few exceptions those of you reading this book wish to become lawyers. Going to law school is a worthy goal. At the present time it is difficult to be accepted. In this closing chapter it seems fitting to offer some general advice pertaining to how to think about career choices. I propose to offer this advice in the form of general principles. Many of you will find that a career in law is consistent with many of the decision making principles that I am suggesting. Advice can be given only in the context of the world that we are moving into. Hence, I begin with some basic assumptions.

The Future - "It Ain't What It Used To Be!"

- a famous baseball manager

In "The Graduate", (a movie from the 60s) Benjamin Braddock returned home with his B.A. and was expected to start a career. A family friend said: "I just want to say one word to you." What's that", asked Benjamin. "Plastics" answered the friend. If a modern day Benjamin returned home today the friend would probably say: "telecommunications!" Telecommunications and the internet are fueling a revolution in every aspect of the way that we live. It is now easy to communicate at low cost to every corner of the globe. In fact, it now can cost more to make a local call from a pay phone than it does to make a long distance call to the U.K. The world is getting smaller and smaller. Businesses in North America now face competition from every corner of the world. Computers have made it possible for people to live almost anywhere and participate in many kinds of global activities. Your careers will not look anything like the careers your parents may have had. The realities of the more global and competitive world include:

- global competition will ensure that capital will gravitate to the country that offers the best return and the lowest costs and impediments to doing business. Certain products will no longer be able to be produced competitively in North America - resulting in the loss of jobs and industries. On the other hand, North America may attract new industries where it has a competitive advantage;

- in an era of personal mobility people will gravitate toward the countries with the lowest tax rates. Have you heard of the brain drain?

- countries with high levels of debt (of which Canada is one) will find it hard to lower taxes. Nevertheless, it will be politically difficult for governments to increase taxes;

- governments that have difficulty increasing taxes will have difficulty providing a high level of government services. Therefore, people must learn to take more responsibility for their physical, emotional and financial health;

- taking care of oneself may require having more than one job or business at the same time;

- long run success requires the ability to learn new skills, change careers and otherwise adapt overnight. Your most important asset is your brain;

- the concept of a job is likely to become obsolete. Therefore, when you think about careers, don't think in terms of getting a job. Think in terms of creating opportunities;

- although English is rapidly becoming the international language of the world, the days of North American economic and cultural dominance may be coming to an end. The most successful North Americans will be those who are fluent with the cultures and languages of other countries.

Emotional and mental flexibility and the ability to be self-sufficient will be the most important attributes for success in the new millennium.

How do these changes impact on career choices in general and the law school admissions decision in particular?

The Essential Principles Of Career Choice Mastery

 Principle 1 : If you like your current course of study, consider staying in it.

Commentary - It is amazing how many people see their undergraduate careers as some kind of "pre-law" holding period. In choosing a career the most important consideration should be whether it makes you happy and fulfilled. You will have many careers during your life. You should think of your undergraduate years as training for any of a number of different careers.

Principle 2 : Consider doing a graduate degree.

Commentary - There are two reasons for this. The first is simply that if you like doing something there is no reason not to continue. The second is that certain fields of law are becoming extremely specialized. To be effective in that area may require very specialized background knowledge.

 Principle 3 : Take courses which will force you to learn to write!

Commentary - Writing is the stock and trade of all law students and some lawyers. I have never known a good law student or good lawyer who did not also have good writing skills. **These skills must be developed before entering law school.** I once attended a lecture given by F. Lee Bailey (a famous criminal lawyer). During the question and answer period a student asked for some advice about what courses to take prior to law school. Mr. Bailey replied:

English, English, English, English, and English!

 Principle 4 : Take courses that will teach you how to learn and how to continue to learn.

Commentary - Your mind and your learning skills are your most important assets. Your undergraduate years are a special time when you have the opportunity to develop them. Don't blow this opportunity!

 Principle 5 : Learn at least one foreign language.

Commentary - Most North Americans do not speak more than one language. The days of North American world dominance are over. Citizens of most other countries (including our biggest trading partners) speak a number of languages. The more languages you speak the more competitive and employable you will be! Business is becoming increasingly international. If you do not speak at least one foreign language you will be at an extreme disadvantage. In many parts of the world people speak more than four languages.

Principle 6 : Career choices are serious business. They should be re-searched thoroughly.

Commentary - There are a number of books about law school and the legal profession. Read them. Talk to lawyers. Talk to law students. Many undergraduate schools have "Pre-Law Clubs." Join them. They frequently have very interesting speakers and events. Every year I organize an event which I call "Pre-Law Forum." I bring together admissions personnel, lawyers, law students, and law professors for one tremendous information day. In addition, I run a complete educational program for pre-law students.

 Principle 7 : You will invest time in your career choices. Make sure that you choose a career because you and only you wish to pursue it.

Commentary - I have encountered many students who have no real interest in law school. They are preparing for the LSAT because of parental pressure or pressure from another source. You owe it to yourself to resist this kind of pressure. After all, you must live with your decisions. Your parents don't.

 Principle 8 : Don't ever think in terms of one career. Never say: I have to decide what one thing I want to do the rest of my life!

Commentary - The world is in a period of turbulent change. It is unlikely that any of you will be able to or will want to stay in one career your whole working life. Never exclude anything you like to do! Think of law as being one of your many careers. Try to incorporate other careers into law. Life and careers should be thought of as a period of continual growth and change.

 Principle 9 : The only good reason to attend professional school is because you would like to study the subject that is being taught!

Commentary - Going to law school is one thing. Becoming a lawyer and practicing law is another. Many people attend law school and never become lawyers. Law school is not trade school, but is an academic experience. It is important that you enjoy it. The chances are that if you don't like law school you won't be a good enough lawyer to ever enjoy being lawyer.

Principle 10 : When in law school try to pick up a joint degree.

Commentary - Learn to leverage your time. A joint degree can only help you. A joint degree may be defined as graduating from law school with a joint degree in either two disciplines or two law degrees. Examples of joint degree programs include: Law/MBA, Law/Economics, Law/Environmental Studies, Law/ Social Work, Joint Civil Law/Common Law programs...

Principle 11 : In law school, be adventurous when selecting your courses!

Commentary - Don't view law school as being some kind of trade school. View it as an opportunity to expand your mind and expand your interests. Select courses that you know nothing about! You might realize that you are fascinated by a subject that you never knew existed. Remember the bumper sticker that said:

"When my ship came in, I was at the airport!"

My point is that law school is an opportunity to discover new interests. Make sure that you are paying attention!

Principle 12 : Set and work within the framework of goals!

Commentary - Dreams are important. But, without goals dreams will always remain dreams. The setting of a firm goal is what is required to turn a dream into reality. I once saw a sign that read:

"Goals are nothing but dreams with a deadline."

Successful people always work within the framework of goals!

Principle 13 : Respect and embrace the principle of hard work!

Commentary - The world is full of opportunity. With few exceptions hard work is required to reap the benefits of these opportunities.

I'm sure that you have heard of Clarence Darrow who was a very famous American lawyer. At the end of his career he gave a speech. At the end of the speech a member of the audience asked the following question.

"Mr Darrow, to what do you owe your success?"

Clarence Darrow replied,

"I owe my success to hard work. When I was young my father had me out on the farm growing potatoes. Because the work was so hard, I became a lawyer and haven't worked a day since."

The truth is that nobody works harder than a successful lawyer!

 Principle 14 : Don't focus exclusively on opportunities that already exist. Focus on opportunities that you can create!

Commentary - What if Bill Gates had said, "I can't have a career in computers. There are no software companies that exist!" Bill Gates created an opportunity. He had vision! He created a whole industry! The point is that you should think beyond the opportunities that exist today. Create your own! Look for problems in society. Everywhere you see a problem, there is an opportunity for a new career for someone! It might as well be you!

 Principle 15 : The Most Important Principle!

Make the decision to be a success!

Commentary - A necessary condition for success is that one has made a decision to be a success! Far too many people give up in the face of adversity. Sometimes adversity can take the form of a low grade or a low LSAT score. Most people become discouraged and simply give up. Others make the decision to overcome the adversity and achieve their goals!

One of my best friends is a very prominent lawyer in a large firm. We were good friends during our undergraduate years. He decided that he wanted to become a lawyer. The first time that he took the LSAT he scored in approximately the 20th percentile. (That is a very low score.) Convinced that he had made some errors in filling in his answer sheet, he tried the test again. He received approximately the same score. It was a truly devastating experience for him. But rather than give up, he **made the decision that he was going to score high enough to get into law school.** He worked and worked and worked. He did the test three more times for a total of five times. But, before each test he worked hard and developed the strategies and principles that were the key to success. His third score was higher but still relatively low. His fourth score was average. The LSAT in February of 1981 was his fifth attempt. He scored in the 85th percentile. Why the slow but dramatic improvement? Because, he made the decision that he wanted to do well!

AS A LAWYER, DEAR, YOU CAN
CORRECT A LOT OF INJUSTICE...
AND CLEAN UP DOING IT.

Career Opportunities In The Legal Profession

Law is one of the oldest professions. There always have been and always will be lawyers. What follows are two good reasons to become a lawyer.

First, there will always be a need for lawyers. Law is the language that is used to organize society. There will always be social problems. All social problems eventually become legal problems. There are many different kinds of lawyers. In fact, the practice of law is so diverse that you could change careers ten times in your life and still call yourself a lawyer. As society evolves certain kinds of lawyers will become obsolete and new opportunities will be created for new kinds of lawyers. For example, the advent of no fault automobile insurance schemes will decrease the demand for the services of lawyers who specialize in automobile accident litigation. But, the increasing number of elderly people will increase the demand for lawyers who represent the interests of the elderly. Every major change in society will create a new set of legal problems and will create a demand for the services of lawyers who are willing to work in that area. The Canadian Charter Of Rights And Freedoms did not exist prior to 1982. Now there are lawyers who earn a very good living practicing in this area of law. Most people weren't even aware of the internet until 1994. Now many lawyers make a "good living" practising the "law of the internet." Many of you could find yourself practicing in an area of law that doesn't even exist today.

Second, there are always plenty of opportunities for good people. Relax! Those who choose to the things that they like always find that they are successful. One of the reasons that people are attracted to certain kinds of work is that they like it.

Conclusion

There is **unlimited opportunity in the world!**
Take advantage of some of it!
If that means going to law school then do it!
If it means something else, then do that!
Be positive!
Be happy!
Be successful!

Chapter Fifteen

Mastering
The LSAT

Where To Go From Here?

I began teaching and developing LSAT programs in 1979. For a long time I have been distressed that many students arrive at my course already having acquired a number of bad habits. My original purpose was to write a short book to be read by students prior to attending my course. When the book was half complete I realized that I had become "carried away." I was now writing a major book about LSAT training. I then decided to make the book available to the general market. **Reading this book is neither a substitute nor prerequisite for attending one of my training programs.** It will, however, help you attain maximum benefits from the program.

I offer a variety of programs for **every LSAT**. They range from as little as one weekend to as long as six weeks. They are available in Toronto and other locations across Canada.

I would like to tell you specifically about my **Mastering The LSAT** program. It is a **specialty program** that I offer at certain times of the year. It is the most extensive program of live instruction available anywhere. Because it is so extensive, I don't run my **Mastering The LSAT** program for every LSAT. (But, I do run other programs for every LSAT.) I run **Mastering The LSAT** for the June LSAT and sometimes for other LSAT administrations. My **Mastering The LSAT** program generally begins about six weeks prior to the LSAT. It is available in Toronto and sometimes other centres.

You might also be interested to know that I have developed a complete pre-law educational program called **"Law School Bound."** It consists of a number of seminars, courses and events which are of interest to pre-law students. They include my annual "Pre-Law Forum" and my "Law School Application Seminar." I also publish a FREE "Law School Bound"® email newsletter. To subscribe, send a request to learn@prep.com

---

My complete contact information is:

(416) 410-PREP®   1 800 410-PREP®

www.prep.com™   learn@prep.com™

Whatever you decide to do, I wish you success! (I would wish you luck, but I don't believe in luck - only in the benefits of hard work.) I hope that you have enjoyed this book and found it to be helpful!

John Richardson

P.S.   If you don't do anything else, at the very least, you should obtain as many actual past LSAT exams as you can! They may be ordered from Law Services. (215) 968-1001 or http://www.LSAC.org

How To Become
A Lawyer In Canada

A license is required to hold oneself out as a lawyer and practice law. In Canada, the legal profession is a self governing profession. This means that the profession governs itself and decides who is entitled to hold a license to practise law. In most provinces it is common to refer to the group of lawyers who govern the legal profession as the "Law Society."

Law Societies are also governed by laws. For example, in Ontario the law that governs the Law Society is called the **Law Society Act.** This is a statute that provides the legislative framework for the regulation of the legal profession. It also specifies the requirements for becoming a lawyer.

Bar Admission In The Common Law Provinces

In order to be admitted to the bar, one must complete the bar admission course in the province in which one wishes to be a lawyer. The bar admission course is administered by the Law Society. In general the bar admission course lasts from nine to eighteen months. It consists of a combination of articling (the development of practical legal skills under the supervision of a lawyer) and classes.

In order to be allowed to attend the bar admission course, one must have already graduated from an "approved law school." The list of "approved law schools" **(for every province except Quebec) includes** each of the Canadian common law schools. In rare instances graduates of foreign law schools may be permitted to enroll in the bar admission course. For further information you should contact the law society of the province in which you wish to practise.

Therefore, the basic procedure is as follows.

1. Graduate from an approved law school. Canada's common law schools are approved in every province except Quebec.

2. Enroll in the bar admission course.

3. Complete the bar admission course.

4. Pay the fees to be admitted to the bar.

Bar Admission In Quebec

Canada has two legal systems. Quebec is based on the civil law system. The rest of the provinces are based on the common law system. A common law degree is required enter the bar admission course in the common law provinces. A civil law degree is required to enter the bar admission course in Quebec. Quebec law schools have civil law degree programs. A number of Canadian law schools have programs that allow you to complete both Common and Civil law degrees in four years. McGill has a program that allows for the completion of both Common and Civil law degrees in as little as three years. This gives you the option of bar admission in both Quebec and the Common Law provinces.

Canadian Common-Law School Addresses and Contact Information

Admissions Secretary
Room 484B Law Centre
Faculty of Law
University of Alberta
Edmonton, Alberta
T6G 2H5
(403) 492-3067

Admissions Advisor
1822 East Mall
Faculty of Law
University of British Columbia
Vancouver, British Columbia
V6T 1Z1
(604) 822-8108

Admission Office
Faculty of Law
University of Calgary
Calgary, Alberta
T2N 1N4
(403) 220-7222

Admissions Officer
Dalhousie Law School
Halifax, Nova Scotia
B3H 4H9
(902) 494-3495

Faculty of Law
Robson Hall
University of Manitoba
Winnipeg, Manitoba
R3T 2N2
(204) 474-9773

Admissions Officer
Faculty of Law
McGill University
3644 Peel Street
Montreal, Quebec
H3A 1W9
(514) 398-6602

Pavillon P.-A.-Landry
Universite de Moncton
Moncton (Nouveau-Brunswick)
E1A 3E9
(506) 858-4000

Admission Officer
Faculty of Law
Ludlow Hall
University of New Brunswick
Box 4400
Fredericton, New Brunswick
E3B 5A3
(506) 453-4693

Office of the Registrar
University of Ottawa
550 Cumberland Street
Ottawa, Ontario
K1N 6N5
Attn: Common Law Admissions
        Officer
(613) 564-4060

Registrar of Law
Queen's University at Kingston
MacDonald Hall
Kingston, Ontario
K7L 3N6
(613) 545-2220

Admissions Committee
College of Law
University of Saskatchewan
Saskatoon, Saskatchewan
S7N 0W0
(306) 966-5874

Office of Admissions
Faculty of Law
University of Toronto
78 Queen's Park
Toronto, Ontario
M5S 2C5
(416) 978-3725

Admissions Office
Faculty of Law
University of Victoria
P.O. Box 2400
Victoria, British Columbia
V8W 3H7
(604) 721-8150

Student Affairs Officer
Faculty of Law
University of Western Ontario
London, Ontario
N6A 3K7
(519) 679-2111 Ext. 8425

Admissions Office
Faculty of Law
University of Windsor
Windsor Ontario
N9B 3P4
(519) 253-4232 x-2925

Office of Student Affairs
Osgoode Hall Law School
York University
4700 Keele Street
North York, Ontario
M3J 2R5
(416) 736-5040

**Visit http://www.LSAC.org for links to all Canadian and U.S. Law Schools
or www.prep.com**

Provincial Law Society Addresses and Contact Information

The Law Society of Alberta
919 11th Avenue S.W.
Suite 600
Calgary, Alberta
T2R 1P3
(403) 229-4700

The Law Society of
British Columbia
845 Cambie Street
Vancouver, British Columbia
V6B 4Z9
(604) 669-2533

The Law Society of Manitoba
201-219 Kennedy Street
Winnipeg, Manitoba
R3C 1S8
(204) 942-5571

The Law Society of
New Brunswick
206-1133 Regent Street
Fredericton, N.B.
E3B 3Z2
(506) 458-8540

The Law Society of Newfoundland
Baird's Cove
P.O. Box 1028
St. John's, Newfoundland
A1C 5M3
(709) 722-4740

The Law Society of Northwest
Territories
4916 47th Street
P.O. Box 1298
Yellowknife, N.W.T.
X1A 2N9
(403) 873-3828

The Law Society of Nova Scotia
1475 Hollis Street
Halifax, Nova Scotia
B3J 3M4
(902) 422-1491

The Law Society of Prince
Edward Island
49 Water Street
Charlottetown, P.E.I.
C1A 1A4
(902) 566-1666

Barreau du Quebec
Maison du Barreau
445, boulevard Saint-Laurent
Montreal, Quebec
H2Y 3T8
(514) 954-3400

The Law Society of Saskatchewan
201-2208 Scarth Street
Regina, Saskatchewan
S4P 2J6
(306) 569-8242

The Law Society of Upper Canada
Osgoode Hall
130 Queen Street West
Toronto, Ontario
M5H 2N6
(416) 947-3300

The Law Society of Yukon
201-302 Streele Street
Whitehorse, Yukon
Y1A 2C6
(403) 668-4231

Visit the Federation of Law Societies at:
http:// www.FLSC.ca
for the appropriate internet links.
Or visit us at
www.prep.com.

How To Become A Lawyer In The U.S.

To put it simply, you graduate from law school and pass the bar exam. U.S. states do not have bar admission courses. In general, in order to receive permission to take the bar exam in a U.S. state one must have graduated from an A.B.A. (American Bar Association) approved law school. A list of A.B.A. approved schools may be found in the **Official Guide To U.S. Law Schools**. You may order it from Law Services. The Canadian schools are not A.B.A. approved. Nevertheless, some states, for some Canadian law graduates, at some times, have given permission to take the bar exam. The rules are different for each state. For specific information you should contact those responsible for bar admission in whatever state you are interested.

U.S. Law School and Bar Admission Web Sites

Specific information may be found at the following web sites:

Law Services - www.LSAC.org - links to all U.S. law schools

The American Bar Association - www.abanet.org - a wealth of information about law schools, U.S. bar admission and the practice of law in the U.S.

The National Conference Of Bar Examiners - www.ncbex.org - basic information about the bar exam in a number of U.S. states and links to the bar examiners in every U.S. state

Richardson - Law School Bound® - www.prep.com™ - links to everything you need to know about becoming a lawyer.

Additional Products And Services

Market yourself into the law school of your choice!

Now that you have trained for the LSAT you need a great application and personal statement!

This special edition of Mastering The LSAT includes as a special bonus ($20.00 value) the complete text of John Richardson's:

Mastering The Personal Statement will completely change the way you think about the application process. It starts on the next page.

Mastering The Personal Statement

The Complete Marketing Manual For
Law - MBA - Med & Grad Schools

Mastering The Personal Statement

The Complete Marketing Manual For
Law - MBA - Med & Grad Schools

RICHARDSON PRESS

JOHN RICHARDSON, B.A., LL.B., J.D.

Richardson Press
P.O. Box 19602, Manulife P.O.
55 Bloor St. W.
Toronto, Canada M4W 3T9

ISBN: 0-9696290-4-4

Cover designed by Bryan Babcock Graphic Design.

Page layout and diagrams by Bryan Babcock Graphic Design.

Manufactured And Printed In Canada

Acknowledgments

I offer my thanks to the students who graciously allowed all or parts of their personal statements to be included in this book. I am grateful to those students who read and commented on this book while it was in draft form. Finally, I wish to extend special recognition to all the people who have worked with me as teachers and in administrative capacities at various times since 1979. You know who you all are!

Outline And Table Of Contents

Introduction

From The Desk Of John Richardson, B.A, LL.B., J.D.

Admission to law, MBA, medical school or graduate school is extremely competitive. Grades and test scores may tell admissions officers much about an applicant's academic abilities, but they reveal little about the person. Professional and graduate schools are very much aware that they are admitting "people". They are looking for an exciting, accomplished and diverse group who will contribute to the class as a whole. Admissions officers use application files as a way of "getting to know" the applicants to their program. In fact, the application file is the equivalent of an "interview" for your seat in the school of your choice. This "interview" must be used to your advantage in order to make the best possible impression. In the same way that you "market yourself" in a job interview, you must use your application file to "market yourself" to a professional or graduate school. Personal statements, the autobiographical sketch and letters of reference are your primary marketing tools.

For many years I have designed and taught test prep programs. As a component to these courses, I have run application seminars and Personal Statement Workshops to help students improve all aspects of their application files. In my experience, students have as much difficulty "Mastering The Personal Statement" as they do "Mastering The Exam."

What are the skills that need to be learned? On the most basic level applicants need to be shown the importance of using their application file as a marketing tool. But, that is not enough. They also need to be shown how to do it!

This book developed naturally out of the many application seminars and Personal Statement Workshops that I have conducted over the years. There are many books that contain samples of personal statements. Although this book contains samples of personal statements, it does much more. It also teaches how to develop personal statements, autobiographical sketches and letters of reference. I have gone further by providing a "Personal Statement Workbook" to help you do it! I have even included guidelines to be used by those who have been asked to write a letter of reference, but don't know how to go about it.

"Mastering The Personal Statement" is a guide and workbook for anybody applying to law, MBA, medical school or any kind of graduate program. Rather than discuss personal statements in general (thus failing to talk about any one type) I have written the main part of the book from the perspective of a law school applicant. This makes sense for two reasons. First, the law school application file is as comprehensive as any kind of application file. Second, the law school personal statement is the most general kind of personal statement - thus making a discussion of it applicable to personal statements of all types. In subsequent chapters I have addressed specific issues relevant to MBA, medical school, and graduate schools.

I have also included a chapter about interviews. Law schools *rarely* use interviews as part of the application process. MBA programs *sometimes* use interviews. Medical schools *frequently* use interviews. Finally, I have included chapters about effective test prep and electronic applications (which are the wave of the future).

In closing I would like to stress that this book is the result of what I have learned "in the trenches" working with real students. I have seen many of them improve their competitive positions quite significantly. The exercises in this book will involve you painlessly in the process of "Mastering The Personal Statement!"

I wish you success in your academic and career goals.

John Richardson

How To Use This Book

Mastering The Personal Statement has been designed to teach you how to apply to any kind of graduate or professional school. It has been designed so that applicants to law, MBA, medical school and graduate school will both know what to do, and be able to do what they know. Part I has been designed so that you will know what to do. Part II - The Personal Statement Workbook has been designed to help you do what you know!

Part I - Because, You Must Know What To Do

Part I develops the general strategy and approach for turning the complete application file into an effective marketing tool. The single most important chapter for all readers is the first chapter - Law School Bound. A consideration of the law school application file is sufficiently general to include other graduate and professional school applications. As a result, I have used an analysis of the law school application as the foundation for a discussion of any graduate and professional school application. Subsequent chapters that deal with MBA, medical school and graduate school applications are best read in conjunction with the general principles of marketing that are developed in the "Law School Bound" chapter. Therefore, it is important that all applicants read Chapter I - Law School Bound. If you are applying to MBA, medical school or graduate school, you should then read (at a minimum), the specific chapter that applies to you. The chapters on Letters of Reference (Chapter 7), Interviews (Chapter 8), Computer Applications and Research (Chapter 9), and Effective Test Prep (Chapter 10) will be valuable to any professional or graduate school applicant. In summary, Part I has been designed to teach you how to design your application file to market yourself effectively. **You will get best results if you read every chapter!**

Part II - Because, You Must Be Able To Do What You Know

Part II - *The Personal Statement Workbook* consists of a series of exercises (The Personal Statement Toolbox) that will guide you through the actual development of your personal statement. In other words, it is not good enough to know what you must do. You will need help actually doing it. The Personal Statement Workbook has been designed to be used by applicants to any professional or graduate school. It is unique to this book.

Mastering The Personal Statement includes sample personal statements and letters of reference. The personal statements are quite good, but are not perfect. They are samples of those used by real people who were successful in their applications. There is no one right or wrong way to write a personal statement. Use the personal statements as examples of different approaches to developing a personal statement. Admissions officers will certainly be familiar with the examples in this book. Do not try to copy them.

PART I

Understanding The Personal Statement And Autobiographical Sketch

"GPA/LSAT figures may provide law schools with quick and handy ways to sort applicants into categories but it is often the personal statement that makes the difference in an admissions decision."

PRE-LAW ADVISORS NATIONAL COUNCIL

"The personal statement is especially important when you consider that most law schools do not include formal interviews as part of the admissions process. Therefore, think of the personal statement as an interview - a chance to tell admission personnel who you are and what you have done that makes you uniquely qualified to study and practice law."

SO, YOU WANT TO BE A LAWYER

"As the Admissions Committee does not grant interviews, the Personal Statement is an applicant's opportunity to inform the Committee about interests, accomplishments and goals."

COMMENTARY FROM A LAW SCHOOL

CHAPTER 1

Law School Bound®

Introduction- Marketing Is Job 1!

Although the preceding quotations all concern the personal statement, they are applicable to the complete application file. The application file in its entirety is your interview for a seat in a law school class. Effective applicants treat the application file as a "marketing tool" which is targeted to the specific requirements and personalities of different law schools. As a good example of targeted marketing, consider the following excerpt from a recent biography of Bill Gates by Stephen Manes and Paul Andrews:

> "Toward the end of the year, Lakeside senior classman Bill Gates took on a different marketing project: the selling of William Henry Gates. Potential customers? College admissions officers. Bill had scored 800 on his math SAT and five achievement tests (although only in the low 700s on the verbal SAT), and he put it, "I wanted to know which personality of mine would appeal to the world at large."

> Witness the transformation! To Harvard, he was Bill Gates, son of a prominent lawyer, someone with connections, "the guy who was into politics ... so my whole page experience was the central part of that application." For Princeton, "I positioned myself as a computer nerd," the programming magician who could hypnotize a minicomputer or mainframe into doing anything he commanded. For Yale, he was a consummate do-gooder and sensitive artist with thespian aspirations, "the guy who did drama, the guy who was Boy Scout." It was one of the earliest displays of his chameleonlike, Thomas Crown-like ability to change his skin, to transform his persona-and eventually, his company's - in order to "do business."

The personal statement and autobiographical sketch are controllable and afford the most opportunity for "direct applicant input." They should be targeted to meet the requirements of specific schools.

Your Complete Law School Application File

The application file is your interview for one of the few seats in a law school class. This interview consists of some or all of the following separate components:

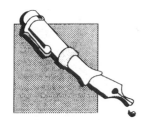

The Covering Letter - Name, Rank and Serial Number

Application form - make copies and practice completing a copy before completing the original.

Third Party Statements - What Others Say

A transcript of your grades - You will not be able to change the numbers, but you may be able to influence the interpretation of the numbers. For example, if a grade of B is the top grade in the class, ensure that the committee is aware of this.

Your LSAT score - Most schools average scores. But, if your second score is higher than your first score, you may have grounds for requesting that the school use only the higher score.

LSAT Writing Sample - Can be compared to the personal statement to determine if the applicant authored his/her personal statement.

Letters of recommendation - Can be enormously helpful. Don't ask somebody to write a letter for you. Ask a potential recommender if he could and would be willing to write a positive letter of recommendation. In this way, you can exercise some control over the content of the letter.

Direct Applicant Input - What The Applicant Says

Personal Statement - Written by the applicant and the most controllable part of the application file. This will either be in the form of one long question or a number of very specific short questions.

Autobiographical Sketch - Many schools (including the Ontario Law School Application Service application) ask for a list of jobs, awards, extracurricular activities, community service, etc.

Direct Applicant Input - Three Types

Grades, test scores, and letters of recommendation are all instances where a third party makes a statement about an applicant. The personal statement and autobiographical sketch give the applicant the opportunity to make his best case in his own words!

Not all schools require a personal statement. However, most schools require some kind of "autobiographical sketch" in which candidates are required to list their activities and achievements. Completing an "autobiographical sketch" in an effective manner requires more than "substance." "Form" matters as well. It must be well written. There can be neither typos nor grammatical errors. It must also be visually pleasing. The way you describe your activities matters as much as what the activities are.

Three Forms Of Direct Applicant Input And Examples

Direct applicant input will take one of the three following forms:

1. **Autobiographical Sketch** - The applicant is asked to list his/her activities, jobs, awards, education, etc. The answers are generally to be completed on a prescribed form. Here are some examples:

   "List in chronological order, beginning with the most recent year. It is important that you complete this section carefully providing details of extracurricular activities, non-academic achievements and community involvement. Indicate the nature and duration of your involvement beginning with the most current activities."

   "List in chronological order, beginning with the most recent year, all post-secondary schools attended. Include all courses completed through professional associations."

2. **Multiple Questions Personal Statement** - Short answers to a number of specific questions. This form of personal statement has the effect of forcing the applicant to think about himself in terms of very specific issues. Some examples of these kinds of questions are:

A. How has your university program aided in your personal development and prepared you for the study of law?

B. Do you think that your employment, business or professional experience will aid you in the study of law?

C. Which of your extracurricular activities have been important to you?

D. Why do you want to study law? What is your career objective?

E. Do you have any special skills or interests that will assist you in law school or in your future career?

F. Are there personal facts or issues relating to your application that you would like the admissions committee to know about?

(Notice that all these questions focus on the applicant.)

Short answer questions are often required to be answered on a prescribed form. **Practice completing copies before completing the original!**

3. **One Question Personal Statement** - The applicant is required to write an essay in response to one specific question (or in some cases to no specific question). This form of personal statement gives more room for the applicant ton determine what is important. Some examples of these kinds of questions are:

A. With specific reference to you r experiences, concerns and values, what is your objective in seeking a legal education?

B. Each applicant is required to submit a brief but reasonably detailed personal statement. This is your opportunity to inform the committee about your interests, accomplishments, and goals. It should include any special facts which should be brought to the attention of the committee.

What Are The Schools Looking For? - Know Your Market

Before attempting to formulate answers you must understand the purpose(s) of the question(s) asked. If you knew how the answer to the question influenced the admissions process, you would know how to better answer the question. How do you learn what the school is looking for?

The Basics - What All Schools Look For

All schools seek applicants who have the tools required to complete the program. The two primary tools are:

Ability - intellectual and academic

Motivation - because intelligence without focus is wasted

Applicants must have the academic and intellectual ability to complete the program. For many applicants their grades and LSAT scores provide adequate evidence of that ability.

Intellectual ability is not sufficient. The world is full of intelligent people who have never achieved anything. A high achiever is motivated to direct his ability in a focused way to achieve results. Hence, schools look for evidence that the applicant is motivated to complete the program.

Beyond The Basics - How They Are Different!

Beyond attracting students with ability and motivation different schools have different objectives in admitting students. Hence, you may wish to emphasize different things about yourself at different schools.

Targeted Marketing - The Importance Of Researching The Schools!

Consider the application process as being analogous to a job search. Imagine that you are applying to ten different jobs. Effective applicants would not send exactly the same resume and covering letter to each potential employer. Effective applicants would research two major issues.

First, what is the business of the employer?

Second, what role does the specific job play in the business of the employer?

The applicant would then design the job application to target the specific requirements of the employer. In the same way that prospective employees must research potential employers, applicants must research the law schools. On the basis of this research, all forms of direct applicant input should be targeted to specific schools. This may mean writing different personal statements for different schools!

Great! But, How Do I Do This Research?

Research each school by asking the following three general questions.

What Is The School's Generalized Policy On Admission?

Different schools have different agendas. Ask, what is the school trying to achieve by admitting applicants to its program? Look for statements about generalized policies on admission. Sources of information include:

For Law Schools In General

- the calendar of information (pay particular attention to the dean's message);

- the application form itself (there is now one common application form for Ontario law schools - U.S. and other Canadian law schools have their own forms);

- most schools now have web sites on the internet;

For U.S. Law Schools

- The *Official Guide To U.S. Law Schools* published by Law Services;

- The *MAPLA Profiles Guide to U.S. law schools*;

For Canadian Law Schools

- The section of the LSAT Registration Book which has information about all Canadian law schools;

- The information about Ontario law schools in the Ontario Law School Application Service (OLSAS) package.

What follows is an example of a generalized policy on admission:

"The purpose of the admissions policy is to admit students from among the many applicants, who will excel at the study of law and, at the same time, contribute creatively and meaningfully to the law school and the community."

What Application Categories (Marketing Avenues) Are Available?

All schools have a "regular applicant" category. In addition, some schools may have categories for "mature students", or students in an "access" or "special circumstances" category. In determining whether an application category is suitable for you, carefully review the requirements of the category and determine how the category furthers the school's generalized policies on admission. Different schools use different applicant categories. Even if two schools use the same label to describe a category, that category may be defined differently at each school.

How Does The School Use The Direct Applicant Input?

Different schools use personal statements in different ways. Try to determine how the school uses the personal statement or other form of direct applicant input. For example, is it appropriate to use direct applicant input to talk about grades and LSAT scores? Take care to respond to the specific question asked.

The most effective direct applicant input is tailored directly to the requirements of a specific school. All other things being equal, any admissions officer would rather admit somebody with a specific interest in their school.

Your Image Isn't Everything...
It's The Only Thing!

Direct Applicant Input As Image Control And Development

Your application file is your interview for law school. Your objective in an interview is to create positive images about yourself. Therefore, all forms of direct applicant input should be aimed at image development and control.

Inside Perspective *- The content and development of many personal statements suggests that the applicant doesn't realize that they serve as a replacement for an interview.*

Think Of The Personal Statement As A Job Interview

Imagine that you are at a job interview. You want to project a positive image of being: competent to do the job, organized, prepared for the interview, capable of following directions, well dressed, interested in that job and company, and "fitting in" with the company. This can be achieved only if you present yourself in a way that the interviewer gets to know ***you***. You would want the interviewer to think that you would be a pleasure to work with. Finally, all information that you convey during the interview must be consistent with any other information that the interviewer has about you! All components of your application file must be consistent and work together to create a positive image where the whole is greater than the sum of the individual parts.

Inside Perspective *- You must use your personal statement to sell yourself to the school. Thorough preparation and thought are essential for a well written personal statement.*

Competent To Do The Job

Law schools are academic institutions. Schools seek applicants with the ability to do their academic work. For most applicants, this will be established by grades and LSAT scores. Do not use the personal statement to simply repeat your transcript of grades and LSAT scores.

> *Inside Perspective - If your numbers place you on the borderline between acceptance and rejection at a school that uses subjective factors in its admissions decisions, then your personal statement will be scrutinized with care for evidence that you can do law school work.*

Organized

We will spend more time later on how to organize personal statements. A well organized file, autobiographical sketch, and personal statement will depict a sensible and clear minded person.

> *Inside Perspective - If your essay is carefully organized and unified, it will be natural for the readers to assume you are a neat and careful person.*

Prepared For The Interview

All forms of direct applicant input should show evidence that it has been written to satisfy the specific requirements of that school. If you are applying in something other than the regular category (for example the mature student category), make it clear why you satisfy the requirements of that category!

> *Inside Perspective - A big mistake made by applicants is not explaining why they are applying in the special category.*

Capable Of Following Directions

Answer the precise question asked. For example there is a difference between a question that asks you to explain why you want to attend law school and a question that asks you why you would make a good lawyer.

Inside Perspective - *Our personal statement requires applicants to tell us why they want a law degree. Too many applicants simply review what they think are their positive qualities for admission without explaining what they think society will get back if a scarce resource is allocated to them.*

Inside Perspective - *A big mistake is failing to read and follow simple directions in organizing the application.*

Pay special attention to any requirements respecting length. George Bernard Shaw once apologized to a friend for having written such a long letter. He commented that he hadn't had time to write a short one. There is no virtue in length.

Inside Perspective - *By far the biggest mistake is that applicants provide statements that are too long. It is a mistake to think that sheer length is an asset; the readers of these statements are more interested in concise presentations.*

Well Dressed

Your personal statement or autobiographical sketch must be beautiful! There is no room for a single typo or grammatical error. Use a font that is visually pleasing. The key is readability. A font size of 11 or 12 pitch is best. Allow yourself plenty of time. The best personal statements are developed slowly and deliberately over a reasonable period of time. They are subjected to numerous revisions and refined to perfection. Have your work reviewed by a friend or associate. Ask, what image(s) does it convey?

Inside Perspective - "... *spelling mistakes and grammatical errors are a personal pet peeve of mine which I find particularly annoying, especially when I read approximately 1200 applications a year.*"

Showing An Interest In That School

Inside Perspective - *One law school admissions director at "school X" revealed that they receive many personal statements in which the applicant says he is looking forward to attending "school Y" the following year. This is a very careless error... Avoid it!*

If a school has a particular program that attracts you to that school make it clear that you are interested in that program!

Will You Fit In With The Student Body?

In the back of the mind of any admissions director is the question: can I see this person at our school?

Is The Reader Getting To Know You?

Direct applicant input is about you. It must be a reflection of your personality. It must make you come to life as a person. Without direct applicant input the admissions director will not have you in sharp focus. A well written personal statement will bring you into focus - bring you to life. An application file without an autobiographical sketch and/or personal statement is like seeing the applicant on black and white television. The personal statement should move the applicant to living color!

Inside Perspective - *A big mistake is that many statements are vague and provide no real information about specific characteristics of the applicant.*

Pleasure To Have Around

How do you know if you have written a good personal statement? If after reading your personal statement the reader thinks:

1. I have a strong sense of who the person is; and

2. I would like to meet that person. Then you have done a good job.

Inside Perspective - A director of a law school admissions committee that interviews applicants once suggested to me that some applicants are given interviews because the personal statement has made the applicant an interesting and likable person.

The Consistency Requirement

The admissions director will look at the complete file for the purpose of trying to get an impression of you. All parts of the file must fit together properly. The Individual components should create a whole that is greater than the sum of the parts. While writing your personal statement and/or autobiographical sketch ask if it fits well with the other components of your complete file.

The Facts Don't Always Speak For Themselves! - How To Make Sure They Do!

Learn to describe facts so that they create maximum impact!

The Autobiographical Sketch - Describe your activities, jobs, and awards in a positive way.

It is your responsibility to tell the committee anything that you want it to know!

> *Inside Perspective - Please remember that the Admissions Committee cannot know what the applicant wishes to have considered unless it is included in the admissions materials submitted.*

When you describe activites, you must be concerned with (at a minimum) both length of time and content.

Length Of Time

The length of time that you have been involved in an activity is strong evidence of your commitment to that activity.

> *Inside Perspective - A big mistake made by applicants is the failure to give meaningful time frames to community service and other activities.*

> *Inside Perspective - If an applicant has worked 40 hours a week but only states that she has worked "long hours" and there is no letter from an employer, the Committee can only guess how long and guess to the applicant's detriment.*

Content Of Activity

Avoid listing only the title of the job, activity or award. In many cases, the title will not be a sufficient description for the reader to understand what you did. After having listed the title, you must describe the responsibilities, qualifications for award, etc. A well written entry can document a history of advancement, achievement and the assumption of greater and greater responsibility. Here are some hypothetical examples that might be found in an autobiographical sketch.

Western Pre-Law Society, 92-94; organized trips to Law Fair; President 1993-94.

Researcher - Department of Justice, Summer 95; was only non law student hired to do legal research in the criminal division.

State University Dean's List; (A- average or higher), 5 consecutive semesters.

Debating Club, 1991-94; Attended weekly meetings, placed second in North American competition 1993, Vice-President 1994.

Big Brothers Organization, 1993; Averaged 8 hours per week providing tutoring and mentoring to two boys aged 8 and 12.

Cambridge Scholarship, 1996; Awarded each year to Cambridge student who makes the greatest all around contribution to the university in the areas of athletics, academics, and university community involvement.

Head Of Orientation Committee, 1996; From an applicant pool in excess of 100 applicants I was selected to plan and organize the orientation activities for 5,000 first year students.

The Applicant Is More Than The Activity!

In each of the above examples, the explanation clarifies the activity and provides evidence of a quality that is desirable in a law student. **The reader will use the descriptive material to infer additional things about the applicant.** For example, the winner of the Cambridge Scholarship (because of interest in athletics and the university community) is much more than an academic. Attending *weekly* meetings of a debating club is evidence of both commitment and discipline. Spending eight hours each week as a Big Brother is evidence of ability to manage time and a commitment to public service. Three years of involvement in the Pre-Law Society is evidence of an interest in law and an interest in working with people. Being elected president is evidence that he is held in high regard by his peers. Notice how much better the summer job with the Department of Justice sounds once you know that the applicant was the *only* non law student selected for the position. The fact that the person was the head of the orientation committee is evidence that the applicant is responsible.

The descriptive material will allow the committee to make inferences about the applicant that extend beyond the activity itself. In this way the descriptive material will assist in the creation of positive images.

Creating Images Through Facts - The Personal Statement

The single biggest mistake applicants make in developing personal statements is that they write a statement rather than a personal statement. A personal statement will help the reader get to know you better. This means that a personal statement must be about you as an individual and NOT about your view of the world in general or law in particular. A statement (in contrast to a personal statement) is not about you but is either about how you see the world or about some other topic.

In order for someone to get to know you, you must reveal something about yourself. Its time to get personal. Don't be abstract. An effective personal statement must talk about you in a very personal way. Focus on the facts. For example you could: write about the best thing that ever happened to you, the worst or the most unusual. You could write about your greatest achievement - making it clear why it is important to you. You could write about your greatest failure or disappointment - saying what you learned from the experience. Go into detail! Be specific! Use concrete examples to make your statement distinctive. Avoid the generalities and platitudes that apply to every law school applicant and will make it impossible for your statement to be distinctive. For example, it does little good to say that you want to make the world a better place. Be specific. What motivates you specifically? Why?

You cannot tell the school directly that you have the qualities it seeks. Rather, you must describe yourself in such a way that the school will infer that you have those qualities. For example, imagine that a law school is seeking applicants with the following characteristics:

Maturity

Disciplined

Hard Working

Honest

Generous

Motivated

Intelligent

Responsible

Well Rounded (diverse interests)

Community Oriented

Sound Judgment

The school requires a personal statement. You cannot write a personal statement that says:

> *"Hello, my name is Stanley Student. I want you to know that I am mature, disciplined, hard working, honest, generous, motivated, intelligent, well-rounded, community oriented and have sound judgment. Please send my offer of admission to:*
>
> Stanley Student
> 123 Main St.
> Anytown, Canada
> A1A 2B2"

Describe specific aspects of yourself that will allow the reader to infer that you have the above qualities. Describe something you have done that will show that you are honest or responsible or motivated, etc. Don't write that you have sound judgment. Describe some event or incident in which you exercised sound judgment.

Your job is to describe specific things about yourself that will convey the kinds of images that are consistent with what the law school is looking for!

A Special Situation - Coming To Terms With Negatives

Every component of your application file should convey the image of a positive person. Avoid emphasizing negatives. If you must mention negatives try to show what you learned from the experience. There may be situations where you wish to place low grades and/or LSAT scores in perspective. The law schools are interested in your ability to do academic work. Your job is to convince the school that such grades or LSAT scores are not indicative of your academic ability.

LSAT Scores

If your grades are competitive, argue that in spite of your LSAT score you have strong academic ability. This ability is proven by your good grades. Under no circumstances should you attack the validity of the LSAT in general.

Grades

You may be able to minimize the effects of a semester of low grades if you can show that they were an aberration. If you have grades that are high, there may be room to argue that the law school should consider only the high grades. This may be possible if you can demonstrate that the low grade(s) were the result of a temporary external problem and that the problem has gone away. Perhaps you started in the wrong academic program. For example, many students change programs (Arts to Sciences) because they didn't like the first program. Poor grades are often the result of a program that is not liked. If the student switches to a new program and the grades improve:

1. The student has a proven ability to get good grades; and

2. The problem that caused the poor grades has gone away.

What follows is a good example of a student dealing with a "false start."

"I am asking the Admissions Committee to overlook the false start I experienced during my initial university studies.

I think of my academic career as being divided into two distinct chapters, the first chapter being when I enrolled at University X in 1986. In my first year of studies I obtained a C+ average in the four credits I completed. The following September I transferred to University Y as a visiting student on a letter of permission for one year. Late planning prevented me from registering in courses that matched my academic interests and my grades suffered. As a result, I decided to leave university life altogether. The next September I enrolled in the two year Financial Management Program at Community College Z. At its conclusion, I was a half credit short of a diploma and had some major decisions to make regarding my future.

During my time at University Y and Community College Z, I was an immature young man who lacked career goals and objectives. While these traits were exhibited by many in my age group I must admit that if this young man were applying to law school today, I would advise the admissions committee to reject his application without delay. Fortunately however, a dramatic transformation occurred in the second chapter of my academic career and I believe that my academic accomplishments during the last three years prove that I have the academic ability to be an excellent law student.

The second chapter of my academic career began with my decision to return to University X in the fall of 1990. I was determined to succeed in my second attempt at university and entered fall classes with a good attitude and the motivation to succeed.

I am now twenty-six years old and will earn my Honours B.A. in the spring of 1993. Maturity and self-direction have vastly increased my academic success and the marks I have achieved during the last three years attest to this change. I know that I will be a first rate law student and would ask with respect that the Admissions Committee disregard or assign less importance to the academic results I experienced during my initial university studies. I know that my enthusiasm, motivation, interest and goals will ensure that I will make a positive influence on the law school and the community."

Okay, I'm Ready To Write.
How To Write, "Right."

Inside Perspective - *A good piece of writing is a good piece of writing; it has unity, force, and coherence. It communicates clearly and persuasively.*

Good writing takes time. Personal statements should be developed over time with great care. What follows are some suggestions for both process and content.

Some Suggestions For Content And Organization

There are no right and wrong ways to write a personal statement. The following are some suggested things to do:

*   **Begin with a strong first sentence.** You can make an instant good impression. You have a greater chance of catching the attention of a bored reader. For example:

    "A wise man (my grade 8 teacher) once gave me the following advice: "try as many different jobs as possible while you are young because it will be of great help in determining what you want to do in life."

    "A #2 pencil and a dream can take you anywhere."

*   **Tell who you are by telling your story.** This will focus the personal statement on you. Write about the best thing that ever happened to you, the worst or the most unusual. Write about your greatest failure or accomplishment. It will make you come alive as a person and make the personal statement more interesting. For example:

    "Although my grades were satisfactory, they did not reflect my abilities. As a result, I decided to work for the summer and travel Japan, Korea and Thailand from September 1994 to December 1994 in the hopes of "finding myself." To my dismay, I found myself out of money and suffering from mononucleosis in early November."

- Use simple language and short concise sentences. Avoid legalese or abstract language. Here is an example of what to AVOID:

  "My rigorous domicile in Russia was the result of a hard fight to obtain a highly coveted work visa which entitled me to enter Russia as one of the few official working residents sanctioned each year by the Russian government."

- Ensure that there are no typos or grammatical errors.

- When listing accomplishments or achievements explain why they are important to you. What role did they play in the development of your personality or your interest in law school?

  "I got involved in rowing in high school. Rowing is an extremely tough sport requiring intense dedication. This sport taught me how to organize my day and use each hour efficiently."

- Work with a plan or outline. Ensure that there is a main idea or theme that you wish to communicate. Pretend the personal statement is a thirty minute interview in which you must make main points.

- If you have been out of school for some time, explain how your interest in law developed through jobs or other activities. For example, a police officer could justify an interest in criminal law because of interaction with the legal system.

- If your interest in law developed as a result of a significant life experience, then describe how that experience contributed to your interest in law. For example, an accident victim could justify an interest in law through interaction with the legal system.

The following are some suggested don'ts:

- Don't write about the law. The audience knows about the law.

- Don't write a resume in prose.

- Don't dwell on negatives.

- Don't draw conclusions. Simply provide facts that will support the conclusions that you want the reader to draw.

The Reader Is A Human Being -
Avoid Upsetting The Reader!

Admissions directors are overworked and read many more personal statements than they would like. It is human nature to experience positive or negative feelings about personal statements and to experience these feelings quickly!

> ***Inside Perspective*** *- The first 40 personal statements that are read are tolerable. But after the first couple of hundred I start to lose interest and read them very quickly. They had better have something interesting to say!*

And Finally

The personal statement is about you. Make sure that everything in the personal statement is for the purpose of making you come to life as a real, breathing, feeling, interesting person who the reader would like to meet! Use concrete examples and facts. In order to accomplish this you must do some thinking about yourself. Part II of this book is a Personal Statement Workbook which has been designed to help you focus your thinking about yourself!

In Summary .....

A personal statement should:

1. be about you

2. ensure that general statements are backed up by specific facts or experiences

3. show that you are a competent, well-rounded, positive and motivated person

4. explain how significant events contributed to the development of your personality

5. be interesting and tell a story

6. explain why you are interested in that specific school

7. be responsive to the precise question asked, the specific requirements of the school and the personality of the school

8. have a theme or organizing principle

9. explain jobs, activities and awards

10. describe facts from which the reader will infer that you have certain qualities or attributes

11. have a strong opening

12. be well written

13. use simple language

14. have no typos or grammatical errors

15. not be too long and respect the directions concerning length

CHAPTER 2

Some Actual Samples Of Law School Personal Statements

Personal statements come in the following two formats:

1. Multiple Questions Personal Statement

2. One Question Personal Statement

This part of the book will provide some actual examples of each type. Each of these examples was written by a real, living, breathing, pre-law student. Most importantly, each of these students was accepted! The examples included here cover a wide range of styles. Each example is quite good but far from perfect. Each is an example of what is achievable by a "mere mortal." I have not included any of the "rare dazzling" personal statements that are crafted by professional writers. You should view them as examples. As you read each one ask how it could be improved? How well do you feel that you are getting to know the applicant? After having read the personal statement, would you be able to describe the personality of the applicant? After having read the personal statement, do you like the applicant?

You will note that these samples have been written by different kinds of applicants, with different motivations, and at different stages of life. This is for the purpose of completeness. A personal statement will be read in the context of what kinds of life experiences the applicant has had. Therefore, don't be upset if you feel that you have not had experiences as varied as some of these applicants.

The publication of this book will guarantee that admissions officers will be familiar with each example. It would, therefore, be a mistake to copy them.

Format 1 - Multiple Questions Personal Statement

(1) How do you think your academic, business, employment and/or professional experience have contributed to your development as an individual and prepared you for the study of law?

As a graduate student in Jurisprudential Philosophy, I have thought in-depth about the purpose of law from a philosophical perspective. My education in Philosophy of Law has lent itself to a consideration of justice and to moral reflection about the law. Philosophy of Law has prepared me in particular to examine the concept of a just legal system, and to consider the appropriate range of judicial discretion. I have spent a great deal of time considering grounds for obligation to obey the law, and what sorts of justifications hold in particular legal systems. For example, do considerations of fairness ground a general obligation to obey the law? What should citizens do in legal systems which fail to meet minimum requirements of justice?

My record as a graduate research assistant and as a tutorial assistant has prepared me to conduct research and to teach. I have always believed that tutorials should be more than a meeting place to negotiate grades, and that graduate students have a special obligation to guide their own students as much as possible. I have worked as hard as I can to foster co-operation and non competitiveness, among my students. I am proud that in a course with an attrition rate of one-third, I have maintained fifty-five of my original sixty students.

On a personal note, being born in South Africa and spending my adolescent years in a legal system which is anathema to the majority of the people has provided me with an acute sensitivity to fighting for justice. I was raised in a family that despised the system, tried to oppose it, and opted to leave rather than devoting the lives of their sons to its defense. That, more than anything, has left a profound impact on me. This upbringing, and my record in academia, researching and teaching, have prepared me for the study of law.

(2) If you have been involved in extra-curricular activities (such as community service, political, religious, social or athletic, etc.), which of these experiences has been most important to you? why?

By far the most important experience has been as a member of the Executive Committee of the graduate program in Philosophy at _____ University. To begin with, it was an honor to be elected to this position as I was the sole student representative. This position was important to me because student representation on committees had been something I was working toward since transferring to School A from School B. I felt that students were not represented in issues that concerned them the most. For example, while I favor preferential hiring policies and believe that concerns of equity should govern hirings, I felt that it was wrong that the formula adopted by the Philosophy Department was instituted largely by tenured faculty members without any input from graduate students. Since the policy would undoubtedly have an impact on our job prospects in the future, I was convinced that it was unjust that we were not consulted. Graduate students at other universities in Ontario shared this opinion and I supported them in bringing forward our concerns to the Canadian Philosophical Association, and in convening meetings at School A to discuss these issues. With student representation in mind, I was instrumental in arguing that graduate students should have a vote on the Search Committee for the Director of the Graduate Program. As a result of my work on the Executive Committee, I was asked to serve as a member of the Search Committee for the Director of the Graduate Program. I worked as one of four people on this committee with the Chairpersons of the Philosophy Department of School A, and I brought forward twelve issues that concerned graduate students. It is no coincidence that this year, graduate students were "invited" to participate on the Admissions Committee, and on the Committee for Scholarship Ranking Procedures, and that I was personally asked by the Graduate Program Director to continue representing the Philosophy Graduate Students' Association in order to maintain continuity. I am the current representative on the Faculty of Graduate Studies, and I am especially proud of my commitment to ensure graduate students' representation, and of my university service that has been helpful in achieving this goal. I have learned just how much one can do with solid, unwavering commitment, and I shall bring that dedication to law school if given the opportunity.

(3) Do you feel that you have developed any special skills or interests other than your university program work experience outlined above? How may these skills assist you in the pursuit of your legal studies and future careers?

As an individual, a young chess player learns that dedication for long periods and concentration for hours on end are rewarded. I learned through playing chess competitively that to perform well requires a tremendous amount of work. The most important lesson came later, however, when I realized that winning as an individual "wasn't everything," and that working with a team or helping young chess players to fulfill their dreams is just as rewarding. Teaching and working co-operatively with groups are special skills which I have cultivated for my own happiness. I did not work for years with Aphasic Stroke survivors twice a week for solely altruistic reasons. To say I did so would be a lie. I volunteered to assist these people because it made me feel good about myself. I saw how people, when severely challenged, can rise beyond circumstances if they have support. I learned how good it feels to provide that support as a friend, and while I cannot classify those lessons as a skill, I believe they are more important than my academic learning. I will continue in my own studies and future career to focus not only on myself, but on others as well.

(4) Why do you want to study law? Do you have a career objective other than the traditional practice of law? Please describe.

I want to study law because I believe in pursuit of justice. I am currently engaged in a doctoral dissertation on equitable health care rationing. Because the dissertation parallels my interest in law, I shall outline its ambitions. My aim is to balance concerns of maximizing human well-being while allowing individual autonomy to pursue health care options which may lie outside the scope of a national health care plan. Jumping ahead on waiting lists and "quality health care" should not be synonymous with going abroad. I am convinced that national health care plans become minimal plans when people who can afford it have an incentive to go abroad. The result of this incentive means that we have a two-tiered system: Those who need treatment quickly, and can afford it, can get it immediately. I believe that equal access should be a guarantee of primary care, and instead of a constraint at the low end, and, people should be able to get the care they need based on: need, benefit, and an upper level constraint. Provisions must always be maintained for primary care.

My dissertation parallels my interest in law at the University of _____, in particular, through access to justice. My interest in an equitable health care system is in keeping with studying law at the University of_____. I feel well prepared to write on the normative and philosophical issue of equitable health care, but I am not yet well prepared to deal with the legal issue. The Faculty of Law of the University of _____, with its emphasis on access to justice, will provide the legal background and the requisite legal reasoning necessary to complete the dissertation, and enable me to work beyond it to completion. I want to work in public policy and legislation, and it will be essential to have a background in law. I have chosen the University of _____ Law School also because I can obtain a grounding in European Constitutional Law by availing myself of the one year study abroad program. Even more so, though I recognize how competitive selection to the program is, I shall work as hard as I can to have the opportunity to Clerk to the Supreme Court. Access to justice, be it in health care, be it in working in under serviced areas, or be it in fighting against unjust regimes such as South Africa's, is a theme I will commit myself to in law school and out.

I can summarize my reasons for wishing to study law at University of _____ Law School in one word: "Flexibility." I even want the opportunity to gain practical experience. The Law School provides this through the community legal aid plan. The blend of practical and theoretical study promises an enriching education at the University of _____ Law School. I could go on. Having completed a large part of my education in Toronto, I look forward to being at a largely non-commuter school with many students in my own age group. The University of _____ Law School is the one I want to attend most for all of these reasons, but mainly, for the single word which summarizes what it offers. I hope I am given the opportunity.

Format 2 - Single Question Personal Statements

Sample 1

Education and work experience (particularly in the legal profession) have been the two factors which have most influenced my decision to apply to law school at _____ .

My education has allowed me to develop expertise in a wide variety of fields. I completed a Bachelor of Arts (Honors) in Political Studies. I am currently completing a Bachelor of Education at the Intermediate/Senior level. My studies have included a year abroad, at _____ . Studying international relations interested me in the relationships between existing laws and the resolution of politically contentious issues, for example through new or amended legislation. My work as an educator has expanded my understanding of interpersonal relations, social and political systems. Both subject areas have dealt with social and political philosophy, which is relevant to the study of law. Thus, the pursuit of legal studies would allow me to expand upon knowledge and skills I have developed in previous areas of study.

At the same time, my work in the legal profession has given me insight into the nature of the practice of law and the many possibilities open to those who hold law degrees. Having been employed as an assistant in a large corporate law firm, I have found the work is challenging, requires creative problem solving and necessitates dealing with clients and colleagues on a regular basis. Labor law and criminal law hold particular interest for me, and arbitration is an area I would like to explore further. Nevertheless, I am also open to other options, such as teaching at the university level, and other areas of business.

These experiences have taught me that I enjoy dealing with a variety of people; that I enjoy challenging, stimulating work; and that I feel it is rewarding and useful to broaden one's perspectives by considering the social, political and economic structures. Given these interests, I have chosen to apply to the_____ Faculty of Law because it offers strong programs in public law and legal theory.

In conclusion, I feel that law at _____ would be the ideal program to suit my interests, and would enable me to be effective and successful in fulfilling my career goals. My work, and educational experiences have allowed me to develop skills and knowledge which could be best explored by a career in law. If given the opportunity, I will use these skills to make productive and thoughtful contributions to _____'s Faculty of Law, and eventually to the legal community.

Sample 2

I will be completing my undergraduate honors degree in Family and Social Relations in April of 1995. A Bachelor of Law Degree at University of _____ interests me very much because of the learning opportunities provided by the proximity of the Supreme Court of Canada, the Federal Court and federal government institutions. I feel that my academic background, interests, community service, and goals make me an excellent candidate for the study of law at the University of _____.

With regard to my Academic background, the programs of Akademia, and Family and Social Relations have taught me to approach problems from a multidisciplinary perspective. Akademia is a one-year program at the University of Guelph in which students take courses in both the Arts and the Sciences as well as Integrated Courses that examine certain problems using a variety of disciplines. Following the first year, students transfer into another program. I chose Family and Social Relations because it is a program in which students study human interaction from an interdisciplinary approach and I wanted to gain some background for family law. Society in general and legal problems specifically are becoming more complex. Therefore, looking at problems from a multidisciplinary perspective is an asset in the study of law.

Being a well-rounded person, I have many interests outside of academics. I have continued to provide leadership for the Akademia program throughout my four years at Guelph. In my second year, I was treasurer on the Akademia planning council which promotes Akademia and arranges interdisciplinary events for first-year students. In the past two years I have continued to provide leadership for the Akademia program by attending events and program planning meetings.

Religion and athletics are also of interest to me. I have been a member of the University of Guelph Navigators for the past three years. The Navigators is an interdenominational club committed to helping others and examining how religion relates to modern day life. With the Navigators I have also done some community service work. Athletics have been particularly useful to me for two reasons. First, they mentally restore me and allow me to approach my academics with vigor. Second, they give me important social contacts, some of which may be helpful in the future.

Community service also plays an important part in my life. Particularly valuable to me has been my experience with the Big Brothers Association. Through Big Brothers I have been entrusted with a "Little Brother". I have done many activities with him like reading, building models, camping, operating computers, and watching movies. When I am in the Sault I devote an average of six hours a week to my Little Brother. Both his mother and his teachers feel that our relationship has assisted his development. I have also helped Big Brothers run community events such as barbecues, bingos, and bowlathons.

Considerable thought has gone into my career goals. One area of law that particularly interests me is the area of family mediation. Ideally, I would like a married couple who is contemplating a divorce to come and discuss their problems with me. I would try to use the experience that I have gained to help the couple to determine if their problems were irreconcilable. If they were irreconcilable and divorce was inevitable, I would try to work with them to draw up a mutually agreed upon, equitable separation agreement. There is evidence to indicate that couples are happier with this type of arrangement and are more likely to comply with its terms.

On the other hand, my career as a student has not been free of difficulties. During the Winter Semester of my first year I suffered from depression and needed to drop one course to lighten my academic load. Additionally, I am not pleased with my June 1994 LSAT score. Because of the significance of the LSAT and my desire to gain admittance to law school, I put a great deal of pressure on myself and under performed as a result. I would ask you, the admissions committee, to wait to see my February 1995 LSAT score, as I am hopeful that it will be more reflective of my true abilities.

In conclusion, I think that I am an excellent candidate for the University of _____ Law School. I am intelligent and have a strong work ethic. I have developed good research, critical-thinking, and essay-writing skills. I feel that I would be an worthwhile addition to the incoming class of 1995!

Sample 3

My name is _____ and I am twenty-five years old. I am originally from Calcutta, India and my mother tongue is Bengali. I graduated from the University of Toronto with a B.Sc.(hons) in Toxicology and Human Biology, and a M.Sc. in Pharmacy. I am presently working on a part-time basis for the Canadian Armed Forces in the Royal Canadian Naval Reserves. I am training as a Maritime Subsurface and Surface (MARS) officer and working toward a Bridge Watch Keeping (BWK) ticket for vessels of the minesweeper class. This ticket would give me responsibility for the conduct and operations occurring aboard Maritime Coastal Defence Vessels (MCDVs), both under routine operation and in times of maritime or national threat. I am interested in studying law because the study of law would not only enhance my educational and career background, but also my considered career options for the future.

I am interested in pursuing the study of law at the University of _____ because I can offer a significant contribution to the school and in return, the school can provide me with distinct educational opportunities.

My background education has been sound, liberal and intensive. To broaden the scope of my science-based education, I have pursued study in the arts. I studied classical piano at the Royal Conservatory of Music for ten years; participated in cultural functions in the Bengali Cultural Association; studied martial arts and obtained a black belt in five years; worked as a volunteer instructor for two years, with women and children affected by domestic or street violence; and presently I study drums and percussion music in private lessons. I have participated in student government bodies in university, which have included being the vice-president of the Pharmacology Course League in 1991-1992, an active member of the Indian Student Association from 1988-1992, and a member of the Caput Committee in residence in South House at Victoria

College from 1991-1992. I also have four years of experience working with computers and interfacing with internet and "information super-highway" technology.

My ethnic and racial background, diverse educational background, and my military career has given me a strong commitment to social equity and human rights. In seeking social equity and safeguarding of human rights, there are a number of aspects of our legal system which I would be able to contribute to.

My ethnic and racial background has given me insight into many problems in the Indian community, the foremost of these being problems with immigration and the protection of prospective immigrants' rights. Many people that come to Canada from India are coming from a system where justice is available only to the rich or the powerful. As a result, they are afraid to seek retribution for wrongs committed against them and are not trusting of the legal system. Being new to the country, they are afraid of lawyers that are from outside of their own community, as they feel vulnerable due to language and cultural differences. There is a large population of East Indians in Canada, with few Indian lawyers available to represent their interests. By studying law, I would be able to effectively represent interests of members of the Indian community, so that they are not excluded from the process of social justice.

My science and biotechnology background gives me a unique insight into a problem which exists for many Canadians. That is, many Canadians are hurt or damaged by medical products or procedures which are available to them. In order to seek compensation, or to re-enforce their rights which have been violated, they require not only representation by someone who has an understanding of the underlying legal principles, but someone who also has an understanding of the scientific processes and issues involved. This broader understanding would make it possible for victims to become more informed and as a result, be better represented in their quest to resolve their situation. The study of law would allow me the possibility of making a significant contribution in this area.

As a potential UN peacekeeper, I am sworn to uphold the human rights of individuals, by mental, physical and possibly, lethal means if necessary. It is a difficult job which requires not only understanding of the human and ethical issues involved, but the legal issues as well. Canada has a proud history in peacekeeping of understanding well, the human and ethical issues involved, in spite of recent difficulties. However, Canada's ability to assert its legal rights of its peacekeepers has historically been clouded, obscured and essentially impotent. Canada maintains an international voice in humanitarian efforts, but lacks a strong Canadian legal precedent which would allow it to enforce the mandate of the United Nations. As a result, in the attempt to restore human rights and social equity in troubled places, Canadian soldiers, sailors and airmen/airwomen are placed in unnecessary and grave risk. As an officer in the Canadian Armed Forces, legal training would provide me with a dual understanding of the issues involved. It would allow me to pursue the investigation and enforcement of social equity and human rights not only throughout Canada, but on an international scale as well.

The three reasons I have outlined above demonstrate most accurately why I am interested in law studies. I am interested in law studies because I have a number of unique perspectives which I can offer to this field. Accordingly, the University of _____, faculty of law, is well suited to my choice of studies. The school is expanding and is developing its commitment to human rights and equity issues. My diverse and flexible background would allow me to introduce to the school, a number of different perspectives which may not have been previously considered. In return, the schools strong commitment to human rights research and education would not only allow me to broaden and strengthen my educational background, but provide me with the basic tools necessary to make a significant contribution to these areas.

Sample 4

While attending the Law Fair in Toronto, a good friend asked me "Why are you here?". This person was not an existentialist but, rather, concerned about my decision to leave a promising career in order to pursue the study of law. I was taken aback not only by the question, but by the strength of my conviction. A legal education has always been one of my aspirations and I feel that it is a privilege to be earned. As a person raised in the welfare system, I have learned many valuable lessons about privileges and can appreciate them. In addition to being prepared to undertake the task, I believe that my life experiences would greatly benefit the University of _____ as well as the community.

It has taken me a long time to realize that I should be proud of myself for surpassing the limits that the majority of people unknowingly set for *children in poverty. For much of my life I was ashamed of where I lived and what it stood for, namely failure. My mother and I lived in a subsidized housing project, and my father left soon after I was born. Thus it was that my mother, with her limited knowledge of English, began receiving social assistance.*

Life in Moss Park was eventful, to say the least. A large housing area in downtown Toronto, it was plagued by poverty, crime and, most of all, despair. The passivity of the adults was so overwhelming that children were afflicted by it as well. It was solely because of my mother's devotion to my studies that I was saved from the fate of my classmates.

Her determination that I receive the best possible education is what prompted her to transfer me, to a predominantly upper class junior high school. There I was able to see the disparity of wealth in our society, and it was also where I first experienced discrimination. I suddenly had to work twice as hard to meet the higher standards, both academically and socially. Thankfully, I was able to stay on the honor roll and was accepted to an advanced level high school rather than the local general level one. There I was involved with both the yearbook committee and the student body. As a class representative I was able to hone my public speaking abilities and have become a confident and effective speaker.

Attending university was a natural step for the students at my high school. I, however, had to motivate myself to continue on, because I could not see past my situation to the benefits that would eventually come. I was the only one of the children in my community who continued on past Grade Twelve. Unfortunately, due to financial constraints, I had to work not only during the last two years of high school but through the four years at York University as well. The time that I had to devote to my studies often conflicted with my obligations at work. This prevented a sincere commitment and as I grew older I realized that I had cheated myself out of what I wanted the most; a legal education.

In an attempt to pacify myself, I completed the Law Clerks of Ontario program. I did this in one year by enrolling in both first and second year courses concurrently. The classes were an intense study of the practical aspects of Real Estate, Litigation, Estates and Corporate Law. However, instead of satisfying me, they only served to heighten my desire.

Currently, in addition to working over forty hours a week and volunteering at the Daily Bread Food Bank, I am attending a third year social science class involving an in-depth analysis of how the law functions.

My interest in law stems from exposure to both the impoverished and the affluent cultures of society. This unique experience has given me the ability to look analytically at both sides and has become an important aspect of my character. Furthermore, having studied French, Greek, and Spanish extensively, I have gained skills that will aid me in breaking down the barriers that hinder many in our communities, and I believe this will enable me to become an effective link between the legal system and the community.

It is for this reason that I would like to attend the University of _____ . I am particularly interested in the Legal Aid Clinic and I strongly believe that I would make a significant contribution if accepted into your faculty of law. I believe I now possess the maturity to handle the responsibility that accompanies the privilege of law school. I would like to thank you for your time in considering my application.

Sample 5

Born in Jamaica and the son of Jamaican immigrants, I was celebrated within my family as the first to attend university. After first year, it became my goal to earn a degree in International Economics and join the department of External Affairs as a Foreign Service Representative. During my first academic year I held two part-time jobs, one bartending at a campus pub and another with the Council of the Student Federation event coordination staff. This involved organizing speeches, dances and other events held in the student commons. I also made the time to play for the varsity rugby team, volunteer as an event planner for the my College Student Council, and participate in the Caribbean Students Association (CSA).

In my second year I decided to take initiative - and control my finances-by creating my own business. I started a boat care company providing and subcontracting cleaning/servicing at three marinas. By working up to 30 hours per week throughout subsequent school years, I graduated without indebtedness. The financial burden eventually demanded that I lighten my course load and even miss a semester in 1989. This venture took quite a toll on my academic performance but it was also a source of tremendous satisfaction and helped to develop my organizational and communication skills. Regrettably, I was forced to cut back on other activities as well and gave up my jobs on campus, the CSA, and of course, the rugby team. In the summer of 1989, I earned two A's in third year courses when the availability of high school workers allowed me to apply a reasonable amount of time to my studies. I chose X as my educational referee primarily because he was aware of my work schedule and the effort that I was making under the circumstances.

My current career began with a customer relations position at Z Life Insurance Company. I was assured that if I worked hard, showed a unique commitment to achievement, and earned my F.L.M.I., I would advance within the company. The Fellow of the Life management Institute program consists of ten courses that touch on all aspects of life insurance administration. These courses include: maths of finance, Canadian life insurance law, marketing, and information systems.

Over the past five and a half years my career has seen three phases. In the first phase, I represented the company in the customer service department. This responsibility provided the occasion to polish my interpersonal skills. I learned to quell situations by listening intently and analyzing issues in a logical order. Besides plenty of patience, success as a service representative requires strong research and writing skills and the ability to deal with the often complex issues of the Insurance Act.

After eight months, a second phase began when I was chosen among fourteen staff members to represent customer service in an information systems project. Representatives from each division of the company spent a year designing and testing the data processing software. My responsibility was to ensure the accuracy of all calculations and documents made by a new computer system. The project stressed the importance of cooperation and demanded very strict attention to detail. By this time, I had earned my F.L.M.I. diploma in an uncommonly short nineteen months.

The third and final phase began when I was promoted to Coordinator of Marketing. In this capacity I am responsible for writing brochures, manuals, and descriptive elements of our computer software. A large amount of my time is spent analyzing the products of other companies and comparing them to ours. I make presentations in our brokerage offices throughout Ontario and in Montreal, in French and English, and represent the company at industry discussion groups. These responsibilities have been mine for the past four years and I welcome the daily challenges to my writing and public speaking skills.

From the age of sixteen I have participated in rugby at the high school, varsity and provincial levels. Having found the rugby club atmosphere extremely supportive, in 1991 I decided to see what I could do to help some boys in trouble and promote the rugby club. I wrote to a probation office and was successful in an application to have work with the club to serve as community service for young offenders. My proposal centered on the importance of community as well as guidance and showed how they can be provided by a team setting. Through my experiences with these young people and subsequent discussions with crown and defense lawyers, I have developed a very deep desire to study law and contribute to a fair and representative system. As a criminal lawyer, I will be in a better position to help assess and influence the ways in which we punish and rehabilitate Canadians.

For me, the University of _____ Faculty of Law is ideal for several reasons. The Community Legal Services program and Clinic courses represent an excellent opportunity to prepare for my career in advocacy. I am drawn to the opportunity to study under a faculty so accomplished in my area of interest such as professors _____

, _____ , _____ and _____ . Also, I will be sure to apply to the _____ / _____ Joint Program to earn my LL.B. in Civil Law as I may eventually seek employment in the federal Ministry of Justice.

While other universities may boast an emphasis on criminal law, I appreciate that the University of _____ shares my belief in the importance of a strong sense of community - an aspect of university that I will not go without again.

I believe that qualified people of all races should be represented in the legal profession and that given my aptitude, experience, and desire to make a positive difference in society, I will make a unique contribution to The University of _____ . By sitting in on law classes and taking the time to discuss the merits of a legal education with lawyers and law professors, I have gained full confidence in the fact that I have not only the motivation but also the ability to succeed in law school.

I have clearly demonstrated my ability to do academic work with first year grades and my studies with the Life Management Institute. I am hard working, motivated, and I have excellent analytical, logical and communication skills as confirmed by my success in the workplace. Active community involvement has been a part of most of my adult life. At the age of twenty-eight, my maturity level has allowed me to carefully consider and pursue this career change with confidence. Finally, I have established the study of law as the right step toward meeting my personal goal of participating in a criminal justice system that serves us all equally. I hope that in the future, exercises such as the Provincial Committee on Systemic Racism in the Criminal Justice System will not be necessary.

Sample 6

First as an undergraduate at Trinity College, then later as a graduate student in the Near Eastern Studies department and as a theological student at the Toronto School of Theology, I pursued my deep interest in the foundations of Judaism and Christianity. In addition to mastering the languages of Syria-Palestine (Hebrew, Greek and Aramaic), which was my main area of interest, I explored the literature, history and archaeology of the whole Ancient Near East. One of the highlights of my studies was a summer spent working on an archaeological expedition in Israel sponsored by Harvard University. I also valued the many hours I spent studying ancient Greek manuscripts as part of my research assistantship. The rigorous discipline required in the analysis of detailed textual material and the necessity of understanding the import of precedents and underlying principles for purposes of arriving at the meaning of a text have provided me with an excellent background for the study of law. Throughout this period, I expressed my equally deep commitment to the community by doing volunteer work during the school year and by choosing summer jobs in the social services area.

In 1980 I married an Anglican clergyman and moved to the Niagara peninsula, where I continued to be involved in various social service and community organizations (Crescent Park Nursing Home, Niagara Women in Crisis, Nova House (a shelter for abused women), Family and Children's Services of the Niagara Region, Fort Erie Palliative Care Association). I was also a leader in an on-going Youth Leadership Training Program sponsored by the Diocese of Niagara.

However, by far the most important preoccupation in my life during the past five years or so has been meeting the special needs of my son,_____ , who was born with a profound hearing loss. After considering the various approaches to educating hearing impaired children, my husband and I decided that the oral method would provide _____ with the greatest opportunity of becoming a fully participating member of society. Our commitment to the oral approach led first to daily trips to Children's Hospital in Buffalo, and eventually to a move to Toronto in order to take advantage of the special programs offered by the Toronto Board of Education and the Auditory-Verbal Therapy Program sponsored by VOICE (a parent self-help organization) at North York General Hospital. I consider it a major achievement that my son is a happy, well-adjusted little boy in a regular Grade 1 class, at home with both his hearing and his hearing-impaired peers.

When we moved to Toronto in the fall of 1986, my husband went back to university and I looked for a job with flexible enough hours to enable me to meet _____ 's needs. In September I obtained a position as a Library Assistant in the Learning Resources Centre at _____ Institute. A few months later I became the supervisor of the Reserve Department, a position which I hold up to the present. My responsibilities include overseeing the maintenance of a collection of some 12,000 items, participating in the implementation of an on-line system in the Reserve area, and training and supervising the Library Assistants. I am actively involved in our union (O.P.S.E.U.), and am a member of the Human Rights Committee of our Local. I am also taking advantage of the facilities at _____ by taking courses in photography.

Now, as a single parent of a school-age child, I intend to develop my own potential by pursuing a career in law, building on the foundation of my previous academic accomplishments and my various experiences over the past several years. I believe that the study and practice of law play a central role in ensuring that the rights of all citizens in a society are advanced and safeguarded and that their obligations to society are guided with fairness, reasonableness and humanity. In my law studies and practice, I would like to focus on the field of regulatory law as applied to either the disadvantaged (particularly the disabled) or labor and labor-related problems. In this way I hope that my career as a practising lawyer will both benefit society and allow me to meet my responsibilities and desire for personal growth.

If I am accepted into the program, I am fully confident I will do well in my studies and complete successfully all the degree requirements. I hope also to contribute in a positive way to the life of the Faculty during my years of study there. I am fortunate to have a supportive family who have always encouraged me in both emotional and practical ways, and I have their assurance of continued support as I embark on this new and challenging enterprise.

Sample 7

A passionate interest in politics, the principles of government, and the values that Canadians seek to live by, motivates my desire to study law at _____ . I was 13 years old and growing up on a farm in rural Ontario when I first attended a constituency meeting for the nomination of our local candidate. The power and influence of the ideas I heard were exhilarating. That experience excited my curiosity about the processes and structures that organize ideas into a framework for the structure of society. I quickly discovered that law is the medium through which human values are articulated. Thenceforth, I have been certain about my decision to study law and make a contribution to Canadian public life.

My interest in politics and political theory led to an undergraduate education in Political Studies at Queen's University. The program is intellectually demanding and has helped me to acquire the knowledge, skills, and habits required for further scholarship. The program requires that students complete 19 credits for a B.A.(H), and I will graduate with 19.5 credits in May 1996. My studies have sharpened my capacity for critical thinking, strengthened the quality of my judgment, and heightened my understanding of interaction between humans and political structures that shape human demands. One of the greatest pleasures of my undergraduate experience has been the opportunity I have had to enjoy learning for its own sake. The challenging academic standards of the program enabled me to prove my intellectual abilities by maintaining a consistent record of academic achievement. I believe that my undergraduate program, with its emphasis on rigorous reading, writing, and thinking, has not only been an excellent preparation for the demands of law school, but also has provided an intellectual foundation that has developed the attributes of effective communication, cultural sensitivity, and an ability to reason critically. My studies have focused on Canadian politics. During 1995-96 I served as a research assistant to Professor_____. In that capacity I have worked on a B.A. honors thesis.

Another important factor in my personal and intellectual growth has been the activities and distinctions I have achieved outside the classroom. Extra-curricular involvement has broadened my experiences and developed my leadership skills. I have devoted a substantial amount of time, energy and creativity to student government and academic issues during my four years at Queen's. My participation in student government has reinforced my interest in law and community service. As my involvement and experience have progressed, I have embraced opportunities to assume more responsibility and face greater challenges. These experiences, particularly my appointment to an office in student government, have strengthened my organizational abilities, enhanced my interpersonal skills, and proven my managerial capabilities. In this position I have demonstrated originality in problem solving, intensified my sense of personal and professional integrity, and emphasized my conviction about the importance of education. One of my goals has been to facilitate the publication of course evaluations in an effort to educate students about the academic opportunities available. I have worked with members of the Faculty and Administration addressing concerns about the availability and accuracy of this information. As a recipient of the Arts & Science Undergraduate Society Achievement Award, my dedication and commitment to student government received public recognition. These academic and extra-curricular achievements have stimulated my passion for life and my appetite for knowledge. I am also proud of the extent and quantity of my employment experiences, which entail a great deal of responsibility and demonstrate the tenacity which has enabled me to finance a major part of my education.

I believe that acquiring an education entails a responsibility to contribute to society. I have realized the need for sensitivity to the social and political environment in which the government operates, and developed an understanding and respect for the history of the Canadian political system. I have faith in the ability of the Canadian government and Canadian citizens to make the changes and decisions that will allow Canada to prosper in the twenty-first century. I intend to apply the knowledge I have gained in my undergraduate experiences to the study of law, to formulate and implement public policy, and to make a contribution to public life. A legal education will develop the analytical abilities and problem solving skills I will need to tackle the challenges and complexities of the modern world in a career in the federal public service. The contributions I have made to community service during my four years at Queen's signify a lifelong commitment to public service. I sincerely believe that my choice of a rigorous undergraduate program, my quest for academic excellence, my achievement in extra-curricular activities, and my success in positions of responsibility in employment exemplify the capabilities and characteristics that will enable me to succeed at law school and in my career as a legal professional.

Sample 8

Any summer evening I would walk onto the grounds of Maranatha Gardens and spend time with its tenants, many of them, friends. The four floor apartment building stands at the end of a gauntlet of thirty well designed townhouses. A few years ago, this patch of land was merely three acres of weeds and garbage in the heart of Simcoe, Ontario. Now it is home to seventy families, many of whom could not previously afford decent housing.

It is difficult to resist a sense of pride. Although the conception and building of Maranatha Gardens was not part of my job description as a Pastor, it became an extension of it. It was one of the accomplishments that made the ministry worthwhile.

Becoming a minister was an unusual move for someone from our home. While we were raised Lutheran (my grandparents immigrated from Iceland to Gimli in 1926), we rarely attended church.

I was born in Winnipeg in 1956, the third of eight children. At the age of thirteen, our family moved to The Pas, Manitoba. Two years later, my parents separated, leaving my father to support and raise all of the children. Perhaps that is why he did not protest too loudly when, at seventeen, I left home and moved to Ontario to become involved in the rock music industry in Toronto as a bass guitarist.

While in Ontario I met and became impressed with a number of evangelical Christians. In the fall of 1974, after committing my life to Christ, I entered a Bible College in Lindsay, Ontario. I attended the three year full time course, graduating in 1977 with a B+ average.

That same year I married my wife, Lynn, and moved back to The Pas, where we lived until 1981. It was then that I was asked to take over a struggling congregation in Simcoe, Ontario. I accepted the invitation and moved to Simcoe in September 1981. I received my ordination in 1984 from the Apostolic Church of Pentecost of Canada, headquartered in Calgary, Alberta.

I was the Senior Pastor of the Full Gospel Fellowship in Simcoe from 1981 to 1996. During that time, the church grew from seven families to over one hundred. It also progressed through two building programs, added additional staff and started other congregations.

Early in my career as a clergyman, I decided that my ministry would be governed by three principles. First, growth (we would resist the trend of declining church interest and would become a noticeable force in our community). Second optimism (we would resist the image of negative legalism and offer people a positive message of hope). Third, relevance (we would resist the tendency of answering unasked questions and, instead, relate to the nitty-gritty of people's lives). Everything we accomplished was guided by these convictions. I believe that we were successful in changing lives because of these principles.

It wasn't always easy. Being the Pastor of a growing congregation, coordinating over seventy staff and volunteers, demanded the continual learning, development and deployment of different skills, many of which will be helpful in the pursuit of law. Some of these skills are as follows.

The skill of administration. I enjoyed the art of forming and chairing boards, committees and organizations. Along with numerous groups within the church itself, I led one Ministerial association, founded another, created a "church planning" organization, was Vice-President of a Missionary Corporation and served in different capacities within my denomination. These endeavors were fulfilling, so long as we accomplished clear goals and objectives.

The skill of research. The constant necessity of writing seminars, messages and manuals sharpened my research and creative abilities. Staying fresh, original, motivational and instructional was a satisfying challenge.

The skill of counseling. A steady caseload of crisis, marriage and behavioral counseling enhanced my interpersonal skills as well as cultivated the areas of problem identification and solving. Although I found counseling to be intense and demanding, it was a high value activity. Many people, from *children to professional adults found direction and encouragement in our offices. It was always gratifying to see the lives of others rebuilt and redirected.*

The skill of leadership training. One top priority was the development of leadership abilities in others. Some people took senior positions within the church. Many of our young people went on to full time ministry. We are particularly proud of that. Also, I have had the privilege of teaching the dynamics of leadership internationally to hundreds of people in colleges and churches. Motivating and instructing others to take ownership of their lives is a rewarding task.

The skill of writing. Writing has also become a very useful talent. Between 1981 and 1996 over five hundred of my articles have been published in newspapers and magazines. Targeting the unchurched, the columns, addressed lifestyle issues in terms that anyone could understand and enjoy. The blend of directness, relevance and humor built a weekly and monthly readership of well over five thousand people. I will endeavor to bring the same mixture of textual integrity and enjoyable style into the practice of law.

Community involvement has been important to me both as a clergyman and as a private citizen. Simcoe is a town of fifteen thousand people with a strong economic base. However, in 1988, the need for affordable housing was brought to my attention. It was then that the dream of Maranatha Gardens was born. I founded Kent Park Community Homes of Simcoe, a nonprofit corporation dedicated to providing housing with dignity to the underprivileged. After forming the corporation, we hired consultants and acquired the appropriate land. Next we attained a government allocation and built a positive relationship with the Ontario Ministry of Housing. Then it was a matter of patiently working with architects, contractors and local groups. Finally, in 1992, Kent Park Community Homes opened the seven million dollar "geared to income" housing facility. Since then, the project, christened Maranatha Gardens, has given young adults a "head start", seniors a decent residence and families an attractive home. As mentioned previously, this accomplishment has been source of pride for myself and my wife Lynn, who also served on the board.

My community involvement also involved chairing committees for the Chamber of Commerce, radio broadcasting and teaching music in local schools.

During my tenure in religious leadership. Lynn and I not only raised up healthy congregations, but, more importantly, two sons, Dallas, 17 and Brady, 15. They have different opinions, different goals, different shoe sizes (13 and 14), but both have exceptional personalities and active social lives.

Music is a large part of church life and became an enjoyable part of our home. I have taught myself piano, keyboards, guitar and bass guitar. I am delighted to see these interests beginning to blossom in our children.

Now, after fifteen years in the ministry, it is time to shift direction. I originally entered the ministry in order to help others and lead our church to success. I feel that I have come as far as I can in my ministry. On Sunday, October 13 (my fortieth birthday) I stood before my congregation and announced that a time of transition had come for myself and for them. It was to become, for all of us, a season of change.

It is my hope that the field of law will allow me to increase my ability to serve others in practical ways. I believe that the skills that I have acquired as a minister will enhance my ability to excel in the legal profession. It is also my intent to expand my leadership into the political arena. I do not feel that I can adequately do this without first being educated in the discipline of law.

Thank you for considering this application. I look forward to the opportunity to study law at the University of _____ and contribute to the class with any sensitivities and perspectives into religious, social and organizational issues that my experience has afforded me.

Sample 9*

In the wee hours of the morning last week, as I was stealing a bit of time to try a few LSAT questions while working overtime at my law firm, a young associate noticed the LSAT book and asked incredulously, "Are you crazy? Why would you want to give up a promising new career as a trademark agent for three years of intense study, followed by one year of very long hours as an articling student, only to be followed by even longer hours as an associate?" I could not answer the question in a few words, so I merely assured her that I considered myself to be in full possession of my faculties. In the following paragraphs, I intend to explain to the Members of the Admissions Committee why I am so determined to continue with my studies.

I was in third year of the Nursing Science program at the University of Ottawa when my son John was born in 1980. At that time, I made the decision to leave my studies to devote all my energies to raising a family. Between 1980 and 1987, I gave birth to five children. By economic necessity, I was forced to start work in 1986, first part-time and then later, full-time. In 1990, a chance encounter lead me to a temporary legal secretarial position at my current law firm. I thoroughly enjoyed the assignment, and have held a contract position there through my company, Cortage Corporation, continuously since then.

After working as a float secretary, having the opportunity to be exposed to and learn about many areas of law practice, I "fell into" the intellectual property department. Due to the nature of this area of practice, secretaries are traditionally given more responsibility than in other areas. Some secretaries advance to become Canadian trade-mark agents. I successfully wrote the October, 1996 examinations, and am now a qualified Canadian trade-mark agent.

My five children are now adolescents, or nearly so. Although each is very much an individual (which makes for some very interesting moments for my husband and me as parents!), we are both very proud of how they are developing as young individuals. We are also pleased with their academic achievements. All three boys have been honours students at high school. The oldest is studying first-year math and science at the University of British Columbia. The two girls are home-schooled, working above their grade-level.

As my children have become older, more independent, and more grounded, I have been able to devote additional thought and energy to my career. During the past year, I have been working on a procedures manual for my department. This project had its inception when I was asked to train a new person with no knowledge of intellectual property, to enter due dates into our trade-mark tracking database. I hope to have it completed by the time I am at law school in 1998!

Last year, when my firm developed an association with a patent agency, I was asked to set up a patent due date tracking system. This involved learning the patent process, worldwide, from filing to expiry, and then programming a set of codes into our existing database to track the flow. The agents have been pleased with the results, given the limitations of the software package. Over the next six to eight months, I have been asked to work with them and our Systems Department to create a new trade-mark and patent database that will satisfy all of us. I am very excited about being able to apply my knowledge and experience to work with this team to create the "ideal" database.

One of our clients needed to track infringers of "knock-off" items or grey market goods, and I created a database. Although we have not yet discovered any common infringers, the client is happy to know that a system exists to "flag" them.

It did not take long for the chair of the IP Department to discover that she could use my French-language skills to translate French-language correspondence or documents, thereby saving our clients time and money.

I was grateful to be given the opportunity to participate in all of these projects and have enjoyed each for its new challenges. However, I still felt that my direction was limited. For this reason (among others), I made the decision to become a trade-mark agent. Studying for the exams, I was exposed for the first time to analysis of case law and applying it to new situations. This greatly aroused my interest in law. It was while preparing for the exams that I made the decision to continue my studies and to become a lawyer.

The University of _____ is an ideal school for pursuing studies in intellectual property. Gordon Henderson's spirit and influence remain there.

Being bilingual, the University is also an ideal program for me. Even though my application is for the English language common law program, I look forward to having the opportunity to take some courses in French. Being a citizen of a province and country with two official languages, I believe there should be more anglophones capable of expressing themselves in French. The University of _____ will prepare me for a career in both official languages.

Members of the Admissions Committee, I trust that I have been able to present sufficient evidence as to why I will be an ideal candidate for the University of _____'s common law program.

* The author of this personal statement was accepted to law school with a weaker personal statement. This sample is a rewrite of the original statement and this rewrite is still in draft form.

CHAPTER 3

MBA Bound!

STOP!! Before reading this chapter you should have read all the previous chapters. Although this chapter stands on its own, it is best read as an "overlay" to the marketing principles previously developed. "MBA Bound" contains supplementary MBA specific information.

Marketing To Business Schools

Our general discussion (although somewhat law specific) is applicable to marketing of all types. The purpose of this appendix is to add some comments that are specifically related to MBA applications.

MBA Advantage - The Background

> "...it's clear that B-schools are in the midst of quite a bull market. At virtually all the best schools, applications, GMAT scores, and starting-pay packages for MBAs are setting all-time records."

> Business Week - October 1996

To put it simply, the MBA degree is getting "very hot." There are quality MBA programs throughout the world. When it comes to an MBA, "The World Is Your Oyster." The long term benefits of an MBA are quite substantial. Hence, you should research your options extensively. MBA options may be considered from the following perspectives:

- *Content of program;*

- *Length of program;*

- *Medium of instruction;*

- *Geographical location.*

First, content. Although there are still many programs that teach management from a general perspective, there are also many "niche" programs. You will find an MBA program designed for almost any subject. Examples include, agriculture, international business, entrepreneurship, science and technology, accounting, hospital administration, arts administration, financial services, etc. Don't think in terms of enrolling in an MBA program. Think in terms of enrolling in a specific kind of MBA program.

Second, length. Where classroom instruction is involved there are three common formats.

1. Full-time: In North America (but not in Europe) the MBA has traditionally been a two year program of full-time study. Many MBA programs have changed to a one year format that requires one year of continuous full time study. For applicants who have completed their undergraduate degrees some years ago, this is a benefit. It is difficult for schools to both require work experience and run a two year program. The opportunity cost to the applicants is simply too high!

> *"Nothing sums up the trend toward shortened programs as much as a comment by Philip Rees, director of Dalhousie University's MBA program in Halifax. When asked about any weaknesses he saw in his school's approach, he answered: `The fact that it's still a two year program.'"*

Canadian Business - October 1996

I predict that the two year full-time MBA will soon become a relic of the past.

2. Part-time: Many applicants elect to pursue the MBA degree on a part-time basis. This has the benefit allowing applicants to continue their current careers. The disadvantage is that part-time MBA programs can take years to complete.

3. Executive MBA: This is becoming a popular option. These programs generally take two years to complete and require one day a week (although it varies from school to school) of full time class attendance.

Third, medium of instruction. Once again, this is limited only by the imagination. As well as the traditional classroom environment, there are correspondence MBAs, online MBA programs, videoconferencing MBA programs, etc. The trend is for MBA programs to be delivered electronically. According to one commentator:

"University-based business schools that don't get ahead of this trend risk losing market share."

Fourth, geographical location. Most applicants apply to MBA programs in the U.S., Canada or Europe. But, there are MBA programs all over the world. For reasons that bear on professional licensing requirements, applicants to law and medical school are likely to be tied to one country. This is not true of applicants to MBA programs.

It is a very exciting time to apply to MBA programs!

Application Strategy

There are hundreds of MBA programs with different application procedures. They differ in terms of application deadlines, number and types of letters of references, the format of the personal statement and GMAT scores. There is no one application strategy. It is vital that you follow the directions for each school. What follows are some comments about various aspects of the admissions process.

Applications And Application Deadlines

Begin early. Research the school and decide if there is a good fit between who you are and the culture of the school. Research yourself. Research the school. Is there a link between the two? Leave ample time to compile your file.

There are many ways to research the schools. In addition to the obvious sources, try to discover the profiles of the current student body. This will provide you with a snapshot of the kinds of applicants the school tends to admit. Most schools have web sites. You may access all of them using the GMAT MBA Explorer at http://www.gmat.org. You may also wish to visit the Marr/Kirkwood web site at www.bschool.com.

The GMAT And GMAT Scores

The GMAT (Graduate Management Admission Test) is part of the admissions process for admission to virtually every MBA program. It is a multiple choice test. The questions are drawn from the following general areas: quantitative (problem solving and data sufficiency), reading comprehension, critical thinking skills and English grammar. In addition, there is a short writing test.

The GMAT may be taken only on computer. This is intended to provide test takers with more options for when they may take the test.

Although GMAT will allow you to take the GMAT as many times as you want (after all there is a fee to take the test) you should understand how schools interpret multiple GMAT scores. Some schools average scores and some will take the highest. The fact that some schools average GMAT scores implies that you should take steps to score as well as you can on the first attempt.

You can and should prepare for the GMAT. There are numerous courses and books available. There are wide differences in the price and quality of courses. Research them carefully. GMAT publishes their own GMAT preparation guide - **The Official Guide For GMAT Review**. It can be located at:

http://www.gmat.org

(See also Chapter 10 of this book - *Percentile Performance - What Is Effective Test Prep?*)

Letters Of Reference

Read the chapter in this book about letters of reference. As a general rule (for MBA applications), letters from employers are more relevant than academic references. (This doesn't mean that an academic reference is irrelevant. Pay close attention to the school's specific culture and requirements.) Employers often have less experience than academics, in writing letters of reference for admissions purposes. Work with your employers and take steps to educate them. You may want to show them the guidelines suggested in this book for how to write an effective letter of reference.

Personal Statements

There are as many different kinds of personal statements as there are schools. In general, you will find that MBA applications are more likely to use the "Multiple Question Personal Statement Format" discussed in this book. In this case the personal statement should be thought of as consisting of a series of short essays. Remember that we are "marketing ourselves to the business schools." What are they looking for? How do they define themselves? What is their "mission statement?"

Mission Statement: The MBA!

"Every B-school dean knows what to confidently promise: The ideal executive of the future - and every one of his school's graduates - will be a leader, not a mere manager. Global in outlook. Facile with information systems and technology. Able to capitalize on diversity. A visionary. A master of teamwork and a coach. Walks on water."

Fortune Magazine - January 1994

Categories Of Commonly Asked Questions

What follows are categories of essay questions that are commonly found on MBA application forms. This list is in no way intended to be exhaustive or representative of any particular school. Notice how each of these topics focuses on a quality that is necessary to succeed in the changing and dynamic world of business. Take further note of how these questions can be directly linked to the "Mission Statement" defined above!

1. Essays on career development - Why MBA? Why now? What do you have to offer to our school? Why are you interested in our school specifically?

Purpose: Have you given sufficient thought to why you are pursuing an MBA? Who are you? Where do you come from? Where do you wish to go? What motivates you? Are you a goal oriented individual? These questions are relevant because effective leadership and management require a high degree of focus.

2. Essays about an ethical dilemma

Purpose: In the long run, businesses can succeed only if they are run by people who can recognize ethical issues. Technology and globalization have compounded the ethical issues of business. The purpose of the question is to see if you can recognize an ethical issue in the first place. What do you see as possible alternatives for solving a dilemma? **Warning!!** An ethical issue is not the same thing as a legal issue. Many ethical dilemmas arise in the context of factual situations that are perfectly legal.

3. Essays about accomplishments or failures

Purpose: The purpose of the question is obvious. It is not the extent of the accomplishment or failure that is important. Its importance lies in how it affected your life and how it affected your decision to pursue an MBA. When you discuss any accomplishment or failure (in addition to describing it), consider:

- How specifically did you contribute to the accomplishment or failure;

- What did you learn from it (remember that every failure imparts a lesson); and

- How did the experience contribute to your growth as an individual and your decision to pursue an MBA.

4. Essays on commitment and leadership

Purpose: There is a vast difference between a manager and a leader. Managers are systematic disciplined planners who make organizations function as they are intended to function. Leaders help create a vision of the future and move the organization into the future as envisioned. As opposed to simply making the organization function as intended, a leader will influence the very intent of the organization. Great managers may be weak leaders and vice-versa. This type of question is aimed at assessing your leadership potential prior to embarking on an MBA. What if you don't have extensive business experiences. You may be able to demonstate leadership in the community.

5. Essays on strengths and weaknesses (or areas where you can be improved)

Purpose: Most people have little trouble identifying various strengths and weaknesses. Try to answer in such a way that you show that an MBA will enhance your strengths and diminish your weakness.

6. Essays on community service and/or extracurricular activities

Purpose: This question will provide you with the opportunity to show that you have a life outside of work and how that life makes you different from other applicants. If you are clever, you will be able to convey information that cannot be easily communicated under other question headings. For example, you may be able to demonstrate that you are a team player and team leader. Working effectively on teams is a skill required of MBAs. Take steps to ensure that you create images of being a well rounded, interesting, and likable person. Remember, those who don't have a life outside of work cannot function at optimal effectiveness in work!

7. Essays on distinctiveness

Purpose: Many graduates of MBA programs say that the most valuable part of the experience was the association with other classmates. Your classmates will enhance your learning experience and expect you to enhance their learning experience. You don't get just an MBA when you graduate from business school. You also join a network of business contacts that can help you throughout your career. By asking about distinctiveness, a school is really asking about what qualities and/or experiences you have had that you can contribute to the class as a whole.

8. Essays on international experiences

Purpose: The business world is becoming increasingly global. There are many niche MBA programs that position themselves as programs in "international business." The better you are able to operate in a global environment, the more suitable you are as a candidate. Operating in a global environment requires a true appreciation of how differently - and equally well - things get done in other parts of the world. International experiences can include work, travel, or study abroad. Don't forget to mention any special language skills you have or experiences in any specific foreign culture.

9. Essays about your capacity to perform well academically

Purpose: This question is directed more towards **effectiveness** than at intelligence. Brains aren't everything. In fact, intelligence without focus is wasted. Your grades and GMAT score will provide sufficient evidence of your academic abilities. What is it about you that demonstrates the specific motivation and focus to excel in this particular program? What can you offer to prove that you are conscientious?

10. Optional essays

Purpose: These essays are designed to give the applicant the opportunity to tell the school anything that is not covered in the other questions or is not evident from other parts of the application file. Avoid repeating things that have already been covered in other essays. Provide the committee with as much additional positive information about yourself as you can. Demonstrate that you have many interests, embrace change, are comfortable with technology and are computer literate. Don't waste this unique marketing opportunity! Make yourself come alive as a living, breathing, interesting person!

In Search Of Excellence! When Viewed Together The Essays Should ...

Remember that all of your essays will be read. They must fit together, be consistent with each other, reinforce each other, and (to the extent possible) be united by a theme that demonstrates an appreciation of excellence! For the truly outstanding MBA "good enough is not enough." Try to show that you have mastered at least one thing (and it can be anything) extremely well. Show that you know the difference between ordinary performance and extraordinary performance. Without an appreciation of excellence, you can't cultivate and appreciate that quality in others. Remember to view your essays both as components that stand alone and as the pieces of a puzzle which make up the complete application file. Remember, the whole is greater than the sum of the parts!

Conclusion

Although the essays are the most complicated and time consuming part of the file, they do provide you with an opportunity to show that you are unique. Use the "Personal Statement Workbook" to derive the information that you will use. Make sure that you leave yourself sufficient time. Personal Statements (particularly of the multiple question variety) always take far longer than your original estimate. I suggest that you budget up to 100 hours for the complete application file. Target your applications to the specific requirements of individual schools!

Chapter 4

Medical School Bound

Marketing To Medical Schools

STOP!! Before reading this chapter you should have read chapters 1 and 2. Although this chapter stands on its own, it is best read as an "overlay" to the marketing principles previously developed. "Medical School Bound" contains supplementary medical school specific information.

> *"Right from the beginning there is a reason that doctors are not specialists in prevention. The admission requirements for medical school are usually driven by marks. If an applicant has perfect marks in biology, physics, and chemistry, he or she can be assured of a place in almost any medical school. While these marks may measure intelligence, surely one important criterion of being a doctor, they do not assess personality. There is little credit given in the screening process for communication skills, for being an athlete, for participating in school plays, for doing volunteer work, or for getting the joke. Yet the medical student is about to enter the one job that requires the most "people" skills of all."*

> Dr. Peter G. Hanson in Counter-Attack

The Importance Of The Medical School Application Itself

A small number of people are "such superior applicants" that they simply "walk into" medical school. There are very few people in this group. For the vast majority of applicants, "getting into medical school" is a challenge. Most members of this vast majority - who have trouble getting in - have the ability to do medical school work. So, why do some applicants succeed and others fail? Consider the following comments from the University Of Toronto Pre-Med Society:

"Some people claim that medical school admissions are based mostly on merit. They believe that the medical school admissions committees are rational entities that carefully weigh the qualifications of the applicants and select the best candidates. Sure, there's some subjectivity in the process, but for the most part, the better the applicant, better the school he'll get into.

Others argue that medical school admissions are random. They feel that there being so many qualified applicants, it's impossible to make a rational decision. It's just a roll of the dice. Of course you have to pass certain minimal requirements, but after that, your qualifications cease to matter. We feel that neither of these views are completely correct. Certainly merit does play a role, and in some cases a student is so outstanding that there's no question he should be admitted. But this is very rare, and for the most part, it is indeed difficult to discriminate among the vast majority of applicants. And certainly there's a great deal of subjectivity in medical school admissions.

But are admissions random? No.

Admissions officers are no different than other people. They try hard to base their decisions on logic and reason, but in the end, emotion rules the day. This is especially when the decisions are difficult and logic provides meager guidance. They may call it "gut feeling" or "intuition," but in the end it all comes down to emotion. Do they like the applicant? Does the applicant remind them of themselves? If you sit in on admissions committee meetings, it's almost comical how the officers who were swimmers in college will pull for the swimmer, the ones who are from the Midwest will pull for the Midwest candidate, etc. It's often unconscious, but it happens all the time.

This is a critical point. The decisions are not random. They are based on emotion. Emotion does not equal randomness. If the decisions are random, you might as well send your application to every single school. But if the decisions are based on emotion, you must polish your application carefully. You must take out all the rough spots and burrs that may give the admissions officer a pause. Are you complaining about your college in the essay? Cut it. Whining is not going to make anyone like you more. Is there something fishy about a disciplinary action on your record? You must go to extreme lengths to lay that to rest. Any vague uneasiness that the admissions officer has about you spells rejection. We can't emphasize this enough. You can't give the admissions committee anything to wonder about or anything to worry about.

If the admissions are based on emotion, you should try to establish a common ground with the admissions officers. If you play a sport, even basketball, mention it. If you love food, mention it. Admissions officers are human. The more you resemble them, the more they'll like you. This is particularly key in an interview. Interviewing well is a difficult art, but an art well worth mastering. It can provide a tremendous opportunity to establish that emotional connection, a connection that can be crucial to your admission."

The point is simple. All components of your application file and subsequent interview must be orchestrated to generate the kinds of positive images that the school is looking for. Yes, you must market **yourself** to medical school. Remember, your autobiographical sketch and personal statement must be designed so that:

1. The committee gets to know you; and

2. The committee likes you.

Direct Applicant Input For Medical School Applications

Multiple School Autobiographical Sketch Or Personal Comments

Medical school applicants in both the U.S. and Canada will almost certainly encounter a centralized medical school application service. For the U.S. check www.aamc.org. For Canada check http://ouacinfo.ouac.on.ca. All applicants supply the same information to the centralized application service. For many Canadian schools this information will be elicited in the form of an "autobiographical sketch." A sample question might be:

"List in chronological order all places of residence and a brief description of your activities since the age of 14. For example; occupations, details of school, university and more specifically your extra-curricular activities."

Why would a medical school application form include an "autobiographical sketch?" Consider the following comments from the University of Toronto Pre-Med Society:

"Increasingly today, schools are looking for students who are well rounded, not "glued to the books." Get involved in activities you enjoy, and if you have the time, assume leadership positions in some of them. Leadership skills are interpreted very positively by the admissions committees, since you will have to assume a leadership role once you are a physician. Involvement in activities outside academics shows that you can relate to and deal with people. A word of caution is avoid participating in too many extra-curricular activities at the expense of your grades. Another important factor is working/volunteering in a hospital or nursing home. This provides an exposure to what doctors do, and what sick people are like. Most evaluators interpret your decision to study medicine as more valid due to the experience."

Applicants to U.S. medical schools - who apply through the centralized process administered by the AAMC - will be required to complete a brief "Personal Comments" section. This is a very "open-ended" personal statement. It cannot exceed one page and cannot be submitted in a font smaller than 10 point. Specific schools may require additional personal statements.

Before completing medical school applications, you should review Section 6 of Chapter 1 of this book called "The Facts Don't Always Speak For Themselves - How To Make Sure They Do." Remember to focus on you. Supply detail and concrete examples. This will keep your answers interesting and distinctive! Your job is to write a "personal statement" and not just a "statement!"

Subsequent School Specific Personal Statement

In addition to the information that is part of the common application form (which must be submitted by all applicants), many schools require applicants to submit an additional personal statement or autobiographical essay. The form of the question varies from school to school. Some schools will use the multiple question format. Others will ask a single question.

How To Answer The Questions - Know Your Audience!

In order to answer the application questions successfully, one has to conduct background research. The goal of this research is to determine why the admissions committee is asking the question. What will the answer to the question reveal about the applicant? How does the answer to the question relate to the admissions policy. Every school has a distinctive personality, specific goals for its program and an understanding of what kinds of students are most consistent with those goals. Research the school. Look for statements about the goal of the program, or about the kinds of personal characteristics the school seeks in its students. We will call statements of this type "Mission Statements." A valuable reference to understand the admission committee's perspective and identify "mission statements" is "The Journal Of Medical Education."

(This was formerly called "Academic Medicine" and is an official publication of the Association Of American Medical Colleges. You will probably find it in your university library.)

21 Sample Medical School Essay Questions

What follows are groups of questions asked by three different medical schools. As you read the questions, ask what clues do the questions provide about the ideal applicant. How does the question relate to the school's "Mission Statement" (if any)? All questions must be answered in light of the "Mission Statement." Pay particular attention to words that have been italicized.

School 1

Mission Statement: "Seventy-five students are admitted annually into the first medical year and are selected on the basis of a strong academic record and the assessment by the admissions committee of personal characteristics considered to be most appropriate for the study of medicine and for the subsequent practice of medicine. ... Candidates should emphasize in the autobiographic sketch those areas of extracurricular experience that include particular interest in advisory work, athletics, community work, fine arts, health care, employment, literature, organization, teaching, and travel."

Questions

1. Why do you wish to become a physician?

2. What do you think *people need and expect* from physicians? How do you think that you would be able to fulfill these expectations?

3. Explain in general how *your development and previous experiences* have contributed in your suitability to becoming a physician?

4. Expand on one area described on the autobiographical sketch that has played a significant role in developing *you as a suitable candidate* to become a physician.

5. Identify three personal references used in your application. For each choice state the reason why he/she should be able to provide an *objective assessment of your motivation, commitment to hard work, integrity and social concern.*

6. Provide any other information that would aid the admissions committee in assessing your application.

School 2

Mission Statement: "The overriding objective to be achieved is the demonstrated ability to identify, analyze and manage clinical problems in order to provide effective, efficient and humane patient care. ... Enabling objectives consisting of knowledge, skills and professional behavior comprise the following:

Knowledge: To acquire and put into practice concepts and information required to understand and manage health care problems. The study of human structure, function and behaviors will be guided by an analysis of the determinants of health and illness. A spectrum of factors will be considered in both the external and internal environments of individuals when deciding on preventative, therapeutic, rehabilitative and supportive management.

Skills: To acquire and use the following skills:

1. **Critical thinking skills:** The application of certain rules of evidence to clinical, investigational and published data in order to determine their validity and applicability.

2. **Clinical skills:** The ability to acquire, interpret, synthesize and record clinical information in managing the health problems of patients, considering their physical, social and emotional function.

3. **Self-directed learning skills:** The ability to identify areas of deficiency in one's own performance, find appropriate educational resources, evaluate personal learning progress and use new knowledge and skills in the care of patients.

Professional behavior: To recognize, develop and maintain the professional behavior required for a career as a health professional. Acquiring the authority to intervene in the lives of patients carries with it the obligation to act responsibly:

1. **toward oneself:** to recognize and acknowledge personal assets, emotional reactions and limitations in one's own knowledge, skills and attitudes, to build on one's assets and to overcome areas of limitations;

2. **toward patients and their families:** to be able, under appropriate supervision, to take responsibility for the assessment and care of patients and their families,

3. **toward colleagues:** to contribute to productive communication and cooperation among colleagues engaged in learning, research or health care,

4. **toward the community:** to contribute to the maintenance and improvement of the health of the general population.

Questions

7. What do you think individuals *need and expect from physicians*?

8. Why do *you* wish to study medicine?

9. How have you prepared yourself to deal with the scientific and *non-scientific aspects* of the study of medicine?

10. Discuss with examples, what you have *learned outside of formal education*. What *motivated* your learning and how did you go about it?

11. How have you *contributed to the community or society* and what have you learned from these experiences?

12. Describe one or more situations in which you have worked with others. Explain how you *worked together, resolved conflicts* and evaluated your efforts?

13. Why do you want to study at _____?
    What would you *offer your fellow students* and the program?

School 3

Mission Statement Exercise: Read the following questions and try to construct a 200 word mission statement based on the questions.

Questions

14. Describe how *specific activities and experiences* in your life have influenced you to apply to medicine.

15. Give examples of instances in which you have been *motivated* to learn *outside the context of school*.

16. Describe the most *challenging experience* you have encountered.

17. Provide examples of *personal skills* that will enable you to *work well in small groups*.

18. Describe personal skills that you possess that will help you *communicate with and care* for the sick.

19. Describe *challenges and stressful situations* that you have encountered. What challenges and stressful situations do you expect to encounter in medical school?

20. What problems and *ethical issues* do you foresee in practicing medicine and how will you deal with these challenges?

21. Why do you think that *you* are a good candidate for medicine?

Guidelines For How To Construct Your Answers

What follows is an excerpt from Dr. Brett Ferdinand's **Gold Standard For Medical School Admissions**:

"Most medical schools require autobiographical materials as important components of the application process. Autobiographical materials include essays, letters, sketches, or questionnaires where you are given the opportunity to write about yourself. Autobiographical materials are a sort of written interview. Thus the same objectives, preparation, and strategies apply as previously mentioned for interviews. However, there are some unique factors.

For example, you can begin writing long in advance of the deadline. The ideal way to prepare is to have a few sheets of paper at home on which you continually write any accomplishments or interesting experiences you have had anytime in your life! By starting this process early, months later you should, hopefully(!), have a long list from which to choose information appropriate for the autobiographical materials. Your resume or curriculum vitae may also be of value.

Be sure to write rough drafts and have qualified individuals proofread it for you. Spelling and grammatical errors should not exist.

The document should be written on the appropriate paper and/or in the format as stated in the directions. Do not surpass your word and/or space limit. Ideally, the document would be prepared on a word processor and then laser printed. The document should be so pretty that your parents should want to frame it and hang it in the living room! Handwritten or typed material with "liquid paper" or "white out" is simply not impressive.

Your document must be clearly organized. If you are given directive questions then organization should not be a problem. However, if you are given open-ended questions or if you are told, for example, to write a 1000 word essay about yourself, adequate organization is key. There are two general ways you can organize such a response: chronological or thematic. However, they are not mutually exclusive.

In a **chronological** response, you are organized by doing a systematic review of important events through time. In writing an essay or letter, one could start with an interesting or amusing story from childhood and then highlight important events chronologically and in concordance with the instructions.

In the **thematic** approach a general theme is presented from the outset and then verified by examples at any time in your life. For example, imagine the following statement somewhere in the introduction of an autobiographical letter/essay.

"My concept of the good physician is one who has a solid intellectual capacity, extensive social skills, and a creative ability. I have strived to attain and demonstrate such skills.

Following such an introduction to a thematic response, the essayist can link events from anytime to the general theme of the essay. Each theme would thus be examined in turn.

And finally, keep in mind the advice given for interview since much of it applies here as well. For example, the appropriate use of an amusing story, anecdote, or an interesting analogy can make your document an interesting one to read. And, as for interviews, specific examples are more memorable than overly generalized statements."

Chapter 5

Some Actual Samples Of Medical School Personal Statements

What follows are some sample answers to medical school application essays. In each case the applicant was accepted into medical school. As you read the answers, think about how the answers could be improved. How well did the writer "come to life?" How responsive were the answers to the precise question(s) asked? Did you get to know the writer? Do you like the writer?

Format 1 - Multiple Questions Personal Statement - Directive Essays

1. What do you think individuals need and expect from a physician?

I feel that my background and experience have instilled in me many of the qualities that are important in molding an effective health practitioner. Not only does a physician need to possess knowledge and the ability and desire to learn, he must also be able to interact favorably with the public using his strong interpersonal skills, ability to communicate effectively, patience, problem solving and analytical skills as well as having a caring and personable disposition.

2. Why do you wish to study medicine?

Medicine is not a static field but it is constantly evolving as researchers delve more into the intricacies of the human body. My future goals include a career consisting of both an educational and clinical component. I feel that my scientific training has provided me with an excellent background for this type of career and I am confident that my patients will benefit from the knowledge derived from my research experiences and up-to-date application of techniques. I am committed to furthering education and dedicated to the preservation of medical research in Canada in spite of the health care problems that face us today. I know that I

*can make a substantial contribution to both medical education
and research from which the community will benefit. For these
reasons and given my background and experiences, I feel that an
M.D. is, at this point, appropriate and necessary in order to fulfill
these goals.*

3. How have you prepared yourself to deal with the scientific and non-scientific aspects of the study of medicine?

*My volunteering at the Credit Valley Hospital in Mississauga has
given me the opportunity to interact with a wide variety of people.
Through my interaction with people in the ER, many of whom had
undergone extreme physical and emotional trauma, I experienced
first hand the importance and satisfaction of bonding with the
patients and it is my patience and empathy that allowed me to
overcome the barriers for trust. My experience in graduate school
has been very challenging and not only demonstrates my capacity
to think and learn more difficult concepts on my own but also
promotes my creativity, problem solving and analytical skills. The
work is quite unlike undergraduate courses where the bulk
requires memory of assigned work and not analytical thought. I
have learned how to solve problems on my own by assessing the
situation, pinpointing the problem by analyzing the results in
relation to the protocol, gathering information from various
sources such as colleagues, journal articles and lab protocols and
using creativity to make the changes necessary to solve the
problem. I feel that in this way, research has provided me with the
opportunity to be self-sufficient and self-motivated and that these
skills will be advantageous in the practice of medicine.*

4. Discuss, with examples, what you have learned outside of formal education. What motivated the learning and how did you go about it?

*Outside of school, I sought out many athletic and musical interests
which also demonstrate my motivation to learn, experience and
master new techniques. Although I have participated on
competitive soccer, tennis, football and baseball teams, I have
excelled in basketball where I played for two years on a semi-
professional team. During this time period, through my self-
discipline and competitiveness, I was motivated to continuously
improve and upgrade my skills. My interest in music has also
motivated me to learn two instruments, the piano and the clarinet,
the latter which I played in the school band.*

5. How have you contributed to the community or society, and what have you learned from these experiences?

I have been very active as a basketball/softball coach during my high school and university years and as a biochemistry teaching assistant for the past three years. The repeated success of my teams and my students demonstrates not only my ability to convey my knowledge but also to challenge my players and students while maintaining their interest. To do this, I believe that one has to earn the respect of the students by in turn showing respect for their ideas and thoughts. To be a good teacher, one has to have a good mix of knowledge and communication skills to impart to the students that knowledge, and I observe my skills improving as I gain more experience. My understanding of younger people, what motivates them, what makes them feel at ease and my ability to identify and interact well with them are assets that will prove to be indispensable as a physician.

6. Describe one of more situation(s) in which you have worked or learned with others. Explain how you worked together, resolved conflicts and evaluated your efforts.

In the research field, I have had to work in small group settings. This has occurred at research conferences and in the lab where discussions are held for the interchange and sharing of new ideas. Although work is performed individually, to obtain complete results, one should never work entirely alone since consultation with others is essential to learning from their experiences and ideas in continuing or taking new directions in my research project. Our entire lab group consistently meets at least once a week to discuss in depth the progress of our research and to exchange ideas regarding one another's project in our endeavor for the general advancement, progress and continued success of our group. Through this constant exchange of ideas and mutual support, my group has provided me with exceptional breadth in my learning experience.

7. Why do you want to study at _____? What would you offer your fellow students and the program?

An important aspect of being a physician is the ability to interact with a diversity of people. I feel that the service of the human aspect of medicine should be stressed since it is just as crucial as possessing treatment knowledge. Patient problems are complex and a complete treatment must include getting to know the patient and making them feel comfortable enough to disclose their problems fully so that the proper treatment can be provided. _____ medical program emphasizes this interactive aspect of medicine, both with the patients and in small groups with colleagues, which is a crucial foundation on which to build life-long interpersonal skills.

My experience in graduate school has taught me how to learn more difficult concepts, improve my problem solving and analytical skills, and also to work well in small groups. These skills will be beneficial to both the program and my fellow students because a useful exchange of ideas will ensue during which I can offer constructive criticisms while at the same time, keeping an open mind in considering new ideas, suggestions and different perspectives in order to achieve the most advantageous result. It is only through a group effort that we can benefit from diverse sources of information and experiences to produce the optimal effect.

Format 2 - Single Question Personal Statement

Sample 1 - Thematic Organization

Medicine has been the underlying theme of my life. In fact, as early as kindergarten I would sign my name as "Dr. Nigel" on exams. My teacher interpreted it as my having a sincere interest in medicine (which I did). However, my peers found it to be a bit much in this regard and let me know it in no uncertain manner. As a consequence, I made my first career move: I decided that I would not become a pediatrician!

My elder sister recently stated that she had been inspired in part by my early magnetism towards medicine; consequently, she enrolled in a pre-med program at Ottawa University. Dr. Kate Davidson graduated from the University of Toronto in 1990 and went on to McGill to specialize in, of all things, pediatrics!

Since kindergarten I have spent my years cultivating qualities which I feel are important in order to be a successful doctor. Such qualities are: patience and understanding, creativity, leadership and academic achievement.

Patience and Understanding

I believe that someone who has no predisposition towards patience
and understanding could not be a successful medical professional.

In 1990-1991, I worked for five months as a volunteer at the Montreal Association for the Blind. I spent several hours each week with handicapped blind children. Whether one-on-one or in a group, these children thrive on patience and understanding. Regardless of whether I was teaching a child a new chore or a new game, I remember feeling that just one of their smiles was worth all the patience in the world.

To further put such qualities to work, I began tutoring my peers at the Sandy Hill Community Centre (where I function as a Youth Worker and an attendant.) In the last year I have tutored dozens of students in the sciences. I learn as much from them as they do from me. I have learned to develop interpersonal skills such as being able to adapt to the needs of an individual. Most importantly, tutoring taught me, and still teaches me, patience and understanding.

Creativity

I feel that creativity is an important quality in the study of medicine since it represents the ability to recombine information into new and exciting ways. In this respect I feel that music can serve as a strong analogy.

At the age of twelve, I passed the McGill Conservatory of Music's grade IX examination in classical piano "with honors". With that as a foundation, in 1984 (the Year of the Child), I was offered a fee to compose music and to perform for a theater group in a summer tour of Canada. Thus, I became a member of Children's Creations.

We performed on the steps of Parliament Hill on Canada Day (introduced by then Prime Minister Turner) and we played as the Tall Ships sailed into Quebec City for Les Voiliers '84. From Place-des-Arts in Montreal to the National Arts Centre in Ottawa; from

Klondike Days in Edmonton to the perpetual summer sunlight of Whitehorse; from the metropolis of Toronto to the modesty of Moncton, New Brunswick: we experienced Canada.

While in Toronto, I did interviews for PBS and CBC concerning the tour and its impact on my future. I openly affirmed my desire to enter medicine. I also mentioned that Children's Creations was a beautiful but temporary method to sharpen my creative skills which will one day be used to a greater end.

Leadership

My last medical examination was sound partly due to my affinity with sports. In high school I was quite athletically successful. I was one of the few individuals who qualified for the Quebec Provincials five years in a row for sports such as basketball, badminton and volleyball.

Due to the size of my high school, many students were not given an opportunity to engage in competitive sports. In order to remedy this, a friend and I set up a "farm system" in which students who were not qualified to splay interscholastically, would play on an intramural team until their skills were sufficiently sharpened. This system is still being employed at my high school where I was also president of the graduating class.
It was more than just new sports organization that I brought to high school, I also brought the publisher of, at the time, the world's second largest francophone publication! Through the help of my English teacher, I organized the play "The Golden Pants" which was written and attended by the publisher of La Presse (Roger Lemelin, author of the play). Mr. Lemelin, after seeing the play, commented on my organizational skills by saying: "You will certainly be the next Prime Minister of Canada!".

Although I was later elected to represent pre-science in the Science Student Association (University of Ottawa), the federal parties have nothing to fear! Since in reality, I was only trying to improve my leadership skills.

Academic Achievement

Although I was awarded several academic prizes in elementary and high school, my most valuable achievements came during my university career. Last spring, I was awarded a scholarship from the Association of Professors from the University of Ottawa for the second year in a row. I was chosen for the award based on my first semester GPA of 9.4/10 and an autobiographical letter.

As a result of my average, I was also the recipient of a summer research scholarship from the National Science and Engineering Research Council. I spent last summer doing research in the Neurobiology Department of the University of Ottawa. My supervisor, Dr. C. Pritchard, was so pleased with my work, she has invited me to return next summer with my next NSERC award. She intends to teach me various "patch clamping" techniques which involve some of the most delicate equipment on campus.

I believe academics is important since knowledge is the key to an accurate diagnosis. With this in mind, I decided to broaden my horizons prior to my entry into medical school.

To this end, I will be completing a General B.Sc. with concentration in Life Sciences, though I will be receiving credit for some honors level courses (i.e. neurophysiology). There are fewer than a dozen students registered in my program due to the heavy load of physics and math. However, it is precisely these two subjects which form two of the three integral components of all theories in the fields I hope to study: neurobiology, neurophysiology and neurology. And for the biology component, there will be no lack of it in medical school! Included in my schedule have been several social science disciplines which have been broadening. Presently, I find this little academic experiment to be edifying, enlightening and successful.

Academic achievements come in different forms - some of which never find their way into school transcripts. For example, last fall I received a 90% in the St. John's Ambulance Course. Also, I have written scientific articles in the school's newspaper; some of these articles will be published in the Canadian University Press.

Conclusion

I have always believed that medicine is the way I could serve society best. Ever since my childhood I have had my eyes focused on medicine. Since then, I have spent much time in many fields, cultivating the qualities I felt were necessary to be the best doctor I could be.

Entering medicine is more than just a childhood dream of mine; rather, it has grown into a lifelong conviction.

Sample 2 - Thematic Organization

Medicine is a humane branch of science where I can connect my divergent interests to an occupation that would express my commitment to scientific training, and my desire to service society. Besides being one of the most rapidly expanding fields, medicine attracted me due to its use for constructive use only.

My decision to study medicine was well thought out and based on numerous discussions and experiences that expanded my understanding of the profession. Initially, scientific readings and studies in Human Biology helped to strengthen my interest in medicine. This interest evolved through the years and motivated me to pursue medical research. During my second year, I was a team member in a research project related to developing a liposome drug delivery system to combat urinary catheter infections. The challenge and responsibility of research stimulated me to integrate skills and resolve the medical problem. In addition, after five years of tutoring individually and in classrooms, I developed a great passion for teaching and continuing education. Through the medical profession, I wanted to fulfill the role of an educator and remain constantly in touch with new, and interesting people, and ideas. In addition, from my volunteering experience in an emergency ward at a local hospital, I found great satisfaction to help relieve patient's suffering, and know that my efforts were put to good use. It was a great opportunity to acquaint myself with the medical field. I hope that my actions and philosophy proved that medicine was the next natural step in my life.

Participation in a research project was a unique experience. Through this, I acquired the ability to analyze problems from diverse angles and work as a team member. During this project, we co-operatively integrated our expertise to achieve common objectives. In order to accomplish this, I exhibited a strong sense of self-motivation, responsibility, leadership and organization skills.

Medicine is not only a science, but also an art that requires constant interaction with people. During volunteering in the hospital, one of the most rewarding experiences was "understanding the importance of sensitivity to the treatment of people rather than diseases." Through careful listening, compassion, and patience, I was successful in sharing a bit of myself with the patients and developing a partnership with them.

Furthermore, teaching experience helped me to acquire a wide range of interaction skills. From this, I could quickly adapt, energetically motivate, and professionally communicate with people of all ages.

A medical doctor is a person who has a diverse background; adapts to new situations quickly, enjoys learning, reading and hard work. In order to be well rounded in all areas of life, I pursued many interests outside formal education. Rapid development in information technology motivated me to study all aspects of computers. To grasp the fundamental principles, I independently experimented, analyzed, and problem-solved systematically. Consequently, I creatively implemented my knowledge to produce tutorial software, internet web pages, and research multimedia presentations. Furthermore, I constantly strive to develop a strong character by reading biographies, creative thinking, and applying concepts in practice. In the past, I faced the greatest challenge in teaching summer school to academically weak grade nine students. Here, I developed a program to instruct computer processing and mathematics to students from three classes. This was challenging because I had to utilize my informally gained computer and character skills, to formally educate students. Furthermore, it was my responsibility to diagnose and motivate the students to overcome their weaknesses and achieve academic success. I worked through this problem in a professional manner with good patience, judgement, and perseverance. In conclusion, through informal self-training and experiences, I developed the essential characteristics of a physician.

The more I read and talked to people about a physician's life, the more the study of medicine excited me. Prospects of grueling physical routine, or lack of leisure time did not repel me. I recognized that arduous study, long hours, physical exertion, emotional strain; moral and financial responsibilities were part of the medical student's, and later a doctor's daily existence. Through experience, problem-focused coping, planning, and social support, I can confidently deal with these stresses. As a result, I am excited by the opportunity to deal with people, to solve problems, and to continue the learning process.

There are a number of general trends occurring in our society that is influencing the practice of medicine. Physicians are becoming glorified civil servants from increasing government control. Due to poor economic climate and budget cuts, all provincial governments are looking at ways to reduce and restructure health care. In turn, this is restricting the freedom and growth of medical practices. From an ethical perspective, medical decisions are becoming increasingly complex due to social awareness, and media publicity. In day to day practice, doctors have to morally deal with terminal care and rights of patients from various ethnic backgrounds. It is imperative for physicians to know how to present an atmosphere of trust, friendship, and uphold a professional manner. I believe that problems in the practice of medicine can be dealt with on an individual and team basis. Individually, I am willing to make short term sacrifices to achieve long term stability and development of the medical field. By growing up in three countries, I have also developed a good understanding of multicultural issues. With a strong moral sense of commitment and desire for social welfare, I can effectively make ethical decisions. As a team, we can unitedly resolve these problems through understanding, cooperation, and conscientious judgement.

I strongly feel that my background has made me mentally, emotionally, and physically prepared to commit my life to medicine. I am an intelligent and adaptive individual and I have the capacity to manage the new challenges of medicine. My philosophical approach is, "to contribute more than what I take." In fact, I will derive great satisfaction from knowing that my skill will benefit society and future generations will reap benefit from my good work. Thank You.

Sample 3 - Chronological Organization

Since my first year of high school in 1988, I knew that I would soon have to make tough career choices. To help me with my decision, I chose a variety of subjects, and participated in many extra-curricular activities. The math and computer science clubs provided opportunities to solve logical problems, while the Reach For The Top team competition tested my knowledge and stimulated my interests in a broad range of topics. The debates set up by the History Department brought out the competitive nature in me, which was also beneficial as a member of the school tennis team. However, this competitive nature was not beneficial in other aspects of my life, especially at the part-time job that I held throughout my high school years.

I started working at a local McDonald's restaurant at age fifteen and by age seventeen, I was a member of the management team. My responsibilities as an assistant manager demanded an ability to communicate and organize. At first, I stumbled, as the competitive nature that I had acquired was becoming noticeable in my work. But gradually, due to experience, and training courses in leadership, I improved. I discovered that working with my fellow employees, and not above or against them, was not only efficient, but also enjoyable. I also began to work more effectively at school, and I started to enjoy team sports such as handball and volleyball.

My interest in science increased throughout my high school years. When it came time to choose a university program, I decided to pursue a B.Sc. In physiology at McGill University. I tried to make my program as variable in content as possible given the restrictions imposed by the program itself. I also decided to participate in a student volunteer program at the Montreal Neurological Hospital with many of the friends that I met in my first year. We talked to several patients each week to try to help relieve some of their loneliness during long hospital stays. The most important thing that I learned from this experience was that, simply listening to and understanding the concern of patients can often make them feel more at ease with their situation. Although, we were able to make some people feel better, I could not help feeling that I wanted to do more. It was at this point that I started to seriously consider medicine as a career.

The many people that I met in my first years to university stimulated a multitude outside interests that I have today. In particular, the appreciation of many forms of music such as folk, reggae, classical and others. Eventually, I learned to play piano and joined a choral ensemble. I also started enjoying many different sports, participating on various intramural teams, cycling regularly, and joining the McGill Tennis Club. Other interests such as snooker, darts and chess can also be attributed to my college experience.

During my second and third years at McGill, I joined a student phone hotline. I received several calls from people trying to adjust to the stress of university life. These conversations further developed my listening and problem-solving skills. I also received calls involving crisis situations, which I feel have helped me react more calmly and constructively when faced with stressful situations.

In my third year at McGill, I was hired as a demonstrator for a first year gross anatomy course. My task was to review with a group of fifteen students, the theory presented in the lectures, while showing them the actual structures inside the human body. The job was easy at first, but as the semester progressed, I had to work several hours each week in order to keep myself one step ahead of my students. Although the work was hard, I discovered that I enjoyed demonstrating immensely and hope to have more chances to teach again in the future.

As I neared the end of my undergraduate work, I still had many tough choices to make. I chose several interesting courses to take in my final year. Many of the courses that I had already taken had given me the opportunity to do many interesting papers and experiments, and I was finding that research could be very creative. Therefore, I considered doing graduate work leading to a Ph.D. in Physiology. I also knew that I had a love for teaching, and so, the idea of becoming a high school teacher was also very appealing. As well, I considered becoming a doctor since I discovered through my volunteer work that helping people could be very rewarding. However, as a result of a personal tragedy, before the start of my final year, I was not prepared to write the MCAT Since this eliminated my chances of being accepted to McGill's Medical School, I decided to put off applying for one year.

This postponement allowed me the opportunity of taking a closer look at my other career options. After careful consideration, I realized that medicine would allow me to pursue my interests in teaching and research, while at the same time allowing me to utilize and develop the leadership and organization skills that I have been building upon during my school and university years.

I am now convinced that medicine is the right career choice for me, and I have decided against seeking admission to graduate

school and Teachers College. Instead, I am spending a year away
from school, working full time as a security guard in Toronto. I
miss McGill a great deal, and I hope to be back again in
September.

Conclusion

Marketing **yourself** to medical school should be taken very seriously.
Allow yourself enough time and enlist the aid of others in reviewing your
application material. Use the autobiographical sketch and personal
statement to demonstrate that you are competent, likable and interesting.
Make sure that you come to life as a living, breathing human being. Use
the Personal Statement Workbook in Part II of this book to organize your
content and process.

Chapter 6

Grad School Bound

STOP!! Before reading this chapter you should have read all previous chapters of this book. The principles discussed are applicable to marketing yourself to graduate schools. This chapter has been designed as an overlay to show how those principles apply to graduate school applications in general.

The Application File

In general, your graduate school application file will contain:

- the application form

- your transcript of grades

- letters of reference

- personal statement, statement of interest, letter of intent, etc.

- possibly a writing sample

- possibly a GRE score for the general test

- possibly a GRE score for one of the GRE subject tests

What follows is a sample of a personal statement for admission to a graduate program in architecture. You should also read all of the samples for law school and medical school.

Statement Of Interest To Apply To The School Of Architecture

To The Admissions Committee:

I was born in Germany and lived there until the time that I graduated from high school. Until the end of the eighth grade I attended German schools. For high school, I had the good fortune to attend a Canadian high school in Germany. This allowed me to learn English, meet many life long friends, and develop many interests. My interests range from soccer (I played competitively and currently coach high school students), to music (I play the piano) to literature (in German and in English), to carpentry (the design and construction of pine furniture), to water colors (the ultimate expression of creativity), to travel (as evidenced by my coming to Canada).

When I was a 16 year old high school student I decided that I wanted to study architecture and become an architect. But, what is architecture and why did I want to study it?

> **architecture** *1. the art or science of building, including plan, design, construction and decorative treatment. 2. the character or style of building; the architecture of Paris. 3. the action or process of building; construction. 4. a building. 5. buildings collectively. The American College Dictionary*

Architecture is both an art and a science. The creativity involved in the design of buildings, with emphasis on character, style and decoration appealed to my creative side. The precision involved in construction and the fact that a building is tangible and of practical use to its occupants appealed to my practical side. The process of building and construction appeals to my need for accomplishment and to see the growth and development of my work.

During my last year of high school I applied to the School Of Architecture at the University Of Waterloo. The bad news is that (I was crushed) I was not accepted by the School Of Architecture. The good news is that I was accepted into the Faculty Of Science which led me along the road to the study of landscape architecture. I believe that an understanding of landscape architecture is necessary for a true understanding and appreciation of the study of architecture. I have just finished my degree in landscape architecture. But, I am not satisfied. My background in landscape architecture is further driving my interest in architecture. My hunger to study architecture is now stronger than it ever has been.

My study of landscape architecture has taught me that one cannot understand landscape architecture without understanding architecture and vice-versa. Therefore, I feel that the completion of my degree in landscape architecture is like completing the first chapter of a two chapter book. The study of architecture will be the second chapter of my academic career. A degree in architecture, coupled with my degree in landscape architecture will give me a "cross-professional" education. This will be of great value in today's marketplace.

Both, landscape architecture and architecture are concerned with the development and maintenance of our precious environment. My studies in landscape architecture have demonstrated to me that all construction in our environment can and should be a creative process. For architecture to be healthy, powerful, and pleasurable, it must be intelligent, practical, and creative. In fact, the health and growth of our society is a function of the amount of creativity involved. Creativity blossoms wherever a holistic approach to life is nurtured. Although computers have their role in design, they are good servants but bad masters. Ultimately buildings should be built:

"By the people, for the people and be of the people!"

On a practical note, I have ample work experience in the design and construction of residential renovations (4 major renovations totaling an approximate value of $300,000). Each of these experiences was a challenging and wonderful learning experience. During each project I encountered problems (sometimes relating to landscaping and sometimes relating to building) where I simply did not know what to do. But, I adopted the attitude that:

"When the going gets tough, the tough get creative!"

And get creative I did. Whether it was the relationship with the client, the problem solving work, the building blocks, or the actual design process, I brought each of my projects to successful completion. Each project had its own unique lesson to teach me. I am proud of what I learned and accomplished from each of these projects.

The 4 renovations have also been important to me for financial reasons. Since arriving in Canada the responsibility for my financial support has been my own. As a result, I have had many part time and summer jobs. I have delivered pizza, shoveled snow, distributed advertising materials, worked in a pub, pumped gas and managed the 4 residential renovations previously described. Although each of my part time jobs has been important to me, it has been my experience with the renovations that has taught me about the construction business and whetted my interest in design and architecture.

I know many students currently enrolled in the School Of Architecture at The University Of British Columbia. As a result I know that the community is exceptional and the school has a strong emphasis on the creativity and design process. Furthermore, in the Faculty Of Architecture, personal friendships and life enhancing experiences (through study abroad) are actively promoted. I am excited about the prospect of attending UBC. Furthermore, with my background in landscape architecture I will be able to contribute to the program.

I am now 26 years old. For 10 years I have wanted to study architecture. I am anxious to begin this second chapter of my academic career. Thank you for considering my application. I hope to begin the Master Of Architecture program at UBC this fall!

CHAPTER 7

Effective Letters Of Recommendation

A Guide For The Applicant

Some schools use letters. Some don't. Some of those who don't will read them if sent. Others won't. But, each of you will be applying to at least one school that requires at least one letter of recommendation.

Although letters of recommendation are third party statements they are very controllable. Actually, the phrase "recommendation" may be a misnomer. Few "recommendation" writers will compromise their personal integrity. As a result, I have seen many letters that are either neutral to the point of being useless or go so far as to suggest that the applicant be rejected. At the other extreme, I have seen many letters that are certain to enhance the applicant's chances of receiving an offer of admission. This part of the book has been designed to help get the most out of the "marketing opportunity" that letters of "recommendation" afford.

From Whom Should You Seek Letters?

You should seek letters from someone who is in a **position to comment** on something **that the school considers relevant.** In most cases, the prestige of the writer is irrelevant. Applicants often seek letters from famous graduates of the school, famous professors, lawyers, politicians, judges, etc. Unless the person can comment on factors that the school considers relevant you will have wasted an opportunity to market yourself effectively.

Who Is In A Position To Comment?

In a perfect world one could say that the best recommenders are people who:

1. Are Objective - Avoid getting a letter from someone too close to you.

2. Know You Well - Seek a recommender who can comment on the most important activities in your life.

3. Have special skills or experiences that make them good judges of applicants. Examples may include employers who have been able to observe your job performance and can comment on your motivation, ability to work, and level of responsibility. Coaches and trainers who know you well from frequent contact can often comment on your drive, dedication, and persistence. Some professors and teaching assistants will also qualify. But remember every recommender must comment on **matters that the school considers relevant**.

So, What Does The School Consider Relevant?

"Remember that law schools are academic institutions interested in your academic potential. University and college faculty are the people whose judgments tend to carry the most weight with admissions personnel. Therefore, try to have at least one letter from a professor in your major field of study (even if you have been out of school for a while)."

The Right Law School For You

Academic ability is not the only consideration. Schools also want to know that you will bring your academic ability to bear on your professional or graduate program. Hence, letters that comment on drive, dedication, and other similar qualities will be helpful.

(In the case of MBA applications, applicants may have been away from school for some years. A letter from an employer who can comment on the current state of your life is often more helpful. Academic ability is likely to be presumed from previous grades and GMAT scores.)

Academic References

All schools are interested in your ability to do their academic work. Therefore, many schools require that at least one of the letters be an academic reference. A professor is a logical choice. Those of you who do not know professors may want to consider teaching assistants. (Often the teaching assistant knows you in a way that the professor does not.)

Remember that an academic reference is for the purpose of hearing what a professor says about your ability to do university work. Therefore, you should do your best to ensure that the letter comes from a university professor.

Those applying in the residual categories (mature student, etc.) may have more difficulty getting a current academic reference. The schools understand this. If you cannot get a current academic reference ask yourself what qualities are consistent with and lead to superior academic performance. (Examples may include: discipline, strong writing and organizational skills, motivation, etc.) Consider getting a reference from someone who can comment on these qualities. (See particularly Sample 4 of the samples I have provided. It is a good example of how to get an academic reference from a non-academic source.)

Every applicant should do his best to ensure that there is at least one strong academic reference in the file. Non-academic references should be used as a supplement to and not a substitute for academic references!

Non-academic References

In selecting non-academic references ask: can this writer comment on something in which this particular school has an interest? Remember, beyond academic ability, different schools may be looking for different things. For example:

- If community service is relevant then you may want to get a letter from someone who has worked with you in that capacity.

- If employment history is relevant then you may want to get a letter from an employer.

- If your medical history is somehow relevant then you may want to get a letter from a doctor.

How Unorthodox Can A Non-Academic Reference Be?

There is no right or wrong answer to this question. Ask: what are you trying to contribute to your application file by using a certain letter? Remember that the application file is greater than the sum of its parts. Consider whether the inclusion of the letter (in conjunction with other parts of the file) improve or diminish the overall effect?

An Exercise In Determining Suitability

Consider the following example.

Imagine that you are opposed to the death penalty and that your reason for attending law school is that you want to do "death-penalty work." Imagine also that you have spent a great deal of time working with an inmate who has received the death penalty and is waiting for his execution. You consider this particular inmate to be articulate and intelligent. **Should you get a letter of recommendation from him?**

This question was posed to a number of experienced pre-law advisers in the U.S. Here are samples of the answers received.

> "Our committee would be happy to receive such a letter on your behalf."

> "If I were you I would try to demonstrate your qualities in more traditional ways. This would ensure that the letter will not be ignored."

> "The letter would be attention getting and would distinguish you from other applicants."

> "I would use this as an additional letter and not as a substitute for the required ones. Some admissions officers will find it helpful but others will ignore it."

> "The schools want academic references that compare you to other applicants. This person could not write such a letter."

Authors opinion: I have the following thoughts.

1. If used, it should be used as a supplement to the academic reference(s).

2. If used, it should be used only if your interest in working with death row inmates is relevant to your application to a particular law school. It could be relevant in two ways. First, it is arguably evidence of community service for a lengthy period of time. Second, it could improve the effectiveness of your personal statement by lending additional credibility to the claims made in it.

3. Use of this letter does have a degree of risk. Experienced pre-law advisers have given different advice about the suitability of this letter.

How Many Letters Should You Send?

In general, you should not exceed the required number of letters. Consider this question from the perspective of the admissions committee. First, you are burdening the committee with extra work. Second, you are not following directions. Finally, you will find it difficult to obtain two good letters. The more letters you submit, the greater the chances of the positive impact of the good letters being diminished by weaker letters.

Select Your Referees To Avoid Repetitive Information

Every letter should be thought of as an **additional** marketing opportunity. Therefore, you should try to obtain letters that complement each other rather than repeat each other. I have already alluded to the possibility of using letters to enhance certain parts of your personal statement.

Avoid a recommender who will simply repeat what is already on your transcript. Example:

To The Committee:

"Stanley Student was in my political science course. He got an A."

Yours Truly,
Professor X."

This letter simply repeats something from another part of the file. It is repetitive and is therefore a wasted marketing opportunity.

How To Qualify People To Write Letters For You

You are now at the point where you have decided who you are going to ask. You have no right to see the letter and the letter should be sent directly by the writer. Obviously you must be careful. Never ask somebody if he/she would be willing to write a letter on your behalf. Remember, they might write an unhelpful letter. In most cases you will not have the opportunity to see the letter before it is sent. So, you must protect yourself by asking the right qualifying question. The right question is:

"Do you feel that you could **and** would you be willing to write me a positive letter of recommendation?"

If the person answers "yes", then the person has agreed not only to write the letter but to write a positive letter. The person is now qualified.

Qualification Isn't Enough - The Person Must Now Be Educated!

You now have a willing partner in the letter writing process. Your next job is to help the writer do the best that he/she can. Schedule an appointment with the writer. Show the writer your personal statement and all other parts of your application file. Specifically you should bring:

- your transcripts;

- personal statement;

- resume and/or autobiographical sketch;

- photocopies of anything you want the writer to specifically refer to.

Suggest the importance of all parts of the file working together. Alert the writer to any special programs to which you are applying. Tell the writer who else is writing on your behalf. In short, give the writer as much information as you can. All of these things should be done well before the deadline date. It takes the better part of a full day to write an effective letter of recommendation. Be respectful of this. Make sure that you thank the writer for his/her hard work. You should offer to pick up any out of pocket costs. Don't forget to notify the writer where you were accepted.

How To Deal With Standard Form Letters

Many schools or application forms include "standard forms" for recommenders to use. Frequently these "forms" are not a required form of letter, but rather a convenience for the writer. In most cases your recommender will be able to do a better job for you by writing his/her own letter and attaching this letter to the standard form. First, ensure that a "non-standard form" letter is allowed. Then encourage the recommender to NOT use that "standard form" and attach the letter to the "standard form."

The Necessity To Follow Up

Ultimately it is your responsibility to ensure that your file is complete. It is important that the letter be sent directly from the writer. (Some writers will allow you to see the letter and others will not.) Take steps to ensure that the letter(s) has actually been sent and received. Make sure that you thank the writer and notify the writer where you have been accepted.

A Guide For The Recommender

Those in the academic community generally know how to write letters of recommendation. These comments are not directed toward them. But, potential recommenders in the non-academic community may have never written a letter of this type. For example, an employer or clergyman may be very anxious to help, but simply not know how. These suggestions are primarily for them. In addition, these suggestions are just that - suggestions. There is no one way to write an effective letter of reference.

If you have read this far, I assume that you have been asked to write a letter and are seeking some guidance. Begin by reading the sample letters included in this book. Look at both the academic references and the non-academic references and see how they supply facts, convey enthusiasm and help the applicant come to life.

I would like to offer two sets of guidelines for the letter writing process. First, guidelines for an initial meeting with the applicant. Second, guidelines for the actual writing.

Guidelines For The Initial Meeting

The applicant should supply the recommender with all the other components of the application file. Ask the applicant to bring a current resume. Review these documents with the applicant. Try to determine how your letter is to fit in with the marketing of the applicant as a whole. Ask if there are any special considerations that should be discussed at any specific law school. Agree on whether the applicant will have an opportunity to see the letter. Ask who else may be writing a letter in support of the applicant. Clarify deadline dates, number of letters, addresses, etc. Remember that the complete application file is the "marketing tool." Your job is to add a specific component to the file so that the whole file has an effect that is greater than the sum of the individual parts.

Guidelines For Actually Writing

Your meeting with the applicant is complete. Now you are ready to collect your thoughts and write. Here are some suggestions.

1. Introduce yourself and describe your qualifications to assess the applicant.

2. Explain how you know the applicant, for how long and under what circumstances.

3. Supply specific factual evidence that will support the conclusions that you want the reader to infer.

4. Compare the applicant to other people you have observed.

5. Try to make the applicant come alive as a person by:

   A. writing in such a way that it is clear that you know the applicant;

   B. writing so that you convey your enthusiasm about the applicant.

6. At all times imagine that you are a witness in a trial. You must show that you are qualified to make judgments about the applicant, have had the opportunity to observe the applicant, have actually observed the applicant and support the applicant both as an individual and in comparison to others that you have observed.

Good Writing Is Like Good Cooking - It Takes Time

Ensure that you leave yourself enough time to write, put it aside, reflect on what you have written and rewrite. An effective letter has the potential to make a difference in the applicant's life. The applicant will appreciate your efforts.

SOME SAMPLE LETTERS OF REFERENCE

Samples - Academic References

Sample 1:

Dear Sir/Madame:

RE: **Stanley Student**
     John Franklin University

For a number of years I taught a part-time course at John Franklin University entitled Introduction to the International Law Of Human Rights - Political Science 410. This was a challenging course intended for second and upper year students during the course of which students were required to read, analyze and digest a large number of judicial decisions as well as participate in the classes/seminars. Evaluation was on the basis of a term test, a major paper and final examination.

I recall Stanley Student from the 1993 fall session as having been in regular attendance, always obviously prepared and an active and able participant in the class. He wrote an excellent paper for the course dealing with the complexities of the law of citizenship as it is influenced by the International Covenant On Civil And Political Rights.

Based on my experience of him in my course, I am of the opinion that he clearly has the ability and diligence to successfully complete a course of studies in law and would advocate his admission to the school.

Yours very truly,

Stephen H. Adjunct, LL.B.

Author's Comments: This is not a particularly helpful letter. I am left with the impression that the writer has neither the knowledge of, nor interest in, the applicant to do a good job. There is no enthusiasm in this letter. Compare this letter to the next two.

Sample 2:

Members of the Admissions Committee:

Re: Stanley Student

Stanley Student has asked me to supply you with a letter of reference in support of his application for admission to your program. Stanley has been a student of mine in Labor Economics (fall 1993) and advanced econometrics (fall 1994). I have been teaching at John Franklin University since 1971 and before that as a doctoral student, I taught at the University of California for 4 years. I am one of 9 full professors in our department of 39.

Stanley Student would fit into the top 100 students I have taught, measured against approximately 12,000 students. He may not have all the theoretical courses as background that some of the other top 100 would have, but he has the logic, the maturity, the clarity, and the communication skills, all of which I view as extremely important in his planned career.

In my labor economics class, students participated in debate and in the advanced econometrics class, there were presentations. Stanley excelled in both. Without being loud or interruptive, Stanley was a ready and regular participant in class discussion and always added value to such discussions, a rare occurrence indeed. His writing skills are similarly strong.

Stanley Student participated as a representative of the class and the University at the Foundation For Economic Education and was selected there to attend a session on investment and free market economics. He readily shared what he had learned when he returned to campus. Despite the age difference (6 to 8 years), I found Stanley to be held in high regard by his peers and indeed there was close cooperation instead of a coldness often accorded excellent students.

Economics is extremely demanding and I am not noted as an easy grader. Stanley topped both classes that I taught. Economics also has a reputation for forcing students to use logic, the same logic which is a necessary characteristic of "excellent" lawyers.

I am aware of and share Stanley Students ethical concerns. I believe he would be a highly professional individual, both as a student and as a member of the bar.

It has been a pleasure to write for Stanley Student. I hope you take account of the demands of the earliest period of his enrollment (carrying a full-term job and many related activities) and look at his full-time marks as being more representative of his ability. I cannot think of another reference to law school that I have written where I felt as strongly about the student's ability to complete law school. That may be seen by the A+ and A which I assigned him as first in both my classes.

Sincerely yours,
John M. Keynes, Ph.D.
Professor of Economics

Author's Comments: This is a superb letter. The author demonstrates that he is well qualified, writes with enthusiasm and compares the applicant to other students. The author uses lots of very specific examples to provide independent evidence in support of his claims. In summary, this letter provides lots of detailed evidence that the admissions committee can use.

Sample 3:

The Registrar
Faculty of Law
Justice Law School

Dear Sir:

I am writing a letter of reference for Sarah Student who is a student in my Russian literature course.

Ms. Student is an outstanding student. In the first term Ms. Student has received "A" grades in all four written essays (two research essays and two test essays) and "A" grades in both oral reports. In these essays as well as in her oral reports, she has demonstrated superior analytical and communicative skills. I am impressed with her exceptional ability to identify the central thesis and to develop her argument with clarity and with well-chosen and well-documented examples.

The literature course which I am teaching is an intensive seminar with a heavy reading list of nineteenth century Russian literary texts in English translation. The texts in the course present complex moral, philosophical and social issues. This course is also very demanding and students must participate actively. Sarah Student is always well prepared for class and participates enthusiastically in class discussions. In class discussions as in her written work, she identifies major issues and presents her arguments persuasively and lucidly.

Sarah Student also has excellent skills in interacting with other students in the seminar. Clearly her extensive experience in community work and human rights issues as well as her work in administration, management and education have been an asset and have provided her with valuable insight and skills in interacting with other people.

Ms. Student is one of the best students that I have ever taught. My qualifications include a Ph.D. in Comparative and Slavic Literature and twenty years of teaching experience.

Yours sincerely,
Dr. Shelia Wisdom
Associate Professor

Author's Comments: This is a superb letter. The author demonstrates that she is well qualified, writes with enthusiasm and compares the applicant to other students. The author uses lots of very specific examples to provide independent evidence in support of his claims. In summary, this letter provides lots of detailed evidence that the admissions committee can use.

Samples - Non-Academic References

Sample 4:

To The Admissions Officer
Any Law School
Anytown, Canada

To The Admissions Committee:

Re: **Stanley Student**

Stanley Student has asked me to write as a referee as part of his application for law school. In my judgment, Stanley is educationally, intellectually and emotionally well suited for the study of law. I am very pleased to write in his support. Frankly, I know of nobody whom I could more enthusiastically recommend for the study of law. Allow me to elaborate.

My background is in law. I hold both U.S. and Canadian law degrees and am a member of the bar of the Province Of Ontario and the states of Massachusetts and New York. In addition, I teach and work with a number of pre-law students. As a result, I have extensive and regular contact with "would be" law students. I first met Stanley in 1987 when he was a student in one of my courses. I have kept up with him since that time. For the last year Stanley has assisted me in instructing a course that I teach to prepare students for the Law School Admission Test. You can see from his transcripts and academic achievements that Stanley is a gifted scholar. In addition to his being a first rate scholar, he is a first rate teacher!

When Stanley approached me to write on his behalf, I asked him why he wanted to study law. As you can see from his academic records Stanley is completing his Masters Degree in the philosophy of law. His dissertation will discuss the rationing of health care from a sociological, ethical and philosophical point of view. My many conversations with him reveal that Stanley realizes that social, ethical and philosophical problems are intimately connected to legal problems. In addition to an independent interest in the study and practise of law, Stanley sees a law degree as a way of improving his work in the area of philosophy of law in general and his dissertation topic in particular. A law degree will equip him to consider constitutional and other legal issues relating to the right to health care.

I recognize that there are a finite number of spaces in your program.

Hence, it is in your interest to ensure that students you accept will benefit from your program and that participants in the program will also benefit from other students. As well as being intelligent and an accomplished student, Stanley is **intellectually suited to the study and practice of law.** From my many conversations with him I have learned that he has a fine mind for discerning and developing general principles and determining to what extent these principles apply to specific factual situations. Stanley is a "natural" at legal reasoning and has an agile and inquiring mind. I expect that he will be a first rate legal scholar.

Stanley has the maturity and discipline that required to excel at law school. During his work with me as a teaching assistant, I have observed that he understands the value and necessity of hard, consistent and disciplined work. Furthermore, he puts his understanding into practice. To put it simply, Stanley has the values and work ethic that are needed to excel at law school.

Finally, Stanley is generous with his time and talents. On numerous occasions, I have seen him assist both his peers and students. (In many cases going far beyond what one would reasonably expect.) Should Stanley attend your school, I have every reason to believe that he will enhance the lives of his colleagues. Certainly, he has been a positive influence in my life.

In closing, I repeat that I enthusiastically support Stanley's application to law school in general and the University of _____ in particular. His academic qualifications are evident from his transcripts. His values, ethics, character, effectiveness and belief in hard work make all those around him perform better!

Sincerely yours,
John Robertson, LL.B., J.D.

Author's Comments: This is a cross between an academic and non-academic reference. It is in part an academic reference from a non-academic person. Applicants having difficulty getting a real academic reference should take note!

Sample 5:

To The Admissions Officer
Any Law School
Anytown, Canada

To The Admissions Committee:

Re: **Stanley Student**

Please accept this as a letter in enthusiastic support of the application of Stanley Student to the faculty of law.

I have known Stanley's family for approximately 20 years. Stanley's older brother and I were roommates at University. At that time Stanley was approximately 3 years old. I am currently a Chartered Financial Analyst and have developed a financial planning company. Beginning in 1990 I began the process of franchising the Financial Planning Offices.

Although I have been a friend of Stanley's brother since 1974 I did not meet Stanley until 1983. In 1989 he immigrated to Canada from Germany. Since that time he has been employed in my business (full time in 1994 and part time prior to 1994). He is a likable young man who I also consider to be a personal friend.

The process of franchising my financial planning business has required the planning and marketing of seminars aimed at potential franchisees. Over the years Stanley has been involved in every aspect of this. He has designed promotional material, arranged for its printing, handled its distribution, been the contact person for those attending the seminars, and handled every other aspect of this business. This has always been a big job. But, what is most significant is that he accomplished these tasks with a minimum of direction. He always took the initiative to ensure that what needed to be done was done. During my 20 years in business I have worked with a number of students and young adults. To put it simply, Stanley has been the best, most responsible, effective and trustworthy employee with whom I have had the pleasure of working. Although he is in his early 20s, he has the maturity and common sense of a person much older.

During 1994 Stanley worked with me on a full time basis. It was also the best growth year that I have had. The spectacular growth during 1994 was largely attributable to Stanley's work. During this time period, Stanley reorganized our whole marketing program. He recreated both our promotional material and its method of distribution. Stanley has a unique ability to put a "new spin" on old ideas and the ingenuity and ability to see a project through to completion. Many of his ideas are still being used by my company.

Stanley has demonstrated that he is a highly intelligent, competent, and effective person. But he is also a pleasure to be around. He interests range from soccer to piano to history to simply being around people. His experience growing up in Germany has given him a cross-cultural perspective that should serve him well in later years. In addition to his accomplishments, integrity and strengths of character, Stanley is a "nice guy."

I enthusiastically support his application to the faculty of law.

Yours truly,
James R. Wealth III, CFA

Author's Comments: As you can see this is a letter from an employer. Notice that the letter includes more than a statement about the applicant as an employee.

Chapter 8

The Interview As A Marketing Tool!

What Is An Interview?

Interviews for professional schools are the same as interviews for jobs. In a job interview your job is to market yourself to an employer. In an interview for a professional school your job is to market yourself to the school. In other words, an interview is a "sales call." The interview and the other parts of your application file are for the purpose of "selling yourself" to the school.

Why Would A School Interview Applicants?

A good question. Interviews consume a great deal of time. They are difficult to organize. Therefore, a school will conduct an interview because they think that a live interview will provide information that is not available from other parts of the application file. The application file is a careful and deliberate marketing initiative. Applicants have time to think about how to respond to the questions. Some applicants develop the file over a period of months. The interview will reveal how you respond to questions spontaneously. The way you answer questions and the content of your answers will assist in the process of image creation. These images will either confirm or contradict information in your file. Your "live performance" will reveal a great deal about you!

Any live contact with the school will leave an impression. This includes any telephone call or entry into the admissions office. Take steps to ensure that every time the school has any contact with you that you leave a positive image. I know of one law student who had been placed on the waiting list. During the summer she called to ask about the status of her application. During this conversation she had a lengthy discussion with the admissions officer. She left the admissions officer with a definite impression about what kind of person she was. The next day she received an offer of acceptance. She feels that her informal conversation with the admissions officer was part of the reason she was admitted. Therefore, you should treat any interaction with the school as being part of an ongoing interview!

Interviews - What Kinds Of Schools Interview?

Law schools rarely conduct interviews. Business schools sometimes conduct interviews. Medical schools are likely to conduct interviews and they are an important part of the process of applying to medical school.

Law Schools

Applicants In The Regular Category

I am aware of only one law school that interviews applicants in the regular applicant category and that school does not interview all applicants in that category. At this particular school many applicants are admitted without an interview. An invitation to an interview is no guarantee of acceptance. Many applicants who are interviewed are rejected. For *most* applicants in the "regular applicant" category, interviews are not part of the application process. Some U.S. schools invite applicants on the waiting list to an interview.

Applicants In One Of The Residual Categories

Many applicants in the "mature" or other residual categories can expect an interview to be part of the admissions process. Interviews are not granted to all applicants. Therefore, the interview is something that is achieved based on the strength of the application file.

MBA

It is impossible to generalize. There are MBA programs throughout the world. Interviews are part of the process at some schools and not at others. The schools that hold interviews may interview only some or all applicants. At some schools applicants may request interviews.

Medical School

Interviews are a part of the application process at most medical schools. Few applicants will be invited to interviews. Therefore, an interview is something that an applicant to medical schools *achieves* by virtue of having a stellar application file.

The Steps To A Successful Interview

Imagine yourself to be a lawyer who is required to argue a case before a court made up of judges. The court requires that you first submit your arguments in writing. You then have the opportunity to make an oral presentation which is to be largely based on your written material. The judges will have read your written material in advance. They may begin by asking you questions about it. Although these questions will control the direction that the hearing will take, through your answers you are anxious to control the content. Although you are anxious to answer any questions that you are asked, there are some specific facts that you want to ensure the court hears about. You are given one hour to make your oral arguments on a fixed day at an appointed time. On that day your job is to deliver the most effective presentation possible and to answer the judges questions in an effective way. You cannot anticipate all the questions. Therefore, it is important that you are sufficiently flexible to respond to anything that might be asked. Furthermore, you know that your presentation will be most effective if you engage the judges in a dialogue. This will keep the presentation more interesting. Not only must you be an effective lawyer. You must look like an effective lawyer. Therefore, you understand that you must be well groomed and well dressed. As the date for your court presentation draws near, you attempt to learn the identity of the judges who will actually hear your case. You learn anything else that you can about the court.

The lawyer's written arguments are analogous to the application file without the interview. The oral arguments are analogous to the interview.

Organizing Yourself For The Interview

Step 1: Know Yourself - The Seller

General

You must know yourself in a general way. Rethink your values, interests and goals.

Career/Academic

Be prepared to answer: Why Law/MBA/Med school? Why at this school? Why at this stage of your life?

Step 2: Know The School - The Buyer

The Specific Type Of Academic Program

Learn about the curriculum in a medical school or MBA program. What exactly is the program about it? How does completion of the program relate to your professional and career goals?

School Specific Opportunities

If the school has a specific niche or area of specialization, you should know about it and be interested in it.

Step 3: Prepare For The Interview

Research

Anticipate possible questions.

Read the papers. Be familiar with current events as they bear on your chosen profession. For example, what are current government initiatives in the area of health care? Should the government cut funding to legal aid?

Practice

If possible do some practice interviewing. Ideally, this should be done with somebody who is experienced in admissions or has been through the process. Doctors, lawyers, MBAs or students who have been on admissions committees are good choices.

Prepare Questions You Would Like To Ask

Think of questions you would like to ask if given the opportunity.

Step 4: Logistical And Tactical Considerations

If given a choice schedule the earliest possible interview.

Know where the building is. Know where the room is.

Arrange to arrive three or four minutes early.

Prepare to dress appropriately. Remember the interview is a "sales call." Be well groomed. Have your clothes laid out the night before.

Bring a copy of every document in your application file.

Step 5: Conducting The Interview

The interviewer will control the *direction* through the questions. You will control the *content* of the interview through your answers.

Respond to the questions asked. Don't *react*. Think about your answer.

Don't sit on the fence. Answer questions decisively. In life it is more important to be decisive than it is to be right.

Be positive. Maintain eye contact. Smile and be animated. Make sure that you display a firm handshake.

Don't disparage anybody or any school under any circumstances.

If you don't know an answer, simply say so.

Appear interested in the interview.

Don't exhibit relief when the interview is over.

And finally,   **Never Interrupt The Interviewer!**

Step 6: It's Over - What Now?

Send a thank you note. In most cases, the interview is a privilege which you have earned.

Some Hypothetical Interview Questions

1.   What characteristics do you have that would make you an outstanding _____?

2.   Tell me about your greatest strength or greatest weakness.

3.   Where do you see yourself 10 years from now?

4.   How do you feel about increasing government involvement in the legal/medical profession?

5.   What appeals to you about our school?

6.   What is your favorite book?

7.   What have you read lately?

8.   What if you found that your friend had cheated on the LSAT/MCAT/

GMAT? Would you report him/her?

9. How did you choose your undergraduate institution and area of academic concentration?

10. How has your undergraduate major prepared you for Law/MBA/Med or Grad school?

11. Why should we choose you over all the other applicants we have?

12. What do you know about our school?

13. You have had an interesting career. Why do you want to go to Law/ MBA/Med or Grad school anyway?

14. Who is your favorite historical figure? Why?

15. What do you think is the strongest part of your application file? What do you think is the weakest?

And Finally - A Picture Is Worth 1000 Words

Interviews, when used, are the final step of the marketing process. If the school goes to the trouble to interview you, the interview will be a major factor in determining your fate!

Chapter 9

Brave New World - Boldly Go!

The Brave New World Of Professional And Graduate School Admissions

Electronic Applications, Testing And Research

In their brief lifetime computers have had a profound effect on all aspects of life. They are beginning to play a major role in the process of applying to professional and graduate schools. Traditionally the application process has consumed lots of paper - most of which is wasted. Think of all the printed application forms, letter of reference forms and calendars of information. Much of this is distributed at great expense to many people who file it in the garbage. Think of the duplication of basic information when applicants apply to a number of schools. Because of computer technology and the internet much of this printing and duplication of effort is no longer necessary. Consider the following four examples of computer aids in the admissions process.

The Computer Generated Application

Applying to U.S. law schools? It is no longer necessary to obtain individual application forms from each school. Law Services (the folks who brought you the LSAT) has developed a CD rom that acts both as a tool to research the individual law schools and also generates specific applications for each of the 179 ABA approved law schools. The applicant saves time by inputting the core information only once. The program then places the information into the appropriate field for each school's application. The program has also been designed to help applicants develop and edit personal statements so that they can be targeted to the requirements of each school. It is inexpensive. The application is then submitted to the individual schools. For information on this product check out the Law Service's web site at www.lsac.org.

There are also two private companies that have developed a similar product.

Download Your Application Form From The School's Web Site

The Faculty of Law at the University of Victoria is an example of a school that will allow you to download the application form from their web site. Why should they print it and incur the expense of sending it out? This is a simple and cost efficient approach. I am certain that all schools will eventually develop the same option.

What About Applying On-Line To Specific Schools?

You can already register for your LSAT or GMAT on-line. The next step will be to apply to the school in the same way. You will see a lot more of this during the next few years.

The Submission Of The Application File On Diskette

Applicants to U.S. and Canadian medical schools apply on one application form to a centralized facility that handles all the administrative work. You can now download a program that guides you through the process of submitting your application file on a diskette rather than on paper. Are you interested to see how this works? Check out the following two web sites: www.aamc.org and http://ouacinfo.ouac.on.ca. Applicants to Ontario law schools also apply on a single application form to a centralized facility. How long will it be before Ontario law school applicants will be submitting their application files on diskette rather than paper?

Computer Adaptive Testing

The traditional "paper and pencil" LSAT, GMAT, GRE and possibly MCAT are on the brink of extinction. GMATs and GREs are now administered on computer. Law Services is currently developing a version of the LSAT to be administered on computer. (This includes certain question types that are not multiple choice.) By the turn of the century the "paper and pencil" LSAT may be a relic of the past.

Researching Schools On The Internet

It is important to research each individual school. This includes reading the calendar of information. Virtually all schools have all of their application information (including the calendar of information) on their web site. This allows applicants to obtain more current information, at less cost to both the school and the applicant.

Richardson-Law School Bound® E-Mail Newsletter

I publish a monthly newsletter for pre-law students. But, I don't print it and I don't mail it out. It is free to anyone with an e-mail account. If you are interested in becoming a subscriber send me an e-mail to learn@prep.com. Check out our web site at www.prep.com!

In Summary ...

I predict that virtually all aspects of the application and admissions process will be handled by computer and the internet. It is even possible to do the interview through videoconferencing. This is the "Brave New World" of professional and graduate school admissions!

CHAPTER 10

Percentile Performance - What is Effective Test Prep?

Multiple Choice Is Your Friend!

"The 23rd Rule Of Life"

"Multiple choice is my friend; I shall not worry.

It maketh me love taking tests and teacheth me what a number 2 pencil is for. It gives my life new meaning (Life is nothing more than a long multiple choice test).

It leadeth me down the right road to the answer in spite of my ignorance.

Yea though I live with the terror of logical games, I will fear no failure.

Thy susceptibility to the power of answer elimination comforts me.

Thy format inspires me because I know the right answer lies before my very eyes.

It giveth me the ability to identify the answer even though I understand nothing.

Confidence and right answers shall follow me through the "test preparation stage of my life" and I will be healthy, wealthy and wise for the rest of my days."

- The Wise Words Of A Test Prep Coach

Percentile Performance! - What Is Effective Test Prep?

Applicants to law school, medical school or business school are required to take multiple choice standardized tests. Law school applicants must take the LSAT. Medical school applicants must take the MCAT. MBA applicants must take the GMAT. Many graduate programs require the GRE as part of the admissions process.

Your test score will play a major role in determining the success of your application. You must take steps to score well. Effective preparation is essential. The purpose of this chapter is to explain how to think about the test preparation process.

But first, where do you get information about the tests?

LSAT   - (215) 968-1001 or www.lsac.org

GMAT   - (609) 771-7330 or 1 800 GMAT NOW or www.gmat.org

GRE   - (609) 771-7670 or 1 800 967-1100 or www.gre.org

MCAT   - (319) 337-1357 or www.aamc.org

Should you prepare?

Yes! Even the test designers acknowledge that preparation improves performance.

For how long should you prepare?

There is no general answer to this question. It depends on you. It depends on your background skills, your initial level of performance and how high of a score you need. Practice testing with real exams will yield realistic score projections.

How should you go about the preparation process?

Everybody buys books. Some people take courses. What books should you buy and what courses should you take?

Books containing real test questions

First, the good news. In each case, the test designer publishes books of actual questions. Since the use of actual questions is essential in the preparation process, you must acquire these books. Examples:

LSAT - Contact Law Services for copies of actual past LSATs. Visit Law Services on their web site at www.lsac.org.

GMAT - Purchase the current edition of **The Official Guide For GMAT Review**. In addition, GMAT publishes software with computer adaptive GMAT tests. Visit GMAT on their web site at www.gmat.org.

GRE - Purchase the current edition of **Practicing To Take The GRE**. GRE also publishes Powerprep software which contains computer adaptive tests. Visit GRE on their web site at www.gre.org.

MCAT - Purchase the materials published by the AAMC. These include official MCAT tests I, II, III, MCAT Practice Items and the MCAT Student Manual. Visit the AAMC on their web site at www.aamc.org.

Now, the bad news. In the case of LSAT and MCAT the sample questions come with answers but no commentary. In the case of the GMAT and GRE the commentary is devoid of any approach to answering the questions. **As a result, most people need additional books or courses to learn systematic approaches for the identification of correct answers.**

"After Market" Books Containing Commentary

Definition - "After market" books are books about the tests that are not written by the test designers.

First, the good news. Some "after market" books contain excellent commentary that will teach you approaches that may be applied to actual test questions.

Now, the bad news. In most cases "after market" books don't use actual test questions. If the acquisition of sample questions, is your reason for purchasing a book, you are better off simply purchasing the actual test questions from the test designer. In other words, "after market" books should be used for commentary and not for practice questions.

Courses - Should You Take One?

A long time test prep instructor once made the point that:

> "A good course will help some people a lot and a lot of people some."

There are many courses all claiming to do the same thing. Some are excellent. Some are terrible. It pays to do research when selecting a course.

How Should You Research And Select A Test Prep Course?

Recently I received the following email from a student:

> "I find that these days there's so many LSAT prep courses that are being offered to students. As a student I find it hard to know which course will prove beneficial to me.... I would appreciate any form of guidance you could offer."

Here is the text of my reply:

> "I know that there are a lot of courses. They all promise the same things and market in the same ways. So I agree, if I were a student, I would have difficulty deciding what to choose as well.
>
> The first point that I would make is that everybody has access to actual past exams. It is essential that you have lots of exposure to actual exams. So, make sure that the course you choose uses actual exams.
>
> The second point that I would make is that you don't take a course from a test prep company (although you do give your money to them), you take a course from a specific instructor. So, you want to go "instructor shopping."
>
> The third point is that your good instructor must be teaching systematic approaches rooted in the design and concepts of the actual test. A systematic approach will teach you how to proceed when you don't know the answer to the question.
>
> Now let's look at your options.
>
> First, there are the companies that try to run courses everywhere (national companies). They tend to be at the more expensive end of the market. These companies are in the position of having to hire a lot of instructors. Although, I am sure that many of these instructors are good, they have so many that you want to inquire about the experience level and ability of the specific instructor teaching the exact section in which you wish to enroll.

Second, you have local, private companies. They tend to be smaller operations, with fewer instructors. The quality of instruction can be very high (especially if the company owner/operator is doing the teaching). It takes a long time to become an effective teacher of test prep courses.

Third, the continuing education divisions of local colleges and universities often run courses. But, they rarely have their own course. They simply put their name on somebody else's course and contract with the other person to deliver the course. I am not judging whether a university course is good or bad. (I have personally taught LSAT and GMAT courses for universities.) I am simply saying that it probably was not developed by the university and has no connection with it.

Fourth, short courses or long courses? In the test prep industry, courses range in length from the convenient weekend format to courses that lasts for months. I have authored test preparation books. I also have taught all variations of courses over the years. Every person has his/ her own learning style. In other words, the question is not: Is a long course better than a short course? The question is: Given the kind of person that I am, will a weekend format be better (which guarantees immersion) or is a longer course better (which puts a strong onus on you to do the work between the classes)?

I hope this helps you think about how to select a course. I wish you well."

John Richardson

Obviously the above principles apply to the selection of a course for any standardized test!

Conclusion

"Success Favours The Prepared Mind." Make sure that you prepare for your standardized test effectively and efficiently.

Developing The Personal Statement - The Workbook

Part I of this book was designed to teach you what a personal statement and autobiographical sketch are about. The purpose of Part II of the book is to help you develop your own personal statement. This will be done in two stages. Stage 1 provides you with a "Personal Statement Gameplan." Stage 2 provides you with the "Personal Statement Workbook" which has been designed to help you research the most difficult and interesting topic of all - yourself.

Stage 1. The Personal Statement Gameplan - The Process

Personal Statement Development - The Eight Essential Steps

(This "Gameplan" will refer to various tools. These tools are part of the Personal Statement Toolbox and will be introduced below.)

1. Begin early. The complete application process can be as much work as an extra half course in university.

2. Research the school. Try to determine what the school is trying to achieve by admitting its first year class. What kinds of students is the school looking for? This information may be found in the school's calendar of information (pay attention to the dean's message), and other sources. (Use Tool 1 in the Personal Statement Toolbox.)

3. Research the application categories available to you. All schools have a "regular category." Many schools have "residual categories." These are called "mature student" or "access", etc. If you are applying in something other than the regular category, think about how to justify your application in that category. How do the various application categories further the school's admissions policies? (Use Tool 2 in the Personal Statement Toolbox.)

4. Research yourself using this Personal Statement Workbook. There are three steps.

   (i) Complete the Comprehensive Applicant Questionnaire (Tool 3 in the Personal Statement Toolbox) provided.

   (ii) Arrange for others to complete the Third Party Questionnaire (Tool 4 in the Personal Statement Toolbox) provided.

   (iii) Complete the Applicant Inferential Imaging Exercise (Tool 5 in the Personal Statement Toolbox) provided.

5. Think about how to link yourself to the application category and the schools general admissions objectives.

6. Write a first draft. Put the first draft away for a few days. Look at it again and write another draft.

7. Circulate the draft of the personal statement along with the Third Party Personal Statement Questionnaire (Tool 6 in the Personal Statement Toolbox) provided.

8. Rewrite and continue to circulate the draft statement along with the Third Party Personal Statement Questionnaire (Tool 4 in the Personal Statement Toolbox) until you are satisfied.

9. Produce a final copy for each school that is suitable for framing. Not only should it be well written, but it should look beautiful.

Stage 2. The Personal Statement Workbook - Getting To Know You!

Applicants often have difficulty writing personal statements because they have not thought sufficiently about themselves, what is important to them, and their goals. It is difficult to think about yourself. In order to assist in this process, I have created six tools to be used during various stages of the development process. Tools 1 and 2 focus on the school. Tools 3 to 6 focus on the applicant.

Introducing The Personal Statement Toolbox

The toolbox contains the following tools:

1. **School Research Exercise** - Purpose: To determine what the schools are looking for in applicants. Try to identify a mission statement.

2. **Category Identification Exercise** - Purpose: To help you determine the appropriate application category for you.

3. **Comprehensive Applicant Questionnaire** - Purpose: To help you focus on yourself.

4. **Third Party Questionnaire** - Purpose: To seek the input of third parties and to learn how they see you and what image you convey to them.

5. **Applicant Inferential Imaging Exercise** - Purpose: to help you identify facts that will result in the reader receiving positive and relevant images about you.

6. **Third Party Personal Statement Questionnaire** - Purpose: to obtain ongoing "feedback" about your personal statement. This "feedback" is to be used to improve and rework successive drafts.

Each of these six tools will be used at various stages in the Personal Statement Gameplan.

Introducing The Tools Individually

These tools are to be used as directed in the process described above.
Each tool is to be used as an aid for a specific step in the personal
statement development process. Tools 1, 2, 3 and 5 are to be completed
by the applicant. Tools 4 and 6 are to be given to third parties to
complete. They are then to be returned to assist the applicant.

Tool 1: School Research Exercise - Getting To Know The Schools

Take a separate piece of paper for each school. By using the calendar of
information, the dean's message, the application form and any other
material you have, identify any:

- statement(s) about how the school sees itself;

- statement(s) about the objective of the admissions policy;

- statement(s) about any special programs that the school offers;

- statement(s) about anything that suggests the school is unique in any
particular way.

**Tool 2: Application Category Identification Exercise - Discovering
Additional Marketing Opportunities**

Different schools have different applicant categories. For example, the
"mature student" category is common. Each different category provides a
new and different opportunity for direct marketing.

Take a separate piece of paper for each school. For each school list:

- the category by label;

- determine exactly what makes one eligible to apply in that category
at that particular school;

- determine how the category further the school's admissions
objectives as a whole;

- assess whether you are eligible to apply in that category;

- consider whether it makes good sense for you to consider applying
in that category (would you be more or less competitive?).

Tool 3: Comprehensive Applicant Questionnaire - Getting To Know You

These questions are to be completed by the applicant. It is impossible that the answer to every question would be directly relevant to every personal statement. Nevertheless, the questions will help you explore the various dimensions of your life. Do not attempt to incorporate the answers to every question into your personal statement.

Geographic Origins

Were you born outside North America? _____

_____

_____

If so, under what circumstances did you arrive in North America? _____

_____

_____

_____

_____

_____

_____

_____

_____

_____

_____

_____

Is your mother tongue a language other than English? _____

If so, at what age and under what circumstances did you learn English? __

_____

_____

_____

_____

_____

_____

_____

_____

_____

Do you speak a language other than English at home? _____

_____

_____

_____

Do you consider yourself to be a member of an ethnic or religious

minority. _____

_____

_____

_____

_____

_____

_____

If so, in what way(s) are you active in that community? _____

_____

_____

_____

_____

_____

_____

How has your minority status made it easier or harder for you to achieve

your goals? _____

_____

_____

_____

_____

_____

_____

_____

_____

_____

_____

_____

_____

Economic Circumstances

What were the economic circumstances of you and your family? _____

_____

_____

_____

_____

_____

_____

_____

_____

_____

_____

_____

_____

_____

_____

_____

_____

_____

_____

Have you had the financial support of your family during your university years? _____

_____

_____

_____

_____

Were you required to work while attending university? _____

_____

_____

If so, how much? _____

_____

_____

_____

Can you think of any way(s) in which your family's economic circumstances created or restricted opportunities for you? _____

_____
_____
_____
_____
_____
_____
_____
_____
_____
_____
_____
_____
_____
_____
_____
_____
_____
_____
_____
_____
_____

General Considerations - The Holistic Approach

How many languages do you speak? _____

What are they? _____
_____
_____

Where were they learned? _____
_____
_____
_____
_____

Do you participate in sports? _____

_____

If so, in what way and how much? _____

_____

_____

_____

_____

_____

_____

_____

_____

_____

_____

_____

_____

_____

_____

_____

_____

_____

Have you been on a university sport team? _____

_____

_____

_____

_____

_____

_____

How much of your time have you devoted to this? _____

_____

_____

_____

_____

_____

Why is participation in sports important to you and how has it contributed to your life? _____

_____

_____

_____

_____

_____

_____

_____

_____

_____

Have you received any recognition in the form of awards? If so, list the award and qualifications for it. _____

_____

_____

_____

_____

_____

_____

_____

What has participation in sports taught you about life in general? _____

_____

_____

_____

_____

_____

_____

_____

_____

_____

Do you play any musical instruments? _____

_____

_____

For how long have you been playing an instrument? _____

_____

Have you received any certificates that recognize your proficiency? _____

_____

_____

_____

_____

_____

_____

_____

In what way does playing a musical instrument enhance your life? _____

_____

_____

_____

_____

_____

_____

_____

_____

_____

_____

_____

_____

_____

_____

_____

Are you a member of or an active participant in any religious organizations? _____

_____

_____

_____

_____

In what capacity? _____

_____

_____

_____

_____

Why is this participation important to you and how has it contributed to your life? _____

_____

_____

_____

_____

_____

_____

_____

Are reading and learning important to you? Why or why not? _____

_____

_____

_____

_____

_____

_____

_____

_____

What is your favourite book and why? _____

_____

_____

_____

_____

_____

_____

_____

_____

_____

Describe a course that made a major contribution to your life. _____

_____

_____

_____

_____

_____

Why was this course important to you? _____

_____

_____

_____

_____

_____

_____

_____

What would be the title of your autobiography? _____

_____

Have you made any contribution to the university community and/or
your community at large? _____

_____

_____

_____

_____

_____

_____

_____

_____

_____

In what capacity? _____

_____

_____

_____

_____

_____

_____

_____

_____

_____

_____

_____

_____

List three things that you have done for the sole benefit of somebody
else. What was your reason for doing these things? Why were they
important to you? _____

_____

_____

_____

_____

_____

_____

_____

_____

_____

_____

_____

_____

_____

_____

_____

_____

_____

_____

Have you had the opportunity to travel? _____

Where and for how long? _____

_____

_____

_____

_____

_____

How did your travel experience help to shape your understanding of the
world and your understanding of others? _____

_____

_____

_____

_____

_____

_____

_____

_____

_____

_____

_____

_____

_____

Is there any way in which your travel experience(s) have contributed to your interest in law, MBA, medical or graduate school? _____

_____

_____

_____

_____

_____

_____

_____

Reflect on your history of employment and/or self-employment. List every job and determine what that job taught you beyond the requirements of the job. (For example, being a sales clerk will teach you things about human nature that extend beyond sales.)

_____

_____

_____

_____

_____

_____

_____

_____

_____

_____

_____

_____

_____

What was your worst job? _____

_____

_____

Why? _____

_____

_____

_____

What was your best job? _____

_____

_____

_____

Why? _____

_____

_____

_____

_____

_____

_____

Are there any special skills that you learned which may help you in other jobs or in law, MBA, medical or graduate school? _____

_____

_____

_____

_____

_____

_____

_____

_____

_____

_____

_____

In what way(s) has your employment history contributed to your interest in law, MBA, medical or graduate school? _____

_____

_____

_____

_____

_____

_____

_____

_____

_____

_____

_____

Each of us has our share of successes and failures. Describe two failures and describe what you learned from each of those failures. _____

_____

_____

_____

_____

_____

_____

_____

_____

_____

_____

Describe two successes and describe what you learned from each of those successes. _____

_____

_____

_____

_____

_____

_____

_____

Have there been any unusually difficult periods in your life? (For example: illness, family problems, divorce, etc.) _____

_____

_____

_____

_____

_____

_____

_____

_____

If so, did the difficulties adversely affect your academic or work performance? _____

_____

_____

_____

_____

_____

_____

_____

Have the difficulties been resolved? _____

_____

_____

_____

_____

In what way did the manner in which you coped with the difficulties teach you something about yourself and contribute to your personal growth? _____

_____

_____

_____

_____

_____

_____

_____

_____

_____

Do you consider yourself to have any skills or abilities that are not common to your peers or beyond those commonly attained by university graduates? If so, what are they _____

_____

_____

_____

_____

_____

_____

_____

_____

_____

_____

Where did you acquire them? _____

_____

_____

_____

_____

_____

_____

_____

_____

_____

What about non-degree academic experiences? _____

_____

_____

_____

_____

_____

_____

_____

Have you taken any extracurricular courses? _____

_____

_____

_____

_____

_____

Have you attained any certificates of achievement? _____

_____

_____

_____

_____

_____

_____

Why did you undertake these courses? (for example was it for general
interest? Was it for self improvement? Was it for advancement in your
employment?) _____

_____

_____

_____

_____

_____

How did these experiences contribute to your life and your interest in
law, MBA, medical or graduate school? _____

_____

_____

_____

_____

Academic And Professional Plans - Why This Goal?

In addition to law, MBA, medical or graduate school, list three opportunities (educational or professional) that you would be interested in
pursuing. (Examples: teaching, jobs, alternative academic experience,
etc.) _____

_____

_____

_____

_____

_____

_____

What is your current area of study? _____

_____

_____

_____

_____

_____

_____

Are you happy in it? _____

_____

_____

_____

_____

If you attend law, MBA, medical or graduate school, will you completely
abandon your current area of study? _____

_____

_____

_____

_____

_____

_____

Will you be able to combine law, MBA, medical or graduate school with
your current area of study? _____

_____

_____

_____

_____

_____

_____

Are you interested in pursuing any joint degree programs? _____

_____

_____

_____

_____

_____

If you are happy in your current area of study and you think that by attending law, MBA, medical or graduate school you will abandon that area of study, why do you want to attend law, MBA, medical or graduate school? _____

_____

_____

_____

_____

_____

_____

_____

_____

At what stage in your life did you decide that you wanted to attend law, MBA, medical or graduate school? _____

_____

_____

_____

_____

_____

_____

Is attending law, MBA, medical or graduate school your primary objective or one of several suitable objectives? _____

_____

_____

_____

_____

_____

_____

What is it about the study of law, business, or medicine that appeals to you? _____

_____

_____

_____

_____

Has your interest in law, MBA, medical or graduate school resulted from experiences you have had in the work force? _____

_____

_____

_____

_____

_____

_____

_____

_____

_____

Will the completion of your studies result in a second career for you? ___

_____

_____

_____

_____

_____

_____

_____

Are you able to point to any significant life event that stimulated your interest in advanced studies or in becoming a professional? _____
If so, what? _____

_____

_____

_____

_____

_____

_____

_____

_____

_____

_____

_____

Emotional Dimensions And Your Mind

What do you consider to be your greatest strength? _____

_____

_____

How has this strength assisted you in life? _____

_____

_____

_____

_____

_____

_____

_____

_____

_____

_____

What do you consider to be your greatest weakness? _____

_____

_____

_____

_____

_____

_____

How has this either strengthened or weakened you in life? _____

_____

_____

_____

_____

_____

_____

_____

Where would you like to be professionally and socially:

In five years _____

_____

_____

_____

_____

_____

_____

_____

_____

_____

_____

_____

_____

_____

In ten years _____

_____

_____

_____

_____

_____

_____

_____

_____

_____

_____

In fifteen years _____

_____

_____

_____

_____

_____

_____

_____

_____

_____

_____

_____

_____

What have you done to begin achieving this? _____

_____

_____

_____

_____

_____

_____

_____

_____

_____

_____

_____

_____

_____

_____

_____

_____

_____

_____

_____

_____

Identify and describe a person who you greatly admire. What do you
admire most in that person and why? _____

_____

_____

_____

_____

_____

_____

_____

_____

_____

_____

_____

_____

_____

_____

_____

_____

_____

_____

_____

_____

What is the one characteristic you have that you value most (integrity, athletic ability, etc.) and why? _____

_____

_____

_____

_____

_____

_____

_____

_____

_____

_____

_____

_____

_____

_____

_____

_____

_____

_____

If you could improve one thing about yourself, what would that one thing be and why? _____

_____

_____

_____

_____

_____

_____

_____

_____

_____

_____

_____

_____

_____

_____

_____

_____

_____

_____

_____

If you were dead and buried, what would you like to have written on
your tombstone? _____

_____

_____

_____

_____

_____

_____

_____

_____

_____

_____

_____

_____

_____

_____

_____

Tool 4: Third Party Questionnaire

People often see you very differently from how you see yourself. What follows is a questionnaire that you can ask third parties to complete. The results may give you food for thought.

I am applying to _____ .
As part of the application process I am required to submit a personal statement. I have included a copy of the specific questions that I am required to answer. The statement is to be about me. I am aware that often other people see me in a different light from how I see myself. I value your judgment and ask that you answer the following questions about me from your perspective. Thank you!

1. Please pick three words that you feel best describe me. _____

_____

_____

_____

_____

2. If you were writing my personal statement, what would be the most important fact about me that you think the admissions committee should know? _____

_____

_____

_____

_____

_____

_____

_____

_____

_____

_____

_____

_____

_____

_____

_____

3. In your opinion, do I have any special qualities that make me uniquely suited for my academic and professional goals? For example, do I have any special qualities that make me uniquely suited for the study of law or becoming a lawyer? _____

_____

_____

_____

_____

_____

_____

_____

_____

_____

4. Is there anything, in general, about my background that you think would be helpful for the admissions committee to know? _____

_____

_____

_____

_____

_____

_____

_____

_____

_____

_____

5. Describe one actual experience that you have had with me that (in your opinion) summarizes my basic character. _____

_____

_____

_____

_____

_____

_____

_____

_____

_____

Tool 5: Applicant Inferential Imaging Exercise

You have completed Tool 3 which was the comprehensive applicant questionnaire. You should have a great deal of information about yourself. Which information should be used? Which should be omitted? Your biographical data is relevant in what it allows the admissions committee to infer about you. Our next exercise will help you decide which facts to use. This exercise will also help you understand what facts you must present so that the reader will infer that you have the characteristics the school is looking for.

EXERCISE: On the left side of the page you will find a list of characteristics that are desirable in many graduate and professional school students. (Note that not every characteristic is relevant to every application.) On the right side of the page you should specify one or more pieces of information about you (look to the comprehensive applicant questionnaire, but don't feel constrained by it) that suggests that you have the characteristic on the left. For example, from what fact about you could it be inferred that you have the ability to work with others? What other characteristic on the left side of the page might this fact be relevant to? For example, would this same fact also suggest maturity or motivation? Ideally, you want each characteristic on the left to be demonstrated by two or more facts or experiences on the right. Completion of this exercise will also give you an idea of where you are strong and where you are weak. You may have time to strengthen your weaknesses. For example, if you have no facts to support the characteristic of being "community oriented" then you can improve in that area.

A Demo

Characteristics*		Facts**
responsible		senior don on my residence floor
motivated		took in excess of normal course load
community oriented		Big brothers organization
work well in teams		President of pre-law society

* In order to learn what characteristics a school values, it is often helpful to look at questions asked of recommenders. In particular you should look at questions that appear on standard letter of reference forms.

** Review your answers to Tool 3 (Comprehensive Applicant Questionnaire) before listing the relevant biographical data.

Applicant Inferential Imaging Exercise

EXERCISE: Describe something about yourself or an event in your life that
would allow the reader to infer that you have the following
characteristics.

Characteristics

Facts or Experiences

Leadership Potential

Ability to Work with Others

Creativity and Imagination

Sense of Humor

Maturity

Disciplined

Hard Working

Honest

Generous

Motivated

Intelligent

Responsible

Well Rounded (diverse interests)

Community Oriented

Sound Judgment

Tool 6: Third Party Personal Statement Questionnaire

After having completed one or two drafts of your personal statement you should circulate it for evaluation. What follows are a list of questions that you may want to ask your outside readers.

Attached is a personal statement that I have written for the purposes of

applying to _____ .

I have also included a copy of the specific question that I am answering. I would appreciate it if you would take some time to read what I have written and answer the following questions. I am particularly concerned with the overall image(s) of me that are suggested by this personal statement. If you find any grammatical errors or typos would you please circle them. Please include any additional comments you have that are not covered by the questions asked.

1. Was my opening paragraph (and particularly the first sentence) engaging and attention grabbing?

2. Did you find any grammatical errors or typos?

3. Did I seem to be a positive person?

4. Was the personal statement responsive to the precise question asked?

5. Was it well written and well organized?

6. Are there any specific words that you think should be omitted?

7. Do I sound like a likable, honest, sincere, interesting person?

8. Can you think of anything that you know about me that I should have included?

9. Was there anything included which you don't think should have been included?

10. Did you learn anything new about me from reading this personal statement?

11. Do you see me in a different way after having read this personal statement?

12. If you didn't already know me, after having read this personal statement, would you want to meet me?

13. Please try to paraphrase the main point of the personal statement as a whole.

Other Products & Services

Courses

Books

Seminars

Newsletter

CDROM

Two ways to keep in touch with the author...

Richardson - Law School Bound®

nE-MAILwsletter

1

The Richardson - Law School Bound® Newsletter is published monthly and distributed by - and only by - e-mail. Best of all, it is FREE to anyone with an email account!

The Law School Bound® Newsletter focuses on the needs and interests of Canadian "Law School Bound®" students.

The topics covered include valuable information and updates about every aspect of the law admissions process, admission to law schools and law as a career.

The Richardson - Law School Bound® Newsletter is also the vehicle used to distribute any updates to the "Mastering The® LSAT" or "Mastering The® Personal Statement" books.

To start your subscription send an e-mail to learn@prep.com

Live Personal Statement

Workshop **2**

Interested in attending the live Richardson - Personal Statement Workshop? They are run several times a year in Toronto, or can be arranged, at your convenience, at your location, for any university, career counseling center, student or private group.

Learn more by contacting John Richardson at learn@prep.com, visit our web site at www.prep.com or call (416) 410-PREP®.

Are you proud of your personal statement?

Are you interested in the possibility of it being published in the next edition of Mastering The Personal Statement? I am interested in personal statements of all types.

If so, send it to the author with your name, address, phone, fax and e-mail to:

JOHN RICHARDSON
P.O. Box 19602, Manulife P.O.
55 Bloor St. W.
Toronto, Ontario M4W 3T9

Alternatively, (and preferably) you may e-mail it to me at:
learn@prep.com

I thank you in advance, but will contact you only in the event that your personal statement is suitable for inclusion.

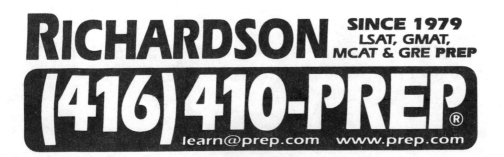